AMERICA'S BEST! 100

C. PAUL LUONGO

Sterling Publishing Co., Inc. New York

Oak Tree Press Co., Ltd. London & Sydney

AMERICA'S BEST! 100 is dedicated to
Richard B. Fisher and Glen R. Johnson of
Pittsburgh, Pennsylvania. They provided the
professional opportunities that enabled me to
create this book.

Library of Congress Cataloging in Publication Data
Luongo, C Paul.
    America's best! 100.
    Includes index.
    1. Consumer education.   2.   Commercial products—
United States.   I.   Title.
TX–335.L85   640.73   79–91375
ISBN 0–8069–0178–0
ISBN 0–8069–0179–9 (lib. bdg.)

Oak Tree ISBN 7061–2689–0

Contents   *America's Best! 100*

All prices in this book are subject to change.

A ✉ appearing with an entry means that the product is available by mail or by freight service.

Special Note: With very few exceptions, I have sampled and visited every subject listed herein, except when otherwise impossible—a statement to which no other guide of this kind that I know can attest.   C. Paul Luongo

Foreword

America's Best! 100 is the ancillary result of a 1974 client press tour that took me to a dozen U.S. cities. When I arrived in my last stop, Chicago, I had two dining experiences, one good and one bad, that I wanted to write about.

Instead, when I sat down at the typewriter I critiqued the entire city of Chicago. Later, I critiqued all twelve of the cities I visited. I distributed my VIP Baedecker informally to the media, friends,

C. Paul Luongo bites into America's best pizza.

and clients. As the project grew in popularity, I was encouraged to include more than just restaurant and travel subjects. *America's Best!* now documents all goods and services that are, in fact, America's best.

The maelstrom of publicity swelled, highlighted by appearances on *The Merv Griffin Show*, NBC's *Tomorrow Show*, and a UPI worldwide feature by Boston Bureau Chief Donald Davis. *America's Best!* was born.

After an investment of $250,000 and more than 150,000 miles of first-class air travel, I have documented 100 of America's best, most charismatic goods and services through the media, Chambers of Commerce, special informants, an exclusive survey of U.S. senators and, of course, my own interviews with the people who provide the best. In addition, *America's Best!* combines the expertise of assistants, epicures, dilettantes, connoisseurs, clients, friends, special contacts, and those who have written to me in response to my TV appearances and the hundreds of newspaper and magazine features written about *America's Best!*

As you'll soon discover, all the subjects I present here are the best in their categories, have a good story, are available to the public, and have that certain scintillating and charismatic quality! For example, even if you don't know anything about banana ice cream, you'll know you've found America's best when you've tried it at the Caffe Pompei in Boston's North End.

My publisher and I have made every effort to make this book as current as possible. But remember, between the time the book is published and it appears on the shelves of your bookstore, a few of the prices and other information may have changed.

I hope *America's Best!* will reawaken in its readers a new appreciation of and demand for quality, as well as a return to the work ethic required to provide the goods and services that discriminating Americans are proud to designate as America's best. I know you will enjoy this book as much as I have enjoyed researching and compiling it. And by all means, let me know what you think of *America's Best!* by writing:

C. Paul Luongo
America's Best!
441 Stuart Street
Boston, Massachusetts 02116
617-266-4210

Thank you, and God Bless!

America's Best! AIR

Honolulu, Hawaii

Director of Environmental
    Programs
State Department of Health
Honolulu, Hawaii 96804

808-548-4139

Lanny Deal
Control Programs Operations
    Branch
Office of Air Quality Planning
    and Standards
Research Triangle Park
North Carolina 27713

919-541-5365

You are in Honolulu, Hawaii, and a soft breeze is blowing. Your rapid heartbeat has calmed down, your cough has disappeared and your eyes have stopped watering because you are breathing America's best air.

Honolulu is the only one of 105 urbanized areas in the U.S. with a population greater than 200,000 that can boast that it has attained the Environmental Protection Agency's national air standards for each of the five pollutants considered most dangerous to human health. The other 104 urban areas are in violation of the standards for at least one, and often for several, of these pollutants.

The five pollutants determined by the EPA to be most dangerous to human health are photochemical oxidants (which can seriously irritate eyes, mucous membranes, and the respiratory system), particulate matter (which can cause breathing problems and respiratory illness), carbon monoxide (which can place serious burdens on the heart to increase blood flow to compensate for reduced oxygen in the blood), sulfur dioxide (which can irritate the upper respiratory tract and cause lung damage), and nitrogen dioxide (which can cause bronchitis and pneumonia).

The 1977 Clean Air Act Amendments passed by Congress require that the federal air-pollution standards be met everywhere for all five pollutants by the end of 1987. Honolulu can relax, but the other 104 urbanized areas have a lot of work to do.

Spokane, Washington, is the only place in the U.S. that comes close to Honolulu. The EPA ranks Spokane as "unclassified" because on one day, on one monitor, one violation was recorded. This one violation is enough to prohibit the EPA from giving

Ocean breezes and the absence of heavy industry make Honolulu's air the best in the U.S.

Spokane a clean bill of health, but not enough of a violation to be recorded as evidence of a non-attainment level.

Why is the air quality index so good in Honolulu? The explanation is two-fold: geographical and industrial.

Honolulu is located on an island. The prevailing ocean winds blow the pollutants offshore. They are so efficient at whisking the pollutants from the island that if the monitoring equipment were placed just seven miles offshore in the direction the winds blow, Honolulu would be in violation of the EPA air quality standards.

Smog, which is made up of photochemical oxidants, is the most widespread pollutant, and heavy industry is the major culprit in contributing to the smog level of a city. Because the most important industry in Hawaii is tourism, the amount of heavy industry is minimal. Even if the amount of heavy industry increased substantially, those prevailing ocean winds would negate any effect it might have on the air quality levels.

So, while you are enjoying the delicious fruit, tropical scenery, and excellent surfing conditions, be sure to inhale deeply, because that's America's best air you're breathing in Honolulu.

America's Best! AIRPORT

Tampa International Airport

P.O. Box 22287
Tampa, Florida 33622

813-883-3400

Walter A. Baldwin, Jr.
Chairman
Hillsborough County Aviation
Authority

George Bean, Director

Paul T. MacAlester, Director
of Information

In 1961, passenger traffic at the Tampa, Florida, airport passed the one million mark—far more people than the outdated facility could handle. So the local aviation authority commissioned the late Leigh Fisher to design a new airport, and ten years later the $83-million complex was completed.

Foreign technical delegations from at least seventy countries and over eighty million people have visited Tampa International Airport since its opening, and every year more than seven million passengers pass through the complex. *South* magazine has reported that Southern businessmen rate it the best in America.

Underlying the praise for Tampa Airport was the decision to abandon any attempt to combine the functions of an airplane docking facility and passenger terminal under one roof. Tampa gave birth to the "landside" and "airside" ideas of airport design. All receiving, baggage, restaurant, parking, reservations, and meeting facilities are centralized in a single building. Thus, no long walks and no problems finding the right terminal, because this is the only building that the public access roads lead to. The maximum walk from the most remote parking facility is only 700 feet. In fact, George Bean, airport director, is especially proud that in 1973 the National Cerebral Palsy Foundation presented the airport with a special award commending the special accommodations for the handicapped.

Ranking twenty-second in the nation in terms of passenger traffic, the airport can handle forty planes at any one time and twenty-million passengers a year, and the design allows for the addition of thirty-two gates. A "satellite" design was utilized to accommodate the quick transport of passengers to the four gate

11

At Tampa International Airport, all attempts to combine an airplane docking facility with passenger terminal were abandoned.

areas, which are separated from the main terminal by 750-foot "arms," through which passengers are comfortably transported in forty seconds from the central terminal in vehicles designed by Westinghouse. The system can transport as many as 20,000 people per hour on its own elevated right of way.

Special access roads to the airport are seldom clogged, and a door-to-door trip from Tampa rarely takes more than forty minutes. The Shriners and Metropolitan Life Insurance Company cited the airport in announcing their decisions to move operations to the Tampa area, as did the National Football League in its establishment of a new franchise in Tampa. The airport's continued success is important to the economy overall, since 35 percent of all visitors to the Tampa Bay area arrive by air.

The airport complex boasts a $15-million, 300-room Host International Hotel with a revolving restaurant on the roof. There are five restaurants, fourteen snack bars, two cocktail lounges, and four bars in the terminal, which is completely carpeted, and spaces for 1,700 cars in the airport garage.

America's Best! ANTEBELLUM HOMES

The Natchez Pilgrimage

P.O. Box 347
Natchez, Mississippi 39120

601-446-6631

Mrs. Homer A. Whittington,
  President
Mrs. Hall (Natie-Jo) Ratcliffe,
  Chairman, Stanton Hall
  Governing Board
Mrs. H. I. Stahlman III,
  President, Natchez Garden
  Club

601-442-6672

The Burn
Buzz and Bobbie Harper, Owners

601-445-8566

Tony Byrne, Mayor, City
  of Natchez

Candlelight Walk: $10 per person

Confederate Pageant: $5 per
  person

Experienced guide available for
  $5 per hour

Half-Day Mini-Tour:
  3 antebellum homes, city tour,
  coffee served in antebellum
  home, $7.50 per person

One-Day Tour: 5 antebellum
  homes, luncheon, city tour,
  including Grand Village of
  Natchez Indians, $20

Deluxe Tour: 1 or 2 days,
  4-6 antebellum homes, elegant
  candlelight dinner in
  antebellum home (dress
  optional), time to shop and
  rest, tour of other historical
  sites, $35 per person

Pilgrimage Day Tours: $12 per
  person, variety of 7 tours,
  includes 5 antebellum homes

With its two-story porches, gardens of azaleas and camellias, splendid willows and oaks, and Georgian columns, Natchez, Mississippi, is the epitome of the antebellum South. In the days before the Civil War, the men who made their fortunes in cotton and indigo built their mansions in this bustling port city on the Mississippi River, and today people come to Natchez from all over the world to see America's best antebellum homes.

Natchez, the oldest settlement on the Mississippi, has carefully preserved thirty-five beautiful homes dating from the 1770s to the Civil War. All of them are on display during the Natchez Pilgrimage each fall and spring, and you can choose between seven tours, each featuring five homes. You can even visit some of the houses

13

by candlelight and watch a Confederate Pageant. If you can't make it to the Pilgrimage, many of the houses are open to the public year-round. All together, the city has fifty properties on the National Register of Historic Places and eight National Historic Landmarks.

While some of the houses are perfect examples of Greek Revival architecture, others reflect Creole and Planter styles. The Oakland House, built in 1835 for the granddaughter of the Spanish Governor of Natchez, is designed like a Spanish Villa. There is also an Italian villa in Natchez, as well as a French-style house built in 1790 on the site of an Indian mound.

Even the largest octagonal house in the U.S. is in Natchez. Called "Longwood," it was never finished because its northern builders went home at the outbreak of the Civil War. Their tools are just where they left them.

Cotton king Frederick Stanton spent seven years and $80,000 building Stanton Hall, which was completed in 1859. (He died the same year he moved in.) Now the house is the headquarters of the Pilgrimage Garden Club, a group of Natchez women that has been preserving the town's historic past since 1932. All hardware in the house is Sheffield silver. The hand-sculpted mantelpieces are from New York and the Cornelius and Baker chandeliers from Philadelphia are considered to be the best extant gas fixtures in America. There is a 450-piece, hand-painted, Old Paris porcelain china set in the dining room, French mirrors and 125-year-old Aubusson rugs in the overwhelming ballroom, and antique beds from British Guyana, France, and England in the bedrooms. Lady Bird Johnson has stayed at Stanton Hall as a special guest, and the house is leased to Pilgrimage Club members on special occasions. Daytime tours cost $2.50.

The Eola Hotel, a long-time Natchez landmark that closed in 1973, was recently purchased by the Forrest Germany family and is scheduled to reopen in 1981 with its forty rooms completely refurbished. There are also five motels in the immediate area. However, the best place to stay is a fine antebellum home.

At The Burn—Scottish for brook—your $50 a night includes a room, breakfast, and a tour of this twenty-three room Greek Revival mansion. The suspended spiral staircase and period antiques are magnificent.

Buzz Harper purchased The Burn in 1977 for $300,000, and estimates that the house and furnishings are now worth $2 million.

It took Cotton King Frederick Stanton seven years—and 80,000 pre-Civil War dollars—to build Stanton Hall.

Guest bedrooms are in the *garçonnière*, a four-room wing off the main house. In pre-Civil War days, young men (*garçons*) were sent there when they were seventeen or eighteen for their sexual initiation.

Buzz has a staff of three hostesses, three cooks, five maids, and two houseboys to host and serve you. You can also stay at Monmouth, Linden, Texada, Rabenaside, and several other houses, and many of Natchez's homeowners host special candlelight dinners. The best way to get to Natchez is on the *Delta Queen* or *Mississippi Queen*, two restored riverboats that pull into dock every week on their trips down the Mississippi.

Natchez's historic charm has attracted many movie and television productions, including *The Autobiography of Miss Jane Pittman* and *Raintree County*, as well as a restoration-minded actor. George Hamilton has bought three homes from the Natchez Historical Foundation, and owns another house outside of town at Church Hill.

America's Best! APPETIZERS

Antoine's Restaurant 713 St. Louis New Orleans, Louisiana 70130 504-581-4422 reservations, 504-581-4044 office	Roy Guste, Jr., Proprietor American Express, Diner's Club and Antoine's Credit Card

Antoine's of New Orleans is to the appetizer what the Cordon Bleu is to veal. This time-honored establishment has been serving generations of customers since it was first founded by Antoine Alciatore in 1840. The restaurant remains in its original location, and is run by the fifth generation of the Alciatore family. So satisfied with the menu created for the restaurant's centennial in 1940, Antoine's clientele has demanded that it remain virtually unchanged for the last forty years. With a list of more than thirty appetizers, Antoine's is best known for two: Oysters Rockefeller and Pommes Soufflées.

The Oysters Rockefeller were invented by Jules Alciatore, a second-generation member of this restaurant dynasty. It was originally conceived to supplant the Snails Bourguignon, served by Antoine's in the 1850s. Rather than importing the snails from France, Jules opted for the plentiful, native oysters of New Orleans, and he adapted the traditional snail sauce to blend with the flavor of the oyster. As Roy Guste, Jr., the current proprietor, explains, the dish was named after John D. Rockefeller "because the sauce was so rich (with eighteen ingredients including absinthe) and green, Jules Alciatore named it after the richest man in America." There is no spinach in this original and secret recipe, the mark of all, inferior, imitations. To date, Roy estimates that Antoine's has sold over four million servings of this American delicacy. Oysters Rockefeller are joined by nine other superb oyster appetizers on the menu.

Pommes Soufflées were introduced to America by Antoine Alciatore and began another New Orleans tradition: they were often ordered before the appetizer with cocktails. This succulent dish was actually more of an accident than a planned creation. It was conceived while Antoine was working under Collinet, the great

Antoine's has been serving since 1840.

master chef of France. Collinet was preparing a banquet for King Louis Phillipe, to celebrate the opening of the first railway in France. The train arrived, Collinet put Louis's favorite fried potatoes into the hot fat, but ever fearful of new inventions, Louis did not arrive on the train. Collinet removed the half-browned potatoes from the fat, put them aside, and returned them to the fat upon Louis's arrival in his carriage. The potatoes miraculously rose into small balloons, and Pommes Soufflées were born, delighting Louis and generations of Antoine's customers.

Antoine's even has a unique way of serving these potatoes. They are placed in their own special *paniers*, which are little baskets made of woven strips of potatoes, French-fried, and inserted in a base of bread.

These are but two of the thirty-four appetizers, which also include nine oyster, eight crab, and seven shrimp dishes. Many patrons prefer to order several choices without any entrée at all. New Orleanians who are regular customers love the delicate flavor of appetizers made from crayfish (fondly referred to as "crawdads"), especially Écrevisses à la marinière, in which the crayfish are marinated in their own juices.

The simply decorated establishment, with its white-tiled floors, hatracks, Victorian chandeliers, and original gas mantles, has been patronized by a host of famous connoisseurs and celebrities. Sarah Bernhardt, Enrico Caruso, Florenz Ziegfeld, Cecil B. DeMille, Tennessee Williams and six U.S. Presidents are among those who have doted upon such famous entrées as: Matelotte d'Anguille (eel stew), Frogs' Legs Sautée Demi-Bordelaise, Tortue Malle à la Rupinscoff (a soft-shelled turtle stew), and Jules Alciatore's triumphant creation, Pompano en Papillote, in which the pompano fillet with its wine-flavored shrimp sauce is cooked in a heart-shaped paper bag.

Antoine's is open six days a week for lunch and dinner (closed Sundays, Christmas Day, New Year's Day, Mardi Gras, and the Fourth of July). An impeccably trained staff of 200 is well prepared to help you choose from the copious appetizer selection.

America's Best! ATHLETIC SHOES

New Balance Athletic Shoes

38-42 Everett Street
Boston, Massachusetts 02134

617-783-4000

Jim Davis, President

What do Bill Rodgers, Erich Segal, Senator William Proxmire and former Massachusetts Governor Michael Dukakis all have in common? New Balance Athletic Shoes! In fact, Bill Rodgers, the fastest in the group, won the 1975 Boston Marathon after training in the New Balance 320 (now called the 322). What's more, five of the top ten finishers in the 1979 Boston Marathon wore the *Comp 100* ($39.95), New Balance's ultra-light 7½-ounce nylon racing shoe with nylon leather lining.

The New Balance 620 ($49.95), introduced in June, 1979, was the only shoe to get a Five Star rating from *Runner's World* magazine and the Running Times Gold Shoe award simultaneously. At only eight ounces, the 620 features a special vibram sole imported from Italy and a nylon mesh upper with leather lining. In proportion to its weight, it offers more protection than any other shoe on the market.

From 1906 until the early 1950s, New Balance specialized in orthopedic shoes and arch supports, so the company understands the importance of peculiar pedate qualities. "Today," says Jim Davis, president, "it is width-sizing that distinguishes New Balance shoes from all others." Indeed, each shoe's fit is so unique that you will probably not have to wear socks while training, unless of course you want to add extra cushioning or keep your feet warm. Since the shoes come in sizes 3½ to 15, AA to EEEE, anyone should be able to find an exact fit.

Laces no longer serve solely as width adjusters. Instead, a patented leather "saddle" surrounds the foot, permitting each runner to pull up the longitudinal arch while tightening laces. There are no inseams on the toe, so blistering on the top of the foot, which hampers many runners, does not occur. In fact, the 420, introduced in January, 1980 ($43.95), features the "Lunaris Pillow," a removable, washable insert that molds especially to your foot. It keeps the foot in the "neutral plane" ideal for healthy feet, legs, and back, and weighs only nine ounces.

Ideally, a racing shoe would weigh three ounces or less, but it would not provide enough protection. New Balance has successfully constructed a shoe that is light enough to run in yet supportive enough to absorb an adequate amount of roadshock, and runners are well pleased with the design.

Since Jim Davis bought New Balance in 1972, shoe production has increased from 30 pair per day to 3,500. Sales have more than doubled each year since 1975 and, with a 10 percent share of the $500 million market, New Balance is gaining ground on previously unchallenged makers like Adidas and Puma.

Davis jogs at least thirty-five miles each week, and most of his employees are joggers too. He urges everyone to try it, but admonishes that someone thirty-five or older and attempting to run after ten years of inactivity should first consult a doctor.

New Balance offers shoes for all stages of training and running, including:

322—better counter-heel design than the highly rated 320; "extended saddle" protection for ball (metatarsal region) of foot; extended vinyl achilles tendon pad; 9½ ounces, $36.95;

455—on- or off-road training; rubber wear-plug in heel for longevity; polyester-mesh "upper," with round studded sole; 10 ounces, $44.95;

220—first trainer for light jogging or walking; lightest, most cushioned first trainer available; 9½ ounces, $24.95;

300 Series—beginning to intermediate trainer; basic universal training shoe, with the same upper design as model 420; 9½ ounces, $29.95.

New Balance shoes are available at 3,000 sporting goods stores across the U.S., as well as in France, Belgium, Switzerland, England, and Japan. All shoes sold in the U.S. are American made. New Balance also produces the shoes under exact specifications in Canada and Japan for sale abroad.

America's Best! AZALEAS

Mobile, Alabama

*Bellingrath Gardens
Theodore, Alabama 36582
205-973-2217*

*Open dawn to dusk, every day
(Azalea season from February–
mid-March): adults $3;*

*children under 12, $1.50;
children under 6, free*

*Azalea Trail
For information contact:
Azalea Festival
P.O. Box 2187
Mobile, Alabama 36601
205-476-8828
March–mid-April*

Businessmen, botanists, amateurs, and professionals agree that Mobile, Alabama, has America's best azaleas. Azaleas, which originated in the Orient, were introduced to the U.S. through the port of Mobile and still flourish there with very little care because the soil and climate are ideal for them.

Azaleas thrive mainly on the slightly acid soil, high humidity, and mild weather found in Mobile, and the Gulf Coast location creates a constantly moist and warm environment, the best type

Azaleas in bloom at Mobile's Bellingrath Gardens.

for azaleas. The plants need more than moisture, however. New Orleans, for example, is also located on the Gulf Coast and has all the moisture an azalea could need, but the soil is too alkaline. The slightly acid soil of Mobile is absolutely perfect for azaleas.

The mild and balmy weather of Mobile, which allows for a longer growing season, is another advantage for the outdoor azalea grower. Greenhouses, therefore, are not needed for protection from harsh weather, and the long growing season is an added incentive to the amateur gardener.

The city encourages citizens to plant azaleas, and the plants are obtainable easily. Some of the largest, wholesale azalea nurseries in the country are located in Mobile. The largest one, Flowerwood Nursery, sells a half million azalea plants annually, more than any other nursery in the country. Blackwell's Nursery sells azaleas exclusively.

The city's considerable tourist industry revolves around the azalea. The azalea season from February to the middle of March at nearby Bellingrath Gardens is world famous and attracts a quarter of a million visitors. The Mobile Azalea Festival runs from the beginning of March through the middle of April and is the city's annual springtime celebration. Mobile's public and private gardens are ablaze with extensive azalea plantings, as well as other flowers. The thirty-seven-mile Azalea Trail, marked by a pink line on the streets, leads visitors through the most spectacular public and private outdoor azalea displays of the city.

Azaleas can live over 100 years and grow to be thirty feet high and fifty feet around—as large as some buildings. In Mobile, entire landscaping plans are designed to show these very old, very large azaleas to their best advantage. All varieties of the plant thrive in Mobile—dwarf, standard, and giant, as well as hardy and non-hardy varieties. The ideal environmental conditions, coupled with the civic and commercial support given to azalea cultivation, have made Mobile "Azalea City."

America's Best! BANANA ICE CREAM

The Caffe Pompei   617-523-9896, 523-9438

280 Hanover Street   *Mario Marino, Proprietor*
Boston, Massachusetts 02113
                                        7 days a week: 8:00 A.M.–
                                            4:00 A.M.

Not many ice cream shops stay open from 8:00 A.M. until 4:00 A.M. Then again, not many offer America's best banana ice cream. Devotees pour in from all parts of the country to discover this exquisite taste treat at Boston's Caffe Pompei.

The Pompei's banana ice cream has eight to nine fresh bananas in each quart. About half a banana, therefore, goes into each dish. Like most virtuosos, proprietor Mario Marino is reluctant to reveal all of the secrets of his special creation. "It's made with fresh bananas, real cream, and special flavors from Italy," he says. But he refuses to divulge the nature of these ingredients, although he acknowledges that they are shipped directly from Italy every two or three weeks.

All of the Pompei's ice cream is made in a $7,000 Italian machine Mario designed. There is no American equivalent. It turns faster than most other machines and makes ice cream that is smoother and more delicious. "But," says Mario, "it's not just the machine, it's a combination of machine with special refrigeration that can keep bananas fresh within the ice cream for three to five weeks."

Mario discovered his banana ice cream through experimentation, and at first it was just one of the regular Pompei offerings. Now, he sells twice as much banana as any other flavor. Each day he makes three to four gallons of this special treat, and even Texans have travelled to Boston for it. A cone costs 75¢, a dish $1, and a hand-packed quart $4. Mario's *pièce de résistance* is the Special, three flavors of ice cream topped with Amaretto, strawberries, whipped cream, sprinkles, and a cherry—all for $2.50.

With these treats Caffe Pompei is riding the crest of America's $6-billion ice cream business. Ice cream is served in over 80 percent of America's households and consumed at a per capita rate of 47.12 pints each year. It's worth noting that even though there are 300 to 400 calories in a cup of ice cream, it is a good source of protein, calcium, phosphorous, and vitamins A, B1 and B2.

Although ice cream is generally believed to be an Italian invention, its origins are unclear. Legend has it that Marco Polo observed the Chinese eating ice flavored with exotic fruits in the 14th century. Another tale portrays Nero sending his slaves scurrying up to the Alps to gather snow so he could put fruit juices on it. These desserts, however, would come under the category of ices, not proper ice cream. By the 1600s, ice cream as we know it had become the jealously guarded privilege of European royalty. Charles I of England once had a French chef beheaded for revealing his private ice cream recipe. It was a Sicilian named Francisco Procopio who brought ice cream to the masses when he began selling it in Paris about 1660.

The colonists brought ice cream to America, and the first American to buy an ice cream machine was George Washington. On May 17, 1784, he paid one pound, thirteen shillings, and four pence for a "cream machine for making ice." The first American patent on an ice cream freezer was recorded in 1848. Ice cream parlors first appeared in America during the latter part of the 18th century in New York. Cones didn't emerge until 1904 at the St. Louis Exposition, when an ice cream seller at the Hawaiian booth ran out of dishes for his ice cream and waffle desserts and was driven to wrapping the ice cream in waffles.

For Mario Marino in Boston, the landmark date was 1966, when he opened the Caffe Pompei as an espresso cafe. Two years later, after much planning and hard work, he finished his labor of love—the Italian ice cream machine—and began serving his homemade ice cream. Since then, he's been dishing out ice cream seven days a week, twenty hours a day at the burgeoning cafe, which can now seat 120 people (excluding the backroom pool hall). To complement the ice cream, Mario also serves coffee, cappuccino, café mocha, and Italian pastry. He sells spumoni for $1.25 a slice.

Mario's quality-conscious entrepreneurial traits emerge when he is asked whether he would mass produce banana ice cream if he could. "No, never, I make it the same! I don't care how much ice cream I gotta make. It's gonna be the same or nothing!"

America's Best! BANJOS

The Liberty Banjo Company

2472 Main Street
Bridgeport, Connecticut 06606

203-368-1176

Paul Morrissey, President-Owner

Monday–Friday: 9:00 A.M.–
5:00 P.M.; Saturday: 9:00 A.M.–
4:00 P.M.

Cash only, or COD, plus shipping

Instrument catalog, no charge; parts catalog and custom work manual, $3.50; special packet, containing parts catalog, custom work manual, instructions for cutting and inlaying pearl, heel carving instructions, $6.50

In Bridgeport, Connecticut, far away from the Blue Hills of Virginia and Kentucky and the bayous of the South, the Liberty Banjo Company makes America's best banjos.

Handcrafting, beautiful engraving and carving, the best parts, and the best in quality woods make the Liberty Banjo the best sounding and prettiest banjo in production. Liberty makes every banjo—fifty a year—by hand to exact specifications. "We don't just take a bunch of parts and throw them into a machine," says President Paul Morrissey. It takes from one week to three months to make each one. Prices range from $400 to $4,400. There is a two-month waiting list, and orders come from as far away as Russia.

There are 400 parts on a banjo, and at Liberty many of them are made by hand. All of the metal parts are made in Liberty's workshops or in local foundries. Liberty banjos require special nuts, bolts, metal frets and alloys to get the right sound and appearance. Paul Morrissey is so meticulous about what goes into a banjo that he once had the tone ring around the box of a pre-Civil War banjo analyzed so that he could duplicate the alloy to best reproduce the beautiful sound. He uses this "prewar bell brass alloy" in his banjos.

Many woods can be used to make a banjo, depending upon the desired sound and appearance. For the fingerboard, Paul uses maple, rosewood, or ebony. He uses curly maple, birdseye maple, walnut, and mahogany for the neck, and a hardwood like ebony or rosewood for the resonator, the box that projects the sound. The metal parts in a Liberty banjo are all brass or bronze.

Liberty banjos feature handcrafted mother-of-pearl and abalone inlay work. The pearl must be carefully cut, otherwise it will shatter and turn to useless dust. It must be sliced in very thin layers before being placed on the banjo's fingerboard (for finger markings) or at the base of the neck (for decoration).

All metal parts are intricately engraved by hand. Bob Flescher, who founded the company with Paul, still does much of the engraving himself. His floral leaf designs adorn the tension hoop, flange (the part that holds the strings firm at the head of the instrument over the drum), arm rest, and tailpiece. The name of the particular instrument is hand-engraved on the tension hoop in beautiful script. The neck is a hollow box with a steel rod running down its entire length to prevent any warp or twist.

The three basic types of banjos are the *five-string*, used for bluegrass, classical, and folk music; the *tenor*, a four-string banjo used since the early 1900s for Dixieland jazz and modern music; and the *plectrum*, which also has four strings but is tuned like a five-string banjo.

Because of the exclusively American origin of the banjo, all

Liberty Banjos feature mother-of-pearl and abalone inlay work.

Liberty banjos are named after folk dances popular in American history. They are:

> *The Backstep*—beginner's model, available in five-string, tenor, and plectrum; open back, with no resonator (one can be added), $400;
>
> *The Buckdancer*—available in five-string, tenor, and plectrum; made of curly maple with beautiful inlay work, adjustable tailpiece, geared pegs, no resonator, $600;
>
> *Quadrille*—available as plectrum, tenor, or five-string; mahogany work, resonator, three-ply hardrock maple tone box, $1,400;
>
> *Promenade*—available as plectrum, tenor, or five-string, walnut carving, engraved, gold-plated, $2,200;
>
> *Cotillion*—fancy curly maple neck, flower relief on heel and carving in stained American walnut, inlays of abalone and mother-of-pearl, beautiful leaf reliefs on back of resonator, gold plating, $4,400.

Banjo music should not be considered simply as Country and Western. In fact there are two other types. Old Time music is mountain music that originated in England, Ireland, and Scotland and came to America with the settlers. It was first played with the fiddle, which was later replaced by the banjo. According to Morrissey, "Bluegrass is simply the powerful, 'overdrive' music that succeeded Old Time music."

Paul has been interested in Bluegrass music all his life. He met Bob Flescher at a Bluegrass festival in West Virginia in 1967, and they decided to go into business and manufacture their own banjo parts. By 1977, they had decided they knew enough to make their own banjos and Paul left his job as a pipefitter. Bob, who is a pilot for Eastern Airlines, gave up his partnership a couple of years ago, but he still does all the engraving for the company.

Paul is in the banjo business simply because he likes it. He could make more money as a pipefitter, especially since meticulous hand-crafting limits the number of banjos he can sell. However, he enjoys the freedom of an entrepreneur and has a love affair with the banjo. Only two people work for him full time, along with three part timers. He sells about 200 banjos a year. One of his more recent sales was to a German collector, who paid $4,400 for a banjo Paul was exhibiting at the Frankfurt Music Trade Show.

America's Best! BARBECUE

Kreuz Market

208 South Commerce Street
Lockhart, Texas 78644

512-398-2361

Edgar "Smittie" Schmidt, Owner

Monday–Saturday: 7:00 A.M.–
6:00 P.M., closed Sundays and
holidays

Beef, $5.25 per lb.; pork, $5.25
per lb.; sausage, $1 for 5 oz.
ring, $3 per lb.

"It's not what you put into the meat," says Edgar "Smittie" Schmidt, "it's what you leave out of it." He learned his trick-of-the-trade at Kreuz Market in Lockhart, Texas, where he's been cooking up America's best barbecue for forty-five years.

For the past forty-five years, Edgar "Smittie" Schmidt has been cooking up America's best barbecue at Kreuz market in Lockhart, Texas.

Smittie hand-rubs salt and pepper into choice cuts, rolls and ties them in a string net, then stores them overnight in a dry bin. He barbecues brisket, prime rib, loin steak, rounds, loin side, and huge beef shoulder clods over an eighteen-foot-long pit in full view of his customers. Then he serves the meat by the pound, quarter pound, and even in a three-ounce snack size in brown butcher's paper.

You grab some pickled peppers, hot peppers, avocados, tomatoes, and soda or beer, and devour your delicious barbecue feast in what Smittie calls "friendship dining." You sit at long wooden benches and cut your meat with knives tied to the tables. Although Smittie supplies plastic forks, he says "most folks use the forks mother nature gave them."

Smittie also barbecues German sausage. It's 85 percent beef and 15 percent pork, seasoned with black and red pepper, and wrapped in a beef casing. He serves it in five-ounce rings right off the pit.

Altogether, he goes through 6,000 pounds of beef and pork a week.

He cooks over post-oak fires, which yield the special flavor of mesquite and softer oaks but burn slower and more evenly. He uses 175 cords a year, which he has cut in the winter when the sap is in the roots. The wood is drier then; it will cure properly and won't spoil when stored. Since cement and dirt collect moisture that will spoil wood, Smittie stores his supply on gravel lots next to the market.

"Old Man Charlie" Kreuz bought the original butcher shop in 1900 for $5 down and $5 per week. His family later added the barbecue pits and a sausage shop. Smittie started sweeping floors there when he was fifteen, and within a year he was working the pits and butchering. He bought out the Kreuz family in 1948, and expanded the market to two thirds of a city block. J. D. Fullilove, his son-in-law, now manages the market, which is located twenty-nine miles south of Austin on U.S. Highway 183.

America's Best! BATHROOMS

✉

Sherle Wagner International, Inc.

60 East 57th Street
New York, New York 10022

212-879-9398

Sherle Wagner, President

A priceless Renoir, a fireplace, a crystal chandelier, or an Italian marble tub set with lapis lazuli and solid gold fittings—they're not unusual in bathrooms designed by Sherle Wagner International.

Sherle Wagner believes that a bathroom should be as beautiful as it is comfortable and personalized. It should also serve two, three, or more purposes, so he offers an endless selection of sculpted fixtures, wall coverings, and unusual accessories to suit any taste.

Innovations for which Sherle Wagner is responsible are tile murals, washable vinyl wallpaper, which he invented about ten years ago, and the re-introduction of the 18th century *chaise percée* to cover the commode. Sherle Wagner does not sell toilet bowls. "The functional part is very difficult to make, so a few large companies dominate the field. We offer only a decorative covering for standard toilet bowls." His most recent innovation is sculptured hardware of contemporary design.

Wagner advocates placing great works of art in the bathroom, on a rotating basis. "If you're soaking in the tub, what better place to view your art collection?" he says. "People who own masterworks are often too busy to enjoy them, but in the bathroom they will have both the time and the privacy to appreciate them fully."

Because of the moisture the bathroom is also an excellent place to keep many kinds of plants.

The most striking aspect of a Sherle Wagner bathroom is the use of semiprecious stones in the decor. Wagner covers the walls, floors, and fixtures of bathrooms with such beautiful natural materials as malachite, lapis lazuli, tiger's eye, amethyst, rose quartz, rock crystal, and twelve shades of onyx. He imports marble from Greece, Turkey, Italy, Spain, Portugal, Pakistan, and Argentina. A malachite wash basin will cost upwards of $5,000. Basins are also available in gold and platinum plate, standing on marble fluted pedestals. To cover a bathtub with semiprecious stone would cost $30,000, while a full custom-made bathroom can range in price from $20,000 to $500,000. A single six-inch square tile of tiger's eye alone costs $125.

Sherle Wagner has done bathrooms for Arabian palaces with more than thirty bathrooms. The King of Morocco, Princess Grace of Monaco, Marcello Mastroianni, and Johnny Cash are among the luminaries who have beautiful Sherle Wagner baths. One customer built his house around a Sherle Wagner bathroom. Wagner has five bathrooms in his eight-room apartment.

Sherle Wagner's favorite bathroom was designed for a New York executive's Fifth Avenue penthouse. The walls are covered floor to ceiling with mirrors, behind which are hidden exercising equipment, including exercycle, muscle-toning gadgets, and massage table, and eleven-foot ceiling-high compartmentalized closets. The floor is of marble and malachite (white and dark green) in a pattern that blends at one end of the room with a solid malachite counter. The basin and faucets are overlaid with gold. An antique Waterford crystal chandelier and crystal sconces are overhead. The bath itself is a three-tiered step-down marble (almost white) tub with malachite fixtures and a sophisticated temperature control system. Soaps, shampoos, and other bathing needs are kept in rare antique bottles nearby. Behind the bath is the sauna. The main room also serves as a kitchen, office, and study, and the furniture is antique Louis XV, including a chaise longue upholstered with pale green tapestried silk. There is also a switchboard and telephones with direct lines to many parts of the world where the owner has business interests. In a corner, near a flight of marble stairs, is a collection of exotic plants, including orchids—a hobby of the owner. Upstairs is a solarium. This bathroom costs about $100,000, excluding antiques.

A Sherle Wagner bathroom.

Wagner works closely with architects, builders, and designers to create bathrooms that are perfectly suited to the purposes of those who use them, whether they serve as the family breakfast room, or the only place where busy married professionals run into each other at least once or twice a day.

While catering to the highest elite, Sherle Wagner also aims to serve the upper-middle class professional. Those who do not wish to redesign their bathrooms completely can buy a hand-painted museum design washbasin with matching faucets and wallpaper for as little as $600 or $700. Wagner also offers such minor accessories as soap dishes, towel bars, tumblers, waste baskets, drawer pulls, and door knobs. Many Sherle Wagner accessories cost little more than the standard commercial fixtures. But however modest or inexpensive, every accessory is designed to be beautiful. "Why should something have to be ugly, simply because it's functional?" asks Wagner.

With this in mind, Sherle Wagner and his wife Rose began considering the possibilities of "functional sculpture" in 1945 when they were both space engineers. Their first creations were towel rings and bars made of brass in the shape of dolphins. They met with instant success, and have never since had difficulty in selling their products.

For a long time the bathroom has been a drab, utilitarian area, and has been tucked into whatever space is left over when the rest of the building is designed. Sherle Wagner would like to change all that. His products are available in eighteen showrooms in the U.S., as well as in Europe and Asia.

America's Best! BEATEN BISCUITS

Orrell's Maryland Beaten Biscuits

Box 7
Wye Mills, Maryland 21679

301-822-2065

Mrs. Herman Orrell, Owner

Wednesdays–Fridays
95¢ per doz., plus postage and handling

Senator Charles Mathias, Jr., of Maryland believes there isn't a better way to start the day than with a Maryland beaten biscuit, unless it be with more than one. He even declared in the *Congressional Record* that "the beaten biscuit is to Maryland what the crêpe is to France, pasta is to Italy, and matzoh is to Israel."

As often as possible, the Senator travels to the small Chesapeake Bay community of Wye Mills, Maryland, to stock up on his favorite beaten biscuits, those baked in the kitchen of Mrs. Herman Orrell.

Many Maryland connoisseurs prefer these heavy biscuits aged, hard, and cold. In fact, they are usually eaten at room temperature, explains Mrs. Orrell, undisputedly the foremost authority on beaten biscuits. As they age, their smooth exteriors harden, while the insides remain soft and very chewy. Customarily they are split and eaten with country ham and chicken or butter and homemade preserves and jellies. Those uninitiated to the unique taste may prefer to heat them in a slow (about 275 degrees F.) oven for about ten minutes first. These delicacies sometimes are served with melted cheese and sauces to make tasty hors d'oeuvres. They also freeze well. If they harden too much, they can be used as dumplings or ground into crumbs to make breaded pork chops.

Maryland Beaten Biscuits are beaten—traditionally with a wooden mallet or blacksmith's hammer—until the dough blisters and snaps from escaping air. Making them is such hard, time-consuming work that the practice is practically an extinct culinary art. Elbow grease is the main ingredient, accompanied by lard, flour, salt, sugar, and water or milk. Mrs. Orrell admits, however, that the recipe handed down through her family's generations contains "just a pinch of baking powder" for safety's sake. They've been made this way since the days of plantations and manors in southeastern Maryland. Although no one knows for sure, Mrs. Orrell speculates that the beating was adapted from the way local Indians pounded corn.

The Orrells have replaced the blacksmith hammer with a spiked rolling machine, except when they bake their renowned biscuits at craft and artisan fairs. But even with this machine, it takes half an hour to beat a batch of dough. And the remainder of the operation must still be done by hand, including the kneading of each individual biscuit. Another machine was experimented with for this task, but the results weren't satisfactory.

"I don't know of anyone else who makes them themselves," Mrs. Orrell says. She never planned to bake them professionally, either. It happened accidentally. She started baking biscuits for a nearby store to earn some pin money during the Depression, then found herself baking more and more biscuits to meet the demand. Her popularity grew without advertising, and in 1967 biscuit baking officially became a part-time business.

The ovens are heated only on Wednesdays, Thursdays, and Fridays, when Mrs. Orrell, her husband, daughter-in-law, granddaughter, and several other women go to work to bake a total of 250 dozen biscuits each of these days.

They distribute the biscuits to selected stores and clubs throughout Maryland. The only shop carrying them that's not in the state is just over the line in Washington, D.C. But Marylanders residing elsewhere across the country and even as far away as Canada and Paris mail order their Orrell's biscuits, which are shipped the same day they are baked.

America's Best! BLOCKHEADS

Blockheads Woodcarving
   Company

P.O. Box 3
Pollock Pines, California 95726

916-644-3629

David & Iris Mae Cawthorn,
   Proprietors

David and Iris Cawthorn are the only people in America who are carrying on the great old tradition of the Cigar Store Indian.

In the days of wooden ships, a beautifully carved wooden figurehead on the bow brought good luck to the sailors and assured their safe return to port. In the late 19th century, with the advent of steel-hulled ships, the wood carvers moved inland and began making wooden statues to serve as commercial signs for those customers who couldn't read. Wooden Indians stood outside tobacco shops because the Indians had introduced the early settlers to the pleasures of tobacco. A statue of a man in a top hat and black suit coat, named Jim Dandy, stood outside theatres to let you know that this was the place to have a good time.

For years, these figures sat in museums as representatives of a lost craft. But in 1973, Iris set about reviving this aspect of Americana. Now she and her apprentice husband David Cawthorn are busy creating blockheads (wood sculptures carved out of a single log) ranging in height from one foot to seven feet that represent everything from the traditional Indian and Peg-leg Sea Captain to Joggers and Musclemen. Priced from $90 for the simpler ones

34

to $2,000 for the tallest and most detailed, each blockhead is a unique work of art with a striking personality.

Since 1973, David and Iris have made over 600 blockheads. Living in the midst of a pine forest, they buy their wood for $75 per cord and have it delivered in a firewood truck. "We don't do the logging ourselves, because Iris's hands are too valuable to get hurt," explains David.

Working with freshly cut 500-pound logs of Ponderosa pine, red alder, cedar, or redwood, Iris begins cutting while the wood is still "wet" (full of sap and water), because it is softer and easier to work with then. She starts with a twenty-six-inch gasoline chain saw. David only works on the smaller figures, while Iris does the life-size ones.

After blocking out the general proportions of the body with the chain saw, Iris does the detailed work with mallets and chisels, using over twenty separate tools. You have to be extremely careful, warns David, who works on faces as well, "because one wrong stroke with the mallet can knock off the whole nose."

After carving, the blockheads have to be dried. In the summer, Iris and David place them in the sun, and in the winter they put them next to a wood stove. While drying, the carving cracks a little. "Cracks and grain are part of the characteristic beauty of wood," says Iris. "But we're careful not to let it crack down the front of the carving."

The Cawthorns finish the sculptures with a coating of oil to preserve the natural appearance of the wood, or paint them in appropriate colors. Some of Iris and David's best works include a six-foot Saint Francis of Assisi, holding a bird in his hands and with a deer lying at his feet. He's made of redwood, with a natural finish, and was commissioned by the redwood park "Trees of Mystery" in Klamath, California. They have also carved a seven-foot strongman for Bob's Olympic Club in Eureka. His name is Arnold Schwarzenegger, "but we only used Arnold as the model for the body—the head is Bob's," explains David. A pair of block-heads, Laurel and Hardy, were sold on the game show *The Price is Right*, but none of the contestants could imagine how much such an unusual item should cost. David and Iris have also made cowboys, miners, fishermen, and mermaids, and they're contemplating a likeness of Johnny Carson.

When Iris was twenty-five, she worked in a mill separating knots of wood from chopped-up bark (for gardening use). A friend who was moving gave her a set of carving tools, and she began toying with them, using the burlier knots as her raw material, and made wooden cups, bowls, chopsticks, and soapdishes just for fun. Then another friend asked her if she could make a fireman. She tried it, because her own father was a fireman. She traded her first figure for some work on her car.

She met David in 1974, when he hired her to help with deliveries for his produce company in Eureka. Soon David, who had once worked making furniture, became Iris's apprentice and sold his company to make blockheads. They were married in September, 1977.

Iris's dream is to set up "a little park somewhere up in the mountains where the trees are, where people could come and have lunch and see our carvings on display," perhaps also a museum where old carvings would be exhibited. Iris would also like to carve an ornate circus wagon, load it up with their blockheads, and go on the road.

America's Best! BLUEBERRIES

Wild Maine Lowbush **Blueberries**	*Green Point Farms* *Dresden, Maine 04342*
Vaccinium lamarckii	*207-737-2246*
The Union Blueberry Festival and *Agricultural Fair* *Union, Maine*	*Maine Blueberry Recipes* *Cooperative Extension Service* *University of Maine, Orono 04473*

Blueberries are America's second favorite berry (the less versatile strawberry is more popular). America's best blueberries are the small, sweet, wild Lowbush variety, and Maine produces more of them than any other state in the nation.

Blueberries love the short growing season and the acid soil of New England. They usually have a better taste toward the northern limits of their growing area, where the days are long and the nights are cool during the ripening season. They also grow abundantly on hills near bodies of water. That's why Union, in the hill country of Maine, with six lakes and ponds within its borders, is America's blueberry capital. Union people celebrate this occasion each year during the Agricultural Fair (the last full week in August) with a Blueberry Festival (Friday), featuring a blueberry pancake breakfast, free miniature blueberry pies, pie-eating contests, and even a Blueberry Queen.

Maine Blueberries are one of the very few wild crops left in America. The Lowbush blueberry plants are only six to eighteen inches high, and they simply can't cope with competing weeds or taller shrubbery, which crowd the plants or cast a shade on them. That's why in Maine, where there are over 150,000 acres of blueberry barrens, the fields are burnt over during the spring while the ground is still wet. This process is performed with machines that use oil or liquefied petroleum gas, and it eliminates weeds and underbrush, and prunes the blueberry bushes.

The wild fruit ripens in July and August, and harvesting extends into September. The berries range in color from light blue to black. Some have a grey powdery appearance, others a dark sheen. Most of the crop is frozen, while the rest is canned. Very few are sold fresh.

The best places to look for blueberries are burnt-over places with some low brush, or the edges of scrub-pine groves. Some people like to search under power lines because birds perch on them, and they carry blueberry seeds with them. Most of the berries are on the underside of the bushes. Green Point Farms in Dresden, Maine (one of the few farms that let you pick your own) will provide you with a blueberry rake, and charge you only 40¢ a pound for wild blueberries (they also have cultivated ones for $1 a quart). Their season is very short, only about a week at the beginning of August.

Among berries, blueberries have the most Vitamin A, and they also contain Vitamin C, calcium, magnesium, phosphorus, potassium, and iron. A cup of blueberries contains only eighty-five calories.

Serve blueberries plain, on ice cream, or with a light dusting of sugar and cinnamon. One New England favorite is a Nantucket recipe for brandied blueberries. For more staid suggestions, check out the University of Maine's booklet, *Maine Blueberry Recipes*.

America's Best! BOTANICAL GARDEN

Missouri Botanical Garden

*2101 Tower Grove Avenue
St. Louis, Missouri 63110*

314-772-7600

*Thomas Smith, President, Board
of Trustees*

Dr. Peter Raven, Director

*Nancy von Brecht, Public
Relations Office*

*April–October: 9:00 A.M.–
6:00 P.M.; November–March:
9:00 A.M.–5:00 P.M.; closed
Christmas Day; adults, $2.50;
children 6–16, $1; under 6, free
(Includes all displays,
greenhouses, gardens)*

When Henry Shaw planned his botanical garden in the middle of the 19th century, he envisioned a showcase that would, like his plants, continue to grow and flourish. It has done just that, and today the Missouri Botanical Garden is America's best.

The Scented Garden is a remarkable feature of the Garden. Plantings, including herbs and plants that are highly textured and have pronounced fragrances, are grouped for their smell and touch. All the plants are labelled in print as well as in braille.

The Climatron, built in 1959, is a ½-acre geodesic dome under which lies a lush tropical paradise filled with banana, hibiscus, fuchsia, bird of paradise, and over 1,600 other species of plants. An aquatunnel takes you on an underwater tour of a tropical pond.

Only a few yards south of this steamy setting lies the Desert House. The peculiar life of the plants here attests to the rugged conditions under which they are forced to survive.

The recently opened Japanese Garden depicts an ancient landscape never before seen on such a large scale in this country. Highlights include a four-acre lake, a miniaturized landscape of bluffs, three islands, two waterfalls, "dry gardens," and a delicate teahouse.

In the Mediterranean House, olive, henna, fig, and grape species grow in an atmospheric greenhouse appointed with cobblestone paths, white stuccoed walls, a grape arbor, and a small pool. It is the only greenhouse in America devoted exclusively to species endemic to the Mediterranean region.

The Climatron is a ½-acre geodesic dome.

The Gladney Rose Garden and the expansive Anne L. Lehmann rose garden contain over 500 rose bushes. An English Woodland Garden in the elegant 19th century style of "carefully planned spontaneity" contains two acres of shade trees and lovely meandering paths bordered by boxwoods and azaleas.

The Garden's herbarium and library are housed in the glass-enclosed John S. Lehmann Building. The herbarium is a library for pressed and dried plants. Over three million specimens have been catalogued, including those discovered by such noted explorers as Charles Darwin and Captain John C. Fremont. The library includes over 300,000 pieces of bound and unbound literature.

The Garden's research has gained worldwide recognition. Researchers are currently categorizing plants from Panama and Colombia, and the Garden has been endorsed as the main repository for African plants in the U.S. Researchers here discovered the creosoting process used to preserve wood on such items as telephone poles.

The Garden is strongly committed to preserving the historic legacy of Henry Shaw. In fact, St. Louisans still affectionately refer to the Garden as "Shaw's Garden." Born in 1800, Shaw had earned enough money by the time he was forty to retire and devote him-

Banana, hibiscus, and other tropical plants thrive at the Garden.

self to his first love, botany. The site he chose was a dusty farm an hour's buggy ride from the city. Today the Garden occupies seventy-nine acres in the very heart of St. Louis.

Shaw's Linnean House, the oldest continuously operated greenhouse west of the Mississippi, is filled with ninety varieties of camellias, Shaw's favorite flower. His country home, Tower Grove House, has been preserved in all its Victorian splendor. It too is open to the public.

America's Best! BOUILLABAISSE ORLEANS

Maison Pierre

430 Rue Dauphine
New Orleans, Louisiana 70112

504-529-5521

Pierre Lacoste, Owner

Dinner: 6:00 P.M.–midnight,
closed Monday and Tuesday

Pierre Lacoste, owner of Maison Pierre in New Orleans, is the first to proclaim that his Bouillabaisse Orleans is America's best. The gregarious Monsieur Lacoste is very particular about this dish, which he describes as "a very simple seafood stew, a peasant dish from France—not leftovers, but a variety of fish available in this area." Lacoste's bouillabaisse is different from the Mediterranean bouillabaisse in his choice of fish and spices. (Bouillabaisse Marseille, to be authentic, must contain *rascasse*, a rockfish found only in the Mediterranean. Any *chef marseillais* will sternly tell you, "*La rascasse, sans elle pas de bouillabaisse!*") He even runs his own fish institute to produce fresh seafood for the restaurant and to develop seafood not on the commercial market.

Aside from the more common shrimp, oysters, crab, trout, squid, and redfish, Lacoste uses shark, conch, and stingray (known by locals as "ray"). The institute has its own boats to catch all the fish, so Lacoste doesn't need to use frozen varieties.

Bouillabaisse, which means "quick boil," is fairly simple to prepare, yet Maison Pierre takes painstaking efforts to bring each serving of the stew to perfection. The herbs and seasonings, such as garlic, onions, tomato, olive oil, bay leaf, thyme, and saffron, are first sautéed. Then the stock is added. This ingredient is the most important factor, as it contains all the most potent flavors gleaned from various cooked foods. The seafoods go in last, depending on which cooks the quickest.

For serving, the seafood is removed from the broth and put in a chafing dish. The broth is placed in a sauce container, and served on a rechauffée with the assortment of seafood. This is presented to the customer, and then served individually from the chafing dish and saucepot with garlic croutons and ailloli (pronounced A-YŌ-LEE), a mayonnaise-like sauce made with garlic, olive oil, coarse salt, and lemon juice. The 19th-century Provençal poet Frederic

Mistral wrote of ailloli: "In its essence is concentrated the strength and joy of the Provençal sun."

Maison Pierre is located in an old house and seats seventy-eight. Reservations stream in from as far away as Mexico, New York, California, and Hawaii. A superlative herb gumbo and black bean soup are also specialties of the house.

America's Best! BREAD PUDDING

The Bon Ton Restaurant

401 Magazine Street
New Orleans, Louisiana 70130

504-524-3386, 523-8419

Alvin, Wayne, and Debbie Pierce,
Proprietors

Monday–Friday: lunch, 11:00
A.M.–2:00 P.M.; dinner,
5:00 P.M.–9:30 P.M.

Reservations for dinner

One customer flies from Mississippi to New Orleans for a taste of the Bon Ton's bread pudding! It's been featured in eighteen magazines, and one recipe has appeared in *Gourmet* magazine at least three times.

Proprietor Alvin Pierce describes his bread pudding as a traditional dish from the Cajun country, a province with French influences. He is from an area called Bayou Lafourche near Thibodaux, forty miles west of New Orleans, where bread pudding is a special holiday treat. In Pierce's youth, during the Depression, it was also an economy dish made from stale bread. Today it still sells for only $1 a serving.

The Cajuns could not get to New Orleans for liquor, so they made do with the local bourbon and bathtub gin. Though it is claimed that the Bon Ton's is the only bread pudding on which you can actually get drunk, Pierce defends his recipe: "People think we load it up with bourbon, but the truth is we preserve the flavor of the bourbon during the preparation." He actually only uses two ounces of whiskey per fifteen servings.

The Bon Ton's recipe for bread pudding calls for crusty French bread. The secret is in the special sauce that Pierce's wife created. The whiskey is added to a mixture of sugar and butter (called creamed sugar), and beaten egg. This mixture is cooled first, which is one way of preserving the whiskey flavor. If the whiskey is added to a hot mixture, the flavor will dissipate, leaving only an alcohol taste. The sauce is mixed with the pudding just before serving; if it is added earlier, the bourbon, the lightest ingredient in the recipe, will be absorbed by the pudding. The pudding and sauce are mixed in individual dessert dishes under the flame of a broiler for about five minutes. This preserves the flavor of the bourbon.

The Bon Ton also serves several other incomparable dishes including Gumbo, Crab Imperial, Crayfish Etouffé, and Cubes of Beef Sautéed in Red Wine with Mushrooms. Some Bon Ton customers have been known to eat as many as five helpings of bread pudding. Eighty percent of the clientele is comprised of locals, any one of whom would agree that the bread pudding alone is worth a visit to the Bon Ton.

America's Best! BROWNIES

Rosie's, Inc.

243 Hampshire Street
Cambridge, Massachusetts 02139

617-491-9488

Judy Rosenberg, President

The first recorded brownie was created in Boston, and the first brownie recipe was offered in the Boston-oriented, 1896 edition of *Fannie Farmer's Cookbook*. Today, 1,500 Bostonians are treated each week to America's best brownies, home-baked in Cambridge, Massachusetts, and offered by Rosie's, Inc.

Proprietor Judy Rosenberg began her "brownie-baking" career

on Valentine's Day 1975, baking in her home kitchen amid scorching ninety degree heat. After years of experimentation at home, she started to sell her treats at the Orson Welles Cinema in Cambridge.

Judy closely oversees the entire brownie-making process to be sure that only the best chocolate, eggs, Grade A butter, sugar, and flour are used. "The taste of a good brownie should be chocolatey, not sweet, while the texture should be moist, not dry and crumbly," says Judy. "Each brownie should reveal two distinct tones of color—a light, shiny, cocoa color on top where it has been most exposed to the heat, and a deep brown color inside where moisture has been retained. Watch out for a brownie that is solid black or brown. It either lacks the proper ingredients or is definitely overbaked."

While all of her brownies are good, *The Harvard Square*, a classic chocolate walnut brownie, is the best and costs only 75¢.

Other, more exotic brownie creations included within the daily batch of 200 are:

> *The Chocolate Orgasm* (75¢)—an incredibly fudgey brownie with a rich and creamy frosting;
>
> *Boom Booms* (75¢)—chocolate brownie marbled with cream cheese;
>
> *The Congo Square* (75¢)—a butterscotch brownie made with chocolate chips and nuts that melts in your mouth; Rosie's bestseller.

Regardless of the type, all brownies are fattening (each one is approximately 300 calories), and Judy doesn't recommend more than one a week (she rarely has one). They are especially good with copious quantities of ice cold milk, and The Harvard Square is delicious with a scoop of vanilla ice cream.

A good brownie will easily last for a week or longer. In fact, brownies are best when they are eaten the day after baking, once the flavor has had time to emerge. Beyond a day, though, they should be kept air-tight or refrigerated and warmed before serving.

Judy is constantly experimenting with new concoctions, and is also developing an organic line, but flour and sugar are essential ingredients in the brownie and always will be. "They should be maintained," says Judy, "because they are classic components that can never be duplicated."

When asked whether non-Americans might appreciate brownies more than natives, Judy pondered the idea of opening a bakery in Europe. "An American Brownie in Paris—it'd blow their soufflé-bent minds!"

America's Best! BUS

✉

Executive Suite	312-427-9400
Keeshin Charter Service 705 South Jefferson Street Chicago, Illinois 60607	Paul A. Keeshin, President Rental: 5 hours (minimum), $500; 12-hour day, $800

The *Executive Suite* is a plush traveling conference room, a home away from home, and occasionally a floating gourmet restaurant. Strikingly appointed in complementary earth tones, the bus comes equipped with washrooms decorated in snakeskin design, a dressing room, and a complete kitchen.

The *Executive Suite*, with all the comforts of a private club and seating for twenty-one people, has been chartered by Jackie Gleason, who used the bus for his dressing room while performing in Chicago, the Harlem Globetrotters, and rock stars Elton John and Neil Diamond. One board chairman chartered the *Executive Suite* to take a party to the Indianapolis 500 for the weekend. The Western Open Golf Association uses the bus for transportation during its famous tournament.

Custom Coach Corporation, of Columbus, Ohio, builds about forty *Executive Suites* a year for $200,000 to $250,000 each. (A standard bus currently retails for about $100,000.) The buses use diesel fuel and have a 1,000-mile cruising range. Keeshin was the first charter outfit to buy a bus. Custom sells mostly to big corporations. Chicago millionaire Ray Kroc, founder of McDonald's, owns twenty-one "Big Mac Buses," comprising the largest executive bus fleet in the world. They are used for promotions, executive

The *Executive Suite:* **All the comforts of a private club.**

meetings, and community-relations activities, like hauling scouts to camp.

"It's the natural adjunct to the corporate jet. The *Executive Suite* fills the void between the airport and the boardroom. Its best feature is that it is so conducive to getting work done," says Paul Keeshin, the creator and designer of the *Executive Suite.* Paul, whose father founded the Keeshin Charter Company in 1912, began with the simple idea that the coach would allow executives time to hold meetings en route to their destination. Keeshin's service now boasts twenty buses and brings in annual revenues of just under $2,000,000.

Chicago restaurateur Nick Nicholas rented the *Executive Suite* on its debut. He used the coach for a lavish dinner party. The menu included champagne and caviar, served at the base of the Wrigley Building. Said one guest, "At first I thought, 'oh God, a bus!' until I saw what was inside. Then, I didn't want to get off!"

America's Best! BUTCHER SHOP

✉

M. Lobel & Sons, Inc.

1096 Madison Avenue
New York, New York 10028

212-737-1372

Stanley and Leon Lobel,
  Proprietors

When M. Lobel & Sons, Inc. opened on stylish Madison Avenue in 1954, the neighbors sneered. But now they vie with each other for the privilege of having a Lobel's charge account. (The Lobels allow credit to only 800 customers, and there is a six- to twelve-month waiting list of about 1,000 people at all times.)

The hallmark of M. Lobel & Sons, Inc. is the original cuts of meat. Some of these spectacular achievements have been documented on network TV and in national newspapers and magazines. They include a prime shell of beef prepared to look like a filet mignon, and boned stuffed capons that reassume their natural form and can be sliced like roast beef. On special occasions, such as Valentine's Day, the Lobels prepare special cuts like heart-shaped steaks.

When Jacqueline Onassis' cook quit on the day of a dinner party, the Lobels whipped up chicken paprika. It won rave reviews, and initiated a new aspect of service in their business. Now, many customers ask the Lobels not only to cut their meat, but to prepare it for special functions. For those who want to be chefs themselves, the Lobels are still willing to give special instructions regarding seasoning and cooking time for a particular piece of meat.

The Lobels have also shared their knowledge in the form of books. *Meat* contains 375 recipes and general information about buying, storing, and preparing meat. *All About Meat* has 100 recipes and very specific details about packaging, freezing, cutting, and serving meat. Now, the Lobels are about to publish two more books, *In Praise of Meat* and *Encyclopedia of Meat*.

Leon and Stanley are really "meat dealers," not butchers. M. Lobel & Sons, Inc. offers any meat specialty at the Madison

47

Stanley and Leon Lobel are fourth-generation butchers.

Avenue shop. A trio of steer, six dozen or more shell strips of beef, and perhaps a lamb are in full view at all times. You'll also find quail and pheasant grown on private preserves, venison in the fall, spring lamb at Easter time, calf's liver with a lucid skin that slices like butter, and such exotic meats as wild boar, hippopotamus, and llama.

Five days a week, at 3:00 or 4:00 A.M., one of the Lobels goes to several wholesale markets to examine hundreds of pieces of meat. They usually buy 2,000 to 3,000 pounds of beef, veal, pork, and lamb each day. Sometimes, however, they do not choose to buy any at all, being dissatisfied with the quality of the available meat. No seafood is sold.

The Lobels age their beef for four to six weeks, and veal or lamb for a week. The meat is put into a dry refrigerated room where the body moisture is lost, leaving only the natural juices and causing the meat to shrink. This makes the meat much more tender and flavorful. The process is entirely natural, employing no salts, chemicals, or tenderizing agents. In fact, the Lobels have invented a way to age meat in forty-eight to seventy-two hours, as well as defrost it, and are planning to make the process available for home use.

The Lobels guarantee their meat unconditionally. If a regular customer, even after cooking and eating the meat, is dissatisfied with its quality, his money will be refunded or the meat replaced. A less regular customer may be required to bring back a portion of the unsatisfactory product. They charge twelve to fifteen percent more than other butchers, but customers don't mind. "It's like going into Tiffany's—you know very well that you're going to get a flawless, high-quality product," Stanley explains coolly.

The brothers have recently found time to start a Steak-of-the-Month-Club, which provides gift steaks twelve times a year for their special clientele. In the future, they envision a larger establishment where customers would be escorted, in white aprons, into the freezing room to select their own cuts.

Stanley and Leon bring four generations of experience to their trade. Their great grandfather was a cattle farmer in Austria (and mayor of his town) in the 19th century. Their father, Morris, brought the family meat business to America, opening a shop in Boston in 1903, then moving to Manhattan in the '30s.

Marilyn Monroe was one of the Lobels' first "name" customers. Now they serve any number of well known people. In fact, when the British royal family visits New York, the Queen's chef shops at Lobel's.

America's Best! CABERNET SAUVIGNON

Heitz Cellars Martha's Vineyard

707-963-3542

Joseph Heitz, President

Heitz Wine Cellars
500 Taplin Road
Saint Helena, California 94574

At a recent wine tasting of Cabernets from the 1968 California vintage, tasters for *The San Diego Grapevine* awarded Heitz Martha's Vineyard Cabernet Sauvignon seven out of eleven first-place votes. The wine was said to have "beautiful color," "a complex, earthy, minty nose," and "immense fruit and tannin." The wine has won comparative tastings against Chateau Lafitte-Rothschild and Chateau Mouton Rothschild, as well as other famous Bordeaux wines.

Andre Tchelistcheff, legendary California wine maker, ranks Joe Heitz among those "truly inspired individuals who treat every bottle as though it were a beautiful lady." Heitz consistently produces a Cabernet Sauvignon of the finest quality. He was the first vintner in California to put the vineyard source on the label. The reasons for the success of the Martha's Vineyard are quite simple. The ground is perfect for growing grapes and the clone Heitz uses grows exceptionally well.

For proper tasting of the Martha's Vineyard, Joe Heitz says, "Let it breathe in the glass, twirl it so that the air mixes with the glass of wine. But don't refrigerate it. The wine should be served at room temperature. If it's too cool, warm it in the glass with your hand." He chooses the years '68, '69, '73, and '74 as the peak years from his Martha's Vineyard Cabernet.

It takes four years to make a bottle of Martha's Vineyard Cabernet Sauvignon. In the fifth year, half of the inventory of Martha's Vineyard is available for sale. The wine is modestly priced when first introduced, and as the wine ages and improves the price rises. Heitz's Martha's Vineyard Cabernet might cost more than $50 per bottle in the last year of release, when only thirty cases are left.

Heitz has been running his vineyard since 1961. He began making Martha's Vineyard Cabernet in 1965, when he bought grapes from Tom and Martha May (Mrs. May is the vineyard's namesake). He has kept his operation small, so he's personally familiar with every drop of wine in every cask. Everybody at the winery is involved in each phase of the wine making, from crushing and fermenting to racking, washing barrels, and filtering. Heitz, his son, and his wife frequently taste each of the wines.

The reputation of California wines has soared in recent years due to a massive amount of research in all facets of the wine industry. Heitz need not advertise, as there are 300 shops on his waiting list in California alone. He has a 7,000-name mailing list and a tasting and sales room. Here you can have a free sample of some of Heitz's wines, though the Martha's Vineyard Cabernet is opened only on February 1, the traditional release date for each vintage.

America's Best! CALLIGRAPHER

Thomas Ingmire

Scriptorium St. Francis
845 Lombard
San Francisco, California 94133

415-673-4938

Tuesday–Thursday: 11:00 A.M.–
7:00 P.M.; *Friday:* 11:00 A.M.–
5:00 P.M.; *Saturday:* 9:00 A.M.–
5:00 P.M.

Calligraphers recognize thirty-seven-year-old Thomas Ingmire as the best known American calligrapher. No other U.S. calligrapher can approach his techniques of gilding and illuminating. He now ranks with famous contemporary calligraphers such as England's Donald Jackson, Germany's Herman Zapf, and Austria's Friedrich Neugebauer.

A native Indianan, Tom went to San Francisco in 1969 to study landscape architecture at Berkeley. He enrolled in a four-week afternoon calligraphy course at the Berkeley Arts and Crafts Co-op in 1972, then participated in a week-long workshop in Santa Cruz, which proved to be the turning point in his career.

Donald Jackson, official scribe of Queen Elizabeth (a post not particularly remunerative and taken primarily for the title), conducted the workshop, and emphasized his specialty, the revival of the historic side of the craft—working with the traditional techniques, tools, and materials such as vellum and quills. By the end of the course, Tom and Donald Jackson had developed a firm friendship. Each summer, when Jackson returned to the U.S. to teach classes, Tom enrolled.

As Tom studied with Jackson, he became more and more in-

51

ME THE LEGENDS

Thomas Ingmire's edition of *The Kakevala.*

terested in calligraphy and less interested in landscape architecture. He devoted half of his time to his architecture firm and half to calligraphy jobs. In 1974, he left the firm to work as a planning consultant and as a calligraphy instructor. In 1975, he decided to make his living at calligraphy—he taught classes, took on commercial jobs, and demonstrated calligraphy at fairs.

Ultimately, in 1977, Donald Jackson sponsored Tom's application to the Society of Scribes and Illuminators in England. When the sixty members of the selective organization convened in November, Tom was elected a craftsman of the Society of Scribes and Illuminators by a unanimous vote. He was the first American to be so honored.

Like Donald Jackson, Tom uses traditional tools and materials such as quills and vellum. He buys his goose and turkey feathers from a New York feather merchant and orders his vellum from England.

After he prepares the quills and vellum, Tom makes his ink. He uses a Chinese stick ink, which he buys in San Francisco's Chinatown. The sticks are about six inches long and one inch in diameter. They last for years. The best ones have a sheen and are very black.

Tom estimates the time a job will take and charges an hourly rate of $25. Costly materials such as vellum and gold are charged separately. Tom's most frequent request is for wedding invitations. He does an original and then has a printer do it in quantity. One of his more unusual requests was from a man who sold gold. He ordered 100 business cards made on vellum with a raised, gilded AU (the chemical symbol for gold) and rich blue calligraphy. The businessman disappeared without paying—leaving a bill of $1500— and Tom hasn't seen him since.

Tom's goal is to do fewer commercial jobs and to work on his own calligraphy as an art form. He recently calligraphed individually the 200 books of a limited edition of the Psalms of David. He illuminated five letters in each book in gold and three colors. No contemporary calligrapher has done this sort of work, although it was a traditional task for calligraphers during the early days of printing.

In the U.S., the best collection of calligraphy accessible to the public is the Harrison Collection of the San Francisco Public Library. San Franciscan Richard Harrison started collecting calligraphy in the 1950s, when calligraphers practically gave their work away. Many pieces which cost Harrison $15 or $20 are now worth over $300. The Harrison Collection contains work of the best calligraphers of the period, especially British calligraphers. Harrison is still collecting and donating calligraphy to the library. Among his recent purchases have been works of Thomas Ingmire.

America's Best! CANOE

✉ _____

L. L. Bean, Inc.	*Leon Gorman, President*
Freeport, Maine 04033	*7 days a week, 24 hours a day*
207-865-3111	*American Express, Visa, Master Charge*

_____

When Leon Gorman, grandson of L. L. Bean and president of L. L. Bean, Inc., decided to market a canoe, he made several excursions to the Maine lakes to determine what type of canoe his customers would want. The result is the Touring Canoe, which is

53

suitable for fishing, touring, and shooting the rapids, and performs just as well on rivers as it does on lakes.

Built by Mad River Canoes of Waitsfield, Vermont, according to Bean's specifications, the Touring Canoe is available only at L. L. Bean. The sixteen-foot model is fifteen-inches deep and has a beam of thirty-five inches; it sells for $580. The eighteen-foot model is fourteen-inches deep and has a beam of thirty-seven inches; it sells for $665.

The canoe is a multilaminar construction of indestructible Royalex rubber and has an inner core of naturally buoyant foam. Only a few things might destroy Royalex—slamming into a rock at the bottom of a waterfall is one. The canoe is covered with vinyl inside and out.

The V-shaped hull tracks well on windy lakes and maneuvers quickly in rivers, and the low-profile bow doesn't catch the wind. The canoe performs well in white water because of its enlarged gunwale (a wooden splash rail) and special splash guards at bow and stern. These exclusive features keep the water outside the canoe. The gunwale is also perforated on the inner side, so that water taken in can be disposed of without completely upending the canoe. Another unique feature is an extra rear thwart that is perfectly situated for poling (in areas like swamps where the shallow water makes it difficult to handle a paddle).

The canoe has great control and balance. The recessed seats, a Mad River exclusive, lower the center of gravity, making the canoe less "tippy." They can adjust forward and back, and are made of cane so that you don't end up sitting in a puddle, a common problem with solid seats. The canoe is also easy to stand up in, for poling or fishing, and the inside is coated with a slip-resistant paint. There are carrying handles built onto the ends, so the canoe carries easily. It is also sturdy enough to accept a small outboard motor.

The great advantage of canoeing is that you can reach areas that few people ever get to. If you ask a Downeaster where the best canoeing areas are, he'll tell you Maine. Outside Maine, you can find beautiful canoeing waters in Virginia, the Carolinas, and Georgia.

Leon L. Bean was born in 1872, and began making his Maine Hunting Shoe, Bean's most famous product, in 1912, right across the street from the present location. The store never closes, a tradition that Mr. Bean began because he was bothered at all hours of the night by hunters who wanted to buy ammunition and other provisions. He decided, therefore, to hire a staff and keep the store open all night. Now L. L. Bean employs 750 workers, including those who work in the plant where, among other leather goods, the Maine Hunting Shoe is still made. Annual sales for L. L. Bean exceed $75 million.

America's Best! CHAMPAGNE

Schramsberg Blanc de Blancs

Schramsberg Vineyards
Schramsberg Road
Calistoga, Napa Valley,
California 94515

707-942-4558

Jack and Jamie Davies,
Proprietors

Schramsberg

NAPA VALLEY
CHAMPAGNE
BLANC DE NOIRS

PRODUCED AND BOTTLED BY
SCHRAMSBERG VINEYARDS
CALISTOGA, CALIFORNIA

VINTAGE 1974

ALCOHOL 12.5% BY VOLUME
CONTENTS 750 MLS

Gerald Ford served Schramsberg wines to Giscard d'Estaing, Queen Elizabeth, and the Emperor of Japan. Jimmy Carter has poured them for Marshal Tito and Mexico's Echeverría Alvarez. President Nixon took Schramsberg champagne to China for his famous toast with Chou En-lai.

Jack Davies makes his distinguished champagne at Schramsberg Vineyards in Calistoga, California, by the time-honored and costly *méthode champenoise.* For the second fermentation, which provides the champagne bubbles, he stacks thousands of heavy bottles on top of another. Then, the meticulous aging and riddling operation begins.

Riddling is the classic way to make champagne brilliantly clear. When the champagne is aged long enough and has collected a heavy coat of dust and mold, the rows of bottles are unstacked and individually shaken by hand in order to stir up the yeasty sediment. (Aging on the yeast is a key to champagne complexity.) The bottles are then placed in riddling racks, and each day for four to six weeks, a strong-wristed man deftly turns each bottle, as many as 50,000 bottles per day, a sixth to an eighth of a turn. The bottles are also tipped slowly into a vertical position. The object is to get the yeast to drift into the neck of the bottle.

When the riddling is finished, all the bottles are again moved by hand, upside down, to an icy bath, where the neck is immersed so the wine inside freezes.

A brave soul then pops each cork. (Internal bottle pressure is at 100 psi—pounds per square inch.) The yeast sediment contained in the frozen wine within the neck of the bottle is blown out when the cork is removed, and the bottle is quickly filled with additional wine and corked. The cork is wired down, the metal foil placed over it, and *voilà*—another bottle of America's best champagne.

There is no law in California specifying the grape varieties to be used for sparkling wine, but Schramsberg uses Chardonnay and Pinot Noir grapes, as do the French, for Blanc de Blancs and Blanc de Noir. In most years, Chardonnay is the most expensive wine grape. Pinot Noir is the most difficult to work with. But they impart special character to the wines of Schramsberg.

"Sparkling wines can be the most interesting of wine styles," says Jack Davies. "At Schramsberg, we are not seeking to create a 'sparkling white burgundy' of our Chardonnay. Instead, we're looking for a wine all our own, a complex, balanced, pleasing wine that can be furnished as a delicate, crisp accompaniment to certain foods."

Since there is no "champagne for all seasons," Schramsberg has developed a group of four champagnes, with totally different blends, to complement various moments of entertaining or dining. They are:

    Blanc de Blancs—made from Chardonnay and Pinot Blanc grapes, primarily the former, a very dry wine, of complex flavor and medium body, which develops greatly with added bottle age; excellent as an apéritif or with seafood, soups, poultry, or sautée dishes; approximately $11.50 retail, $18 in restaurants;

    Blanc de Noir—the most traditional of true champagne styles; from the free-run juice of Pinot Noir grapes, blended with Chardonnay; a dry, rich champagne, heavy in body; ages well

Schramsberg cellars cut deep into the hills of the Napa Valley.

into a full, complex wine; approximately $12.95 retail, $22 in restaurants;

Cuvée de Gamay—delicate salmon in color, medium-bodied, dry and fruity; from the free-run of the Napa Gamay grapes, blended with Pinot Noir grapes; recommended for apéritif, and with pasta, richer seafood dishes, game, or fruit; approximately $9.95 retail, $15 in restaurants;

Cremant—Schramsberg's unique dessert champagne; produced principally from the aromatic Flora variety grapes; bottle-fermented to about one-half standard effervescence; a *cremant* (creaming) wine; finished *demi sec* to accompany sweet dishes; approximately $9.95 retail, $15 in restaurants.

Jack and Jamie Davies first saw the Schramsberg property in the summer of 1964 when they were attending a wine-tasting feast in the Napa Valley. Jack had been developing plans for a small, specialized winery. The Schramsberg site, named after wine-making pioneer Jacob Schram, was in disrepair, but boasted good hillside potential and even underground caves dug a hundred years earlier by Chinese workers. The Davies bought Schramsberg and produced only 200 cases of champagne from the first harvest in 1965. Schramsberg now produces about 12,000 cases a year.

Schramsberg Champagne is not readily available. Only selected distributors are appointed to supply it to various regions of the country. What's more, distributors tend to ration their supply to retailers, hotels, and restaurants.

Jack Davies is more concerned with quality than quantity. Now that Schramsberg is well established, he can concentrate on fine-tuning the vineyards, growing better grapes and harvesting them at their very best balance, and blending better cuvées.

America's Best! CHEERLEADERS

Dallas Cowboys Cheerleaders, Inc.

6116 North Central Expressway
Dallas, Texas 75206

214-369-8000

Tex Schramm, President &
General Manager
Suzanne Mitchell, Vice-President
& Director
Clint Murchison, Owner, Dallas
Cowboys Football Club

Suzanne Mitchell, outspoken and protective director of the Dallas Cowboys Cheerleaders, will warn you never to call her girls the Dallas Cowgirls. "That's a gimmick stuck on us by the media, which have given us an image based on sex appeal. That's not it at all! Our reason for existence is the Dallas Cowboys, so we carry their name up front!"

The Dallas Cowboys Cheerleaders are famed as the most beautiful, talented, and popular cheerleaders in America. Their ardent fans easily outnumber the fans of the Cowboys. They receive mail and gifts from all over the world. Although the Cheerleaders discourage gift-givers, they often answer their mail themselves (50 to 100 letters come in each week). They even have a fan club in a London prison. But Suzanne feels that the appeal of the Cheerleaders is not primarily sexual, but rather the clean-cut All-American allure of Texas women.

The Dallas Cowboys Cheerleaders: Clean-cut Texas women.

On the field, the Cheerleaders never stop dancing. Their gyrations are coordinated, according to the action going on in the game. They have routines for touchdowns, field goals, defense, and offense. The Cheerleaders rehearse two nights a week for four or five hours at the studio of choreographer Texie Waterman. They are represented by William Morris, the number one talent agency in America. Their name is copyrighted, and their uniforms are patented—a royal blue halter, white vest with fringe, white hip-hugger short-shorts, vinyl boots, and a silver Windbreaker®. The uniform has been imitated by many other cheerleading squads, and has even provoked a heated competition to take off more and more clothes. Says Suzanne disdainfully, "We'll never do that. We don't want the fans to forget there's a football game going on. We let the Cowboys do the competing."

The girls all have to take care of their own uniforms, which are closely inspected before each game. Suzanne goes about with a pair of scissors trimming the fringe on the vests. And she has been known to keep a girl out of the game because she had a spot on her uniform.

All the girls have their own career objectives. They are waitresses, medical technicians, secretaries, and teachers. Vanessa Baker, who has been with the Cheerleaders for a record eight years, was awarded her M.A. at Texas Stadium before a game. For that occasion she donned a cap and gown over her uniform. Now she's pursuing her Ph.D. in special education to teach the deaf.

In a typical year, over 1,000 girls apply for the thirty-seven positions on the squad. The selection process takes two months, during which each would-be gets a chance to dance for the judges. The current Cheerleaders must defend themselves in the finals—a position on the squad is no guarantee that a better-qualified girl won't come along.

The girls earn extra money by making public appearances at conventions, openings, trade shows, and other functions throughout the U.S. On any given weekend, at least half the squad is appearing somewhere. However, no girl is allowed to appear alone, and they are not allowed to appear in any place where alcohol is served. Proper staging and two uniformed guards are demanded for the girls (once when these requirements were not met a riot broke out), and they must be allowed at least an hour and a half to "take the smile off and be totally alone." In the rare event that the girls must spend the night somewhere, they must be accompanied by Suzanne Mitchell.

At the end of the year, a percentage of the money earned in public appearances is divided evenly among all the Cheerleaders. This eliminates any competition between the girls for the opportunity to appear, because they are all working for each other's benefit. Even so, the girls each make well under $5,000 a year from all their cheerleading activities.

Each year, the Cheerleaders issue an official calendar and poster. You can also buy a deck of Dallas Cowboys Cheerleaders playing cards, tee-shirts, photographs of the individual Cheerleaders in black and white or color, and numerous other Cheerleader paraphernalia. Suzanne's book, *The Dallas Cowboy Cheerleaders*, is available nationwide.

America's Best! CHILI

The International Chili Society	The Rangoon Racquet Club
8899 Beverly Boulevard *Los Angeles, California* 90048	*9474 Santa Monica Boulevard* *Beverly Hills, California*
213-272-2786	*213-274-8926*
C. V. Wood, *President*	*Manny Zwarf, General Manager*
	Monday–Friday, *11:30 A.M.–2:30 A.M.;* *Saturday, 3:30 P.M.–* *2:30 A.M.; closed Sunday*

"I like to start the day with a bowl of chili, washed down with a mixture of Pepsi and milk," says C. V. Wood, president of the International Chili Society. "It's also great over eggs, spaghetti, or rice, and it makes a great filling for tortillas. The fact is, you just can't get a bad bowl of chili, the only thing is that some are simply better than others."

The origin of chili is still under heavy debate. Woody's favorite story, however, is that it was originated by cowboys riding on the range. They discovered that chili peppers could stop the oxidation of meat, so they packed them with their meat. When the meat was boiled two or three days later, it had lots of chili pepper flavor, hence the name *chili con carne*, which means just that—chili with meat.

"Good chili first starts with excellent meat," says Woody. Secondly, the meat must be permeated and broken down just right. The secret to chili is in the eye—knowing when it's cooked just right. Woody insists on using only chili powder, none of the chili blends, which contain other spices of indeterminable proportions.

There are two places to get America's best chili. One is at a chili-do at Wood's palatial estate, and the other is at his restaurant, the Rangoon Racquet Club in Beverly Hills. Even at $10.50 for a dinner-sized bowl, the Club earns very little profit. There are twenty ingredients, including Pepsi, beer, and spices, and each batch takes seven to eight hours to cook, not including the one-day refrigeration time. The recipe is right on the back of the Rangoon menu. "The carbonation from the beer and Pepsi totally changes the value of the spices," says Woody.

The late H. Allen Smith once said nobody knew more about chili than he did. This boast of an upstart Easterner was more than two Texas chili connoisseurs could abide by. Frank Tolbert and newspaperman Wick Fowler challenged Smith to a chili cook-off in an abandoned mine in Terlingus, Texas. Smith lost the contest by committing the cardinal sin for a chili lover: He actually put beans in his chili.

This event, held in 1967, gained national celebrity and blossomed into an annual chili competition. When a rift developed, the International Chili Society was formed, headed by Wood, the president of the McCulloch Oil Corporation. Wood, whose varied achievements include building Disneyland and developing Lake Havasu City replete with the London Bridge, moved the festival to a dusty turn-of-the-century gold mine in Rosamond, California.

Today, the festival is attended by about 35,000 people who jam the Mojave site with thousands of cars and hundreds of campers and mobile homes. Groups walk about bearing such slogans as "Bad Chili is Super," and "Chili Today and Hot Tamale." The competition is held on a weekend in October, which Woody is careful to schedule around the Los Angeles Rams' playing schedule. Contestants are winners of thirty-two state championships, and others come from as far away as Great Britain and Tahiti. All proceeds go to the Los Angeles Children's Hospital.

C. V. Wood is the two-time winner of the International Chili Competition. He's the only unbeaten champ and is, therefore, no longer allowed to enter the contest. The Society has assembled a regular roster of celebrity judges, all of whom are chili afficionados. They include actors Robert Mitchum, Vincent Price, Ernest

Borgnine, William Conrad, Betsy Balsley, food editor of the *Los Angeles Times*, Craig Claiborne, *New York Times* food editor, Wood and his wife, actress Joanne Dru, and Dr. Roy Nakayama, Dean of Horticulture at Mexico State University and the world's leading expert on the chili pepper. Contestants use all sorts of ingredients, more often than not reflecting their native areas. Texans use Texas water, Tennesseans use their native raccoon meat, North Dakotans use pheasant, and New Yorkers use Long Island oysters.

America's Best! CHUCKWAGON SUPPERS

Flying W Ranch

*400 Wilson Road
Colorado Springs, Colorado
80919*

303-598-4000

Russ Wolfe, Owner

*Chuckwagon Suppers plus shows:
May 25–September 20,
7:30 P.M., $6 prix fixe,
children under 9, $3.50*

*Winter Steak House, Dinner &
Show: October–May, closed
January and February; Fridays,
Saturdays and Sundays only,
5:00 P.M. and 8:00 P.M.; $9:50
prix fixe*

No credit cards or checks

Reservations required

No one wears a long gown or a coat and tie to the Chuckwagon Supper and Old Western Show at the Flying W Ranch. The faithful initiates of this uniquely American experience rough it. They sit outside at long wobbly tables in groups of twelve, scald their fingers on their hot tin plates and coffee cups, and down an authentic cowboy meal of beans, potatoes, beef, biscuits, and applesauce.

When owner Russ Wolfe began operating in 1953, he served only about fifteen meals a night. He's served about one million meals since then, and now dishes up 1,400 every summer night. It takes only twenty-two minutes to serve all that food, a point of pride for Russ and his employees.

The centerpiece of the Chuckwagon Supper is the beans, absolutely required in an Old Western meal. Russ Wolfe vouches for their authenticity, saying, "These are the cheapest red beans money can buy. They're pretty much indestructible!" The beans are cooked all day long in a mixture of chili sauce, tomato sauce, brown sugar, blackstrap molasses, raw onions, and smoked bacon ends. The coffee is made by filling long bootsocks with a pound of grounds, and boiling all day. The cowboys used to use sugar sacks, not socks, but nowadays sugar comes in paper sacks, so bootsocks seemed the best alternative.

The beef (500 to 600 pounds each night) is especially lean and sliced very thin in the Western tradition. The potatoes are prepared by a special boiling and roasting process to simulate the Old Western style without the disadvantages. (Cowboys would just bury their potatoes among the embers.)

In place of a green vegetable, and to balance the meal, Chuckwagon diners are served chunky applesauce. Biscuits are baked in authentic Dutch ovens, which are difficult to control. But the Flying W cooks try their best to make their biscuits better than the cowboys'—burnt on top and bottom, doughy in the middle, and served with butter and jelly.

The meal is rounded off with some old-fashioned spice cake and lemonade. The Flying W Ranch serves no liquor with the Chuckwagon suppers, in order to preserve a family atmosphere.

After dinner, Flying W Wranglers present the Old Western Show with their guitars, banjos, fiddle, bass, and percussion, an exhilarating evening of songs, stories, jokes, and jamming. Special guests also give demonstrations of Western culture, such as Indian dances or fancy gunslinging.

The Flying W Ranch is an authentic working cattle and horse ranch of 3,000 acres. A twenty-minute ride from Pikes Peak, it lies just north of the mysterious red rock formation known as the Garden of the Gods, an extension of which crosses the ranch. There's a faithful reconstruction of an Old Western town, complete with a schoolhouse, a jail, a drugstore where you can have an old-fashioned malt or soda, a dry goods store, an underground Indian "kiva" where two Navajo women make beautiful rugs (completing only four each year), a hand-hewn log house, and a combination barber shop-dentist's office-undertaking parlor. A mine has been cut into the nearby rocky hills, and every day at the smithy a horse from a neighboring ranch is shod. The neighbors save $20, and the Flying W gets a fresh horse for each daily demonstration. Horses are booked months in advance for this free service.

During the winter, a more elegant form of western dining goes on at the Flying W Winter Steak House, embellished with the elaborate appointments of the old Ute Theatre of Colorado Springs. On Fridays and Saturdays only, 300 guests enjoy a steak dinner cooked over an open applewood fire and a show by the Wranglers, who double as waiters. Liquor is served.

America's Best! CLOSETS

American Home Accessories Company

212-688-6568

686 Lexington Avenue
New York, New York 10022

Cecil Rhodes, President
Kathleen Brandmeier, Chief Assistant

Cecil Rhodes doesn't think chic habiliments should be stuffed away in a dark, drab closet. Instead, he suggests color-coordinated garment bags, shelf boxes, and padded hangers, shoe racks, hat stands, and lined linen drawers, all in a well spaced closet decorated with quilted satins, chintzes, or cottons.

President of American Home Accessories, Rhodes has brought elegance to the closets of nobility and the stars. He has created glass-faced drawers with shoe racks to match for comedian David Frye, original accessories (all in black) for Frank Sinatra, and padded satin hangers in red and gold for the Duke and Duchess of Windsor.

Typical Cecil Rhodes closets range from $500 to 10,000, and the sky's the limit, according to taste. But the individual accessories are more accessible in price. Shelf boxes start at $25, and hat boxes start at $20. A wooden hanger with blond, black, or walnut finish begins at $3. Some men like them covered with felt or velvet, with braided trim all around, and double or triple brass trouser bars.

Rhodes makes hangers for every different kind of garment, specially shaped to preserve the form of the clothing, which could be damaged by a narrow, angular, conventional hanger. "Men and women should have separate closets," says Rhodes, "and their hangers must be different because of their different physiques."

Among the many types of hangers are wishbone hangers for shirts and blouses, coat hangers with special long necks to prevent the garment from rubbing against the hanging bar, pinch-type skirt hangers, S-shaped slack or pants hangers, and evening-gown hangers with brass buttons to hold the straps of the gown. For those who want to fit lots of clothes in a smaller closet, Rhodes designs thinner padded hangers. (Christina Onassis needed these for her yacht, because of limited space.)

If you are especially small or large, Rhodes will gladly create special sizes of hangers for your clothes. You can have your hangers personally monogrammed for 10¢ apiece, if you buy over 500 at a time. Every year Rhodes sells 11,000 gold-stamped hangers to the Pierre Hotel in New York. Altogether, he sells about 50,000 hangers a year.

When decorating whole closets, Rhodes creates separate compartments for garments, linens, hats, and shoes. "A well spaced-out closet can hold three times as many clothes as another," he says. His shelf boxes are covered with fabric and trimmed with tailored ribbon, braid, or ruffle. When you lift the lid, the front drops open to let you see in. He also designs shoe racks, often as an open box with a brass bar that the heels hang over. "Show biz people have incredible numbers of shoes, so we design shoe racks that let them see all their shoes at once." Shoe racks start at $100, and go up to $500.

Most of Rhodes' patrons have their closet walls covered with wallpaper and vinyl, matching all their other accessories, but he still now and then receives a special request for satin or taffeta quilting. As for the danger of moths, Rhodes doesn't worry about them. "That's not my department," he says.

Rhodes did his most extensive and exotic work in the Newport home of Mrs. Harvey Firestone. He designed a closet for each of the thirteen bedrooms in the mansion. Each closet is done in a different color, and has smartly tailored trimmings and hangers.

He also did her entrance room closet in a blue English print. All this work took many months, and $10,000.

Rhodes' business began in 1935, in Westchester County, New York, when his wife, an interior decorator, made special covered hat stands and hangers for her best customers. Working in the kitchen of her home, she created the first coordinated closet ensemble. They began supplying major department stores all over the country, and in 1939 they exhibited at the New York World's Fair. After the war, they began to do only custom jobs for decorators. Rhodes' work is absolutely unique, unavailable elsewhere, and is still done entirely by hand.

America's Best! COLLEGE CLASSROOMS

The Nationality Rooms

University of Pittsburgh
Pittsburgh, Pennsylvania 15260

412-624-6150

E. Maxine Bruhns, Director,
Nationality Rooms and
Intercultural Exchange
Programs
Wesley W. Posvar, Chancellor

An 18th-century palace hall from Peiping's Forbidden City, a 6th-century Irish Romanesque oratory, an 18th-century home from Damascus, a 16th-century Polish Castle, and London's House of Commons—these locales have all been recreated or restored in the University of Pittsburgh's forty-two story Gothic skyscraper. The building is the only university skyscraper headquarters and the only Gothic skyscraper in the U.S.

Each Nationality Room represents a different ethnic community of Pittsburgh, and in commemoration of the U.S. Constitution, must be designed in a style pre-dating 1787.

The Chinese Classroom, dedicated to Confucius and his democratic ideal of education, simulates a palace hall in Peiping's Forbidden City. Details include a round, lacquered teak table, chairs engraved with the twelve qualities of a gentleman, and the tradi-

The Italian Classroom is modeled on a 15th-century Tuscan Monastery.

tional laughing lions at the door, warding off evil spirits and representing the happy nature of the Chinese people.

Many of the items in the English Classroom, with its Tudor-Gothic architecture and formal bench arrangement, were rescued from the original House of Commons, which was bombed in 1941. These include panelling, a fireplace with the likeness of Queen Victoria, and stone brackets carved with the Tudor Rose design.

One of the largest and most expensive rooms, the German Classroom, is arrayed in carved, painted, and inlaid walnut and oak. It is modelled after the University of Heidelberg, the oldest university in Germany. The stained-glass windows contain scenes and quotations from the *Tales of the Brothers Grimm.*

The Syria-Lebanon Room was originally a library in an elegant Damascus home. It includes linden-panelled walls, built-up with with gesso technique and emblazoned with silver and gold leaf, Persian rugs, and an antique chandelier from a mosque.

In the Early American Room, a restoration of the living quarters of an early colonist portrays the simple, rustic life of the 1600s. Highlights include a nine-foot fireplace, a white-pine seminar table, and wrought-iron candelabra. The small closet contains a

Fittings in the Syria-Lebanon Room were built for a library in Damascus in 1782.

secret staircase to a hidden loft, where colonial women and children took refuge when danger threatened.

The Nationality Rooms were originated by Mrs. Ruth Crawford Mitchell, and planning began in 1924. She went into the ethnic communities of Pittsburgh to rally support and formed a committee of interested citizens. Enthusiasm for the project spread from neighborhoods to the nation and to the mother countries. In many cases, governments responded with generous support, often providing architects, artists, materials, and money. Craftsmen were gleaned locally and imported from Europe. The first rooms were officially opened in 1939. The rooms are now valued at over $500,000 each. Funds are still collected for replacing and adding artifacts.

Up to 30,000 people visit the Nationality Rooms each year. A student organization called the Quo Vadis Society gives tours, including special tours for children, senior citizens, the handicapped, and groups interested in architecture, interior design, art, mythology, and religion.

Over the years, many VIPs have come to marvel at this unique achievement, including the U.S. Secretary General, Queen Fredericka, and Nikita Khrushchev. Mr. Khrushchev was left in awe of the Gothic skyscraper and the classrooms, and was most impressed with one room, designed in Byzantine and Folk motifs of the 16th century—the Russian Room, of course.

America's Best! COLLEGE MUSICAL

The Hasty Pudding Theatricals

12 Holyoke Street
Cambridge, Massachusetts 02138

617-495-5205

1980 Officers:
Charles Milot, Lloyd Thrower,
  Producers
Phil Murphy, President

At The Hasty Pudding Theatricals every spring, a group of Harvard undergraduates, just recovered from their winter exams, give vent to their boisterous creative energy in an original full-length musical comedy—irreverent, bawdy humor, featuring an all-male cast and a famous kick line of Harvard "lovelies." A wig, eyelashes, makeup, and some killing clothes transform a well rounded Harvard man into a femme fatale, named Juana de Boise or Eva Destruction.

The Hasty Pudding is entirely independent of Harvard University, and supports itself with the profits from the annual show, which often come to more than $10,000. The production is the result of a nearly year-long competition for scripts and scores, intensive casting sessions, and a budget of approximately $132,000. There are always at least six scripts and six scores to choose from, and the selection is made by consensus among the five Pudding officers—the president, vice-president, secretary, and two producers. Music auditions take place in September, and casting is done in January, with no shortage of candidates. About 100 students try out for about eighteen roles in three days, and try-outs often go on all day and all night. Finally, to apply a glossy finish to the productions, the Pudding enlists the aid of a professional director, set and costume designers, and a musical director.

Like Harvard's eight exclusive "final clubs," the Hasty Pudding Club admits only those who have been "punched" (nominated) by two current members. But unlike them, it is co-ed, and admits freshmen. Students pay a $50 initiation fee, and $25 dues per term for the use of the Clubhouse, where excellent dinners are served six nights a week. The Hasty Pudding Theatricals, however, are open to the whole student body.

By the Charter of 1844, women are absolutely not allowed onstage, but since 1969, students of Radcliffe College, Harvard's feminine counterpart, may write or compose for the Pudding, produce or direct, play in the band, or work as stage hands.

Harvard regulations virtually prohibit the students from missing any classes, so a lot of hard work for the Pudding Show has to be done during vacations and at odd night hours. Students receive no academic credit for participating in the musical, and no one gets paid.

The Hasty Pudding has sent its writers, producers, and actors to Hollywood, Broadway, and other important places. Alan J. Lerner, Fred Gwynne, Archibald Cox, and Oliver Wendell Holmes were all involved in the Pudding during their Harvard days. Jack Lemmon performed in three productions and in 1948 was the leading lady (he won the role by one vote), but had to appear under a pseudonym because he was on academic probation at the time. His academic troubles resulted from spending too much time with the Pudding. In 1959, Erich Segal (*Love Story*) coauthored *The Big Fizz* with Joe Raposo. J. P. Morgan produced a show that was an economic disaster. Some Pudding members have chosen most unusual professions upon graduation. Mark Szpak, the 1977 president and leading lady, went off to southern Poland to become a shepherd. Barry Sloane, one of the producers of the 1977 show, became president of Boston's Century Banks after

71

graduation. While the Pudding Show has never sent anyone into the Presidency, John F. Kennedy, Theodore and Franklin D. Roosevelt, and John Quincy Adams were members. But none of them ever made it to the Pudding stage.

To announce the opening of the show, as well as to generate maximum publicity, the Club announces its "Man and Woman of the Year" in February. Elizabeth Taylor, Bette Midler, Liza Minnelli, Katherine Hepburn, Rosalind Russell, Beverly Sills, and Candice Bergen have all been honored. The Woman of the Year visits the University a few weeks before opening night, is paraded through the streets of Cambridge, and presented with the Hasty Pudding Pot at a raucous ceremony.

The Man of the Year attends opening night. Recipients include Johnny Carson, Warren Beatty, Robert Redford, Richard Dreyfuss, and Robert De Niro. Men and Women of the Year meet with a delegation of Club members, and sometimes give seminars. Usually they stay in hotels, but Johnny Carson and his wife wanted to be on campus, so they roomed at a master's residence in the Harvard Yard. Carson afterwards remarked, "It's the first time I've scored on a college campus in years."

The Hasty Pudding Club was established in 1770 as an eating club to offer students some relief from the college food. Hasty Pudding was a favorite dessert of the members. In the early 19th century, members led by Lemuel Hayward (class of 1845) began presenting improvisational burlesques and mock trials of famous figures in their dormitory rooms. The first show, *Bombastes Furioso,* was produced in 1844 to satirize a current opera. By 1888, the members could afford to move their productions out of their rooms and into their present clubhouse, and a great tradition was well under way.

In 1929, the Pudding presented what is considered its worst show ever, *Fireman, Save My Child.* The New York audience, consisting largely of alumni, was so offended by the show and by the wild behavior of the performers that it told the Pudding to stay out of New York.

Sensational shows, however, like 1930's *Face the Music,* reconciled the Pudding with its audience, and now Hasty Pudding Shows are greeted by wildly enthusiastic crowds wherever they go. The Pudding puts on as many as thirty-eight shows a year in the 363-seat Cambridge Playhouse, and four in New York, and goes to other cities, depending on the number of graduates who live

72

there. It even performs in Bermuda. The flamboyant energy, scathing satire, and of course the most unusual chorus line this side of Paris, make an evening at the Pudding Show a truly unique collegiate theatrical experience.

America's Best! CRABS

Dungeness Crabs	Bob and Gail DeLorm
	283-3 Crabs
Cancer magister	*Sequim, Washington* 98382
	206-683-3110

Dungeness-type crabs can be found anywhere off the West Coast from San Francisco to Alaska, but if they don't come from Dungeness Bay, Washington, they're not America's best.

"Other areas don't have as good conditions as Dungeness," explains crabber Bob DeLorm. "Our crabs like the gentle tides of the Bay. And food is important. For instance, at Bellingham, they don't have enough of the right food. They don't grow as fast, don't moult as often, and end up covered with barnacles."

Dungeness crabs weigh between 1½ pounds to a record 2 pounds, 14 ounces. If they don't measure at least 6¼ inches across the back, they must be thrown back into the sea. They mature in four years and live as long as eight. Crabbers are only allowed to keep adult males, in order to perpetuate the species.

Crabs are caught in cylindrical "pots" of stainless-steel wire, with one-way trap doors, that lie at depths of eight to twenty feet. The crabs walk into the trap, lured by the smell of the bait inside, which includes clams, cockles, and horseclams. There is an escape ring at the back to allow undersized crabs to go on their way.

The crab season in Dungeness lasts from October 1st to April 15th, with the peak in December and January. (Further out on the ocean, the season runs until September.) The season ends after the females have spawned and the males have disappeared to moult. No one knows where they go.

Bob DeLorm, who has sixty pots, takes in about 200 adult male crabs a day during peak times, and only twenty-five a day during the slower periods. There are only five serious crabbers in Dungeness, most of whom have only about twenty pots, but further south there are commercial fishers who take as much as 90,000 pounds of crab each month.

"You can't make much of a living from crabbing," says DeLorm. A former state highway patrolman, he learned the crabbing trade as a teenager, and continues now full-time "for the love of the Bay and being out on the water."

If you buy Dungeness crabs "green" (that is, alive—actually they're brownish), they cost about $1.10 a pound. Prepare them by boiling for twenty minutes in fresh sea water (salted water doesn't work nearly as well), then cool them with cold sea water to halt the cooking and make the crabs easier to shell. Crabs will keep in the refrigerator only about three days, but they can be frozen for months. Lay them on their backs for freezing to keep the juices from running down into the meat and turning it a yellowish color.

America's Best! CRANBERRIES

Ocean Spray Cranberries, Inc.   *Harold Thorkilsen, President*

Water Street
Plymouth, Massachusetts 02360

617-747-1000

Cranberry World: April–
November, 7 days a week,
10:00 A.M.–5:00 P.M.;
admission free

Brigitte Bardot reportedly bathes in them and considers them something of an aphrodisiac. Ted Kennedy's cooler is always well stocked with them, and the Kennedy White House required weekly deliveries. Writer John McPhee says that when fried, they are the perfect remedy for a sore throat. What is this popular sub-

Knee-deep in cranberries: Ocean Spray harvesters wade through bogs to bring in 2,200,000 barrels of the popular berry each year.

stance? Cranberries, the largest export crop of Massachusetts. America's best are those of the Late Howe variety, grown only in the Bay State.

Ten thousand acres are under cranberry cultivation in Massachusetts, more than in any other state. Ocean Spray, Inc., of Plymouth, Massachusetts, is the largest seller of cranberries in the world. The U.S. sells 75 percent of the world's cranberries, and Ocean Spray accounts for 80 percent of that. Total production is 2,200,000 (100-pound) barrels a year, and the Late Howe is the mainstay of the fresh cranberry market.

Cranberries have accompanied Thanksgiving turkey since they were first served to the Pilgrims by American Indians in 1620. Thanks to Ocean Spray, cranberry sauce has become the most popular accessory for roast turkey. It was originally developed in 1930 as a good use for undersized berries or those of marginal color. Ocean Spray offers two sauces, the more popular jellied sauce and a whole-berry version. Until the early 1960s these products accounted for 90 percent of Ocean Spray's business, and 80 percent were sold between Thanksgiving and Christmas.

Now, however, cranberry juice is the largest seller, and cranberry sales have leveled appreciably. Ocean Spray Cranberry Juice Cocktail is spiced with vitamin C, sweeteners, and water, and is not as tart or as astringent as the pure cranberry juice. The creation of the popular beverage was spurred on by the efforts of Uncle Sam. In 1959, the Department of Agriculture identified a chemical carcinogen that was contaminating the nation's cranberries. Announced just before Thanksgiving, the decision was termed "untimely" and "a grievous error" by Harold Thorkilsen, president of Ocean Spray. Ultimately, the government paid $6 million in reparations, and Ocean Spray sought new marketing directions to reduce its vulnerability. The result was Cranberry Juice Cocktail, which is now the largest component of a booming $200-million-a-year business.

In addition to its cranberry sauce and juice, Ocean Spray markets frozen juice concentrates and fresh, whole cranberries. Only the best Massachusetts Late Howes are good enough to be sold fresh. Ocean Spray also makes Cranapple, Crangrape, Cranorange, Cranprune, and Cranicot drinks and a cranberry relish.

Cranberry juice has become a popular cocktail mixer, and other uses continue to be found. Many doctors recommend cranberry juice for urinary disorders, because of its peculiar quality of remaining acidic in its passage through the body. Cranberries may replace Red Dye Number 40 as the best source of natural red color.

The Five Seasons Cranberry Book, written by Ocean Spray and Better Homes and Gardens, offers cranberry recipes ranging from Chili Cranberry Franks to Cranberry Cheese Frosties. The most widely used recipe is probably cranberry-orange relish, a staple on Thanksgiving and Christmas dinner tables.

What started out as a small grower's cooperative in 1930 has now expanded to include a network of 850 cooperative farmers and a total Ocean Spray work force of 1,500. The Ocean Spray executive offices are located in Plymouth, Massachusetts, where the Cranberry World museum provides displays on the history and methods of cranberry production.

Ocean Spray plans to expand into the world cranberry market. Even now, American-grown fresh cranberries are sold in Fauchon, the elegant gourmet food shop in Paris. In Scandinavia, Ocean Spray hopes to provide a close cousin to the popular lingonberry, which has nearly been wiped out. And wide horizons exist in Japan, where the same farming techniques used for rice could easily be transferred to cranberry farming.

America's Best! DEPARTMENT STORE

Marshall Field & Company

111 North State Street
Chicago, Illinois 60690

312-781-1000

George P. Kelly, President
George W. Love,
*   Senior Vice-President,*
*   Marketing-Sales Promotion*

State Street store: Monday–
*   Saturday, 9:45 A.M.–6:00 P.M.;*
*   Mondays and Thursdays*
*   till 7:00 P.M.*

Marshall Field credit cards only

"Chicagoans have a proprietary interest in our store—that's because we've been here since 1852," says George P. Kelly, president of Marshall Field & Company. There are sixty Marshall Field-owned stores throughout the country, and all of them have earned the reputation for elegance and customer service that has been established over the years by the company's flagship store on State Street.

The State Street store has 160 buyers, more than any other department store in America, enabling Field's to offer the broadest range of merchandise at all price levels. Mr. Kelly estimates that Field's sells 10,000 different items, including antiques usually sold only in specialty stores.

Typical Christmas catalogue offerings, for example, include an 1850 necklace, with "European cut diamonds (approx. 20 ct.) set in an English flower design on 18K gold and silver, with diamond clasp" for $15,000 and an 1803 document signed by President Thomas Jefferson appointing James Monroe Ambassador to Britain. On vellum and in a protective case, it sells for $10,000. Museum-quality Japanese screens, signed by Sadayoshi Ryuensai of the Tosa School, circa 1830, sell for $12,000 apiece.

The State Street store has four floors of workshops which employ 500 people. Field's picks up and delivers all goods it repairs, a policy established in 1872 with a horse and wagon.

Field's exclusive services include:

Oriental rug reweaving and repair;

restoration of heirlooms, antique gowns, tablecloths, antique fabrics, wedding veils, including coloring of threads to match old fabric;

antique hat repair;

hand- or machine-engraving of gold, silver, silverplate, and pewter;

antique jewelry and ceramics repair and redesign;

porcelain patterns perfectly reproduced when repaired;

machine and hand monogramming;

fur coat linings replaced, altered, monogrammed, rare in-and-out fur storage;

dress and suit tailoring;

dry-cleaning;

upholstery, drapery, slipcover work;

chair reconstruction.

Field's also has impressive food services. Two hundred specially trained people make Frango Mints and other candies, bread and pastries, and all the foods served in the State Street store's eleven restaurants, as well as thirty-four retail frozen-food products. To insure Field's quality, the store maintains its own central testing laboratory.

Frango Mints are one of Marshall Field's most popular items. The store sells 360,000 pounds of the chocolates each year. In fact, Frango Mint sales account for half of Field's annual $12-million food revenue. Hand-dipped and hand-filled, they come in seven flavors: rum, coffee, lemon, raspberry, orange, almond, and mint. They were originally called "Franco Mints" when they were made by Seattle's Frederick & Nelson chain, which Field's acquired fifty years ago. The name was changed to "Frango" after Franco's victory in the Spanish Revolution.

"I can't think of any other store so involved with food services, except Harrod's in London," says George Kelly. The store has kept some of the 5,000 recipes for retail and restaurant foods in the corporate vault. There are eleven restaurants at the State Street store, the most famous of which is the Walnut Room. Opened in 1890, the 1,000-seat restaurant is the oldest department store tea-

Field's 1,500,000-piece Tiffany dome is the largest glass mosaic, with unbroken surface, in the U.S.

room in America and a traditional meeting place for three generations of Field's shoppers. Breakfast and lunch are served Monday through Saturday and dinners Mondays and Thursdays until 7:00 P.M. There's piano music on Wednesdays.

Christmas is a special time at Field's. The Display Department spends nine months preparing the full city block of window displays on each side of the building. Real people portray Aunt Holly, Uncle Mistletoe, Marcia Housemouse, Freddy Fieldmouse, and, of course, Santa. Elizabeth Williams, who played Aunt Holly in the display for twenty-one years, was buried in her costume.

The year-round highlight of the store is the 1,500,000-piece Tiffany dome, the largest glass mosaic, with unbroken surface, in the country. It sits atop a rotunda between the fifth and seventh floors. Fifty men worked a year and a half to install the 6,000-square-foot dome, which was unveiled in September, 1907.

Field's has recently spent $22 million remodeling the State Street store, which opened in 1868. The old, obstructive six-foot-high mahogany cabinets have been replaced with pecan wood counters trimmed with brass, polished daily. The marble floors and countertops, long a hallmark, remain.

Field's opened a seven-floor store in 1975 at Water Tower Place, Chicago's chic vertical shopping center. In November, 1979, the new Galleria II store opened in Houston with a gala dinner to benefit the Texas Children's Hospital. The $250-a-plate extravaganza was over-subscribed even before it was publicly announced. Field's plans four more stores for the Texas division, which caters to higher-income families, especially those moving into the fast-growing Houston area.

Marshall Field owns thirteen Frederick & Nelson stores in Seattle and the Northwest; nine Halle Brothers stores in Ohio and Pennsylvania; three Crescent stores in Portland, Oregon; sixteen John Breuner Company stores in Northern California, Western Nevada, and Central Arizona; and sixteen Chicago Division stores, including one store in the Milwaukee area and the flagship stores at State Street and Water Tower Place. Field's also maintains foreign buying offices in London, Frankfurt, Paris, Florence, and Tokyo.

America's Best! DIMENSIONAL PAPER SCULPTURES

Eleanor Stanifer Jacobs   *714-582-8885, 582-2390*

6702 Estrella Avenue
San Diego, California 92102

Eleanor Stanifer Jacobs suffers from insomnia. She doesn't turn on the late-night talk shows, she doesn't pick up a book, and she doesn't take a sleeping pill. Instead, she sets to work on America's best dimensional paper sculptures.

Mrs. Jacobs uses a process called *vue d'optique*, a French phrase meaning "view of the optic." It is a technique of optical illusion developed by artists in Italy and France in the 17th century. They used multilayers of etchings, one upon the other, to create a dimensional effect.

The initial stage of creating a dimensional paper sculpture is the purchase of at least four and sometimes seventeen identical art prints. Mrs. Jacobs first glues a print to a thin board and, after careful study, decides which details will be brought out and given dimension. For example, details such as the feathers of a duck, the ornamentation of a horse's saddle, and the clothing of a Dutch peasant will all be given shape and dimension in the final sculpture.

Eleanor Jacobs is an insomniac turned paper sculptor.

Using a craft knife, curved scissors, straight scissors, and tweezer-like dental tools, Mrs. Jacobs delicately trims the details in order to highlight the sculpture. Next, she applies various types of art glues to the paper cut-outs and assembles the multidimensional paper sculptures. She tries to deepen the effect of the architecture in the picture, while bringing forward the people or the details.

Mrs. Jacobs has sculpted almost everything—Dutch peasant scenes, detailed still lifes, light and airy florals, birds, American Indians, and the Last Supper. She creates many of her scenes using the street scenes of Dutch artist Anton Pieck. Norman Rockwell prints also lend themselves well to the *vue d'optique* process. They are becoming increasingly difficult to obtain, and Mrs. Jacobs once purchased 150 identical Rockwell prints because she was so delighted to find them.

The frames for the sculptures are custom-made. Mrs. Jacobs selects the frames and often paints them herself. She also constructs wooden shadowboxes to house the sculptures. These enhance the multidimensional effect.

Mrs. Jacobs first sold a dimensional paper sculpture in 1973 for

$250. You can buy a simple butterfly or flower for $75, but a much more intricate sculpture of a chamber-music scene will cost $2,500. Mrs. Jacobs does not promote her work, however. Creating a *vue d'optique* is a hobby for her own enjoyment. She never makes more than two paper sculptures from the same print.

Mrs. Jacobs has exhibited her paper sculptures in art shows in the San Diego area, but her work usually adorns her studio and the homes of family and friends.

America's Best! DUDE RANCH

Rancho de los Caballeros	*Dallas Gant, Jr., General Manager*
Wickenburg, Arizona 85359	*Mrs. Edie Hayman, Owner*
	Buford Giles, Resident Wrangler
602-684-5484	*Anne Giles, Sales Director*

In Gold Rush days, Apache warriors terrorized the town of Wickenburg, Arizona, but today it is a serene haven for any city-weary dude. "Rancho de los Caballeros" means the "ranch of the gentlemen on horseback," and this is one ranch that offers every luxury a caballero could possibly desire.

Dallas Gant and his wife, now Mrs. Edie Hayman, opened the Rancho de los Caballeros in 1946. Mrs. Hayman still runs the ranch with her son Dallas, Jr. (Rusty). She prefers to call the resort a "guest ranch," citing Webster's definition of a "dude" as "a fastidious or affected man." The concept of the ranch is to provide the ultimate in comfort and retain the informality of a ranch. Rancho de los Caballeros is an arrangement of twelve *casitas*, small bungalows housing 125 guests in sixty-two double rooms with living areas. The cottages are charmingly decorated in Mexican-Indian decor with hand-painted furniture by an octogenarian artisan, and there are natural wood beams throughout. No TVs or telephones intrude on the peace and quiet, and there's no room service. The attitude at los Caballeros is "let's get up and out!"

The main building is U-shaped around the pool, and all activities occur here to keep the *casitas* as quiet as possible and to create a sense of community. The buildings provide a breathtaking view of the Vulture Mountains. It was in these mountains that Henry Wickenburg in 1863 discovered one of the largest gold mines in America. Grateful townspeople changed the name of the town from Pumpkin Patch to Wickenburg as a tribute.

Dallas landscaped the ranch to create his own desert oasis. The desert blooms with the color of jasmine, bougainvillea, century plants, paloverde, and sprawling lawns, which set the villas apart from the beautiful desert vegetation. The lawns are Australian rye grass, sown and mown in just seven days! They are replaced each year, as watering in the summer would be too costly.

The main attractions of the Rancho de los Caballeros are the perpetual sunshine, dry climate, comfortable accommodations, and excellent food. Activities include riding, tennis, golf, trap shooting, billiards, cattle roundups, and trail rides. To prevent greenhorns from getting saddlesores, Buford Giles, the resident wrangler in the tack room, has devised a unique system of storing each saddle according to horse and rider. You can ride seven days a week (morning rides are $9, afternoon rides $6), and the ranch's 20,000 acres provide excellent terrain and scenery. All rides are limited to only twelve riders per wrangler. There are fast, medium, and slow rides, as well as teen and kiddie outings.

Guests can also go on all-day rides. They ride out on horseback or by car, and are met by the chef who cooks right out on the range. Breakfast is served at Skyline Ridge, lunch at Vulture Peak, and dinner on the South Yucca Flats. It's an unusual treat for those who have never had imported lobster tails among the wild cactus. Each year a group called the "Desert Caballeros" comes to the ranch for a five-day trek through the desert on horseback. There's a raucous send-off and homecoming, and mule races on the trail. Caterers ride along to provide the food, and mariachi bands serenade the campers at night.

Peso Dollar and his Counterfeit Bills provide the music for special events and holidays at the ranch. At Christmas, Santa arrives Arizona-style—on a burro or a golf cart decorated as a sleigh. Throughout the season there are gymkhanas (games on horseback), square dances, and the annual Cattle Rustlers' Ball, where all costumes recall the early days of the West.

The Rancho de los Caballeros is open from mid-October to mid-May. Mrs. Hayman feels the summer months, when temperatures reach 115 degrees, are too hot for a vacation. *Casitas* range from $96 to $116 for two on the American Plan. A 15 percent gratuity is added for the excellent help, who know each guest by name. The ranch will accommodate groups of 10 to 120 from mid-October through the end of January and from mid-April through mid-May. A week after you leave Rancho de los Caballeros, you'll get a card at home that says, "So long amigo, till we meet again."

America's Best! FERRIES

Washington State Ferries

Seattle Ferry Terminal
Seattle, Washington 98104

Richard Berg, General Manager
Ralph White, Deputy General
    Manager

*Newel Hunter, Public Services
    Director*

Information (in Washington):
    800-542-0810; in Seattle and
    the rest of U.S.: 206-464-6400

When was the last time you looked out the window of your commuter bus and saw a school of dolphins or a killer whale? Or even the mountains, for that matter? This is standard fare for the daily passengers on the Washington State Ferries.

Washington has the largest ferry fleet in the world, and the nineteen boats function as America's most unusual bus system, making 500 commuter crossings daily throughout Puget Sound. They also take recreationists and tourists to some of the most remote and unspoiled wilderness areas in America. Monday through Thursday, the system carries 41,000 passengers per day, and on weekends 50,000 per day. The ferries ply 880,000 miles a year and transport eighteen million people.

Technically a ferry is a symmetrical boat that can load or unload at either end, and consequently can come into a dock and

The *Walla Walla* makes a commuter run.

leave it without turning around. Superferries, like the *Spokane*, can carry 2,000 passengers and 210 vehicles. Four hundred and forty feet long and powered with a diesel-electric engine, its maximum cruising speed is twenty-three knots and it can be brought to a standstill from full speed in less than 900 feet. It has two passenger decks, two car decks, six restrooms, and like all the Washington ferries, it is equipped with wall-to-wall carpeting, a grill and dining area (serving beer), fire and water safety apparatus, and is kept spotlessly clean.

Long-time commuters are very vocal about the ferry service, and let the administration know when they want things done differently. The authorities once considered putting televisions on the boats. "But the commuters screamed bloody murder—they thought it would cheapen the experience," says Alice Collingwood, ferries spokesperson.

There is an occasional problem with tourists, who sometimes crowd the residents off the boats and make them late for work. While the Transportation Authority says its obligation is to commuters, commerce, resident recreationists, and tourists, in that order, law does not permit favoritism.

Some Friday nights, the ferries seemingly turn into floating parties as the riders go island hopping. If the party doesn't happen spontaneously, you can start it yourself. The ferries are available for rental on any night but Friday and Sunday, $2,950 for four hours! You can use the system's catering service or bring your own food.

There are about 172 islands in Puget Sound (if you count every rock at low tide), and four of them have no bridges to the mainland. The residents depend entirely upon the ferries for access to the rest of the state. These are the breathtaking San Juan Islands, Lopez, Shaw, Orcas, and San Juan, and a three-hour one-way scenic tour through the narrow straits costs only $1.45 (or $4.50 if you bring your car).

On Shaw Island, the local agents of the ferry system are members of a society of Franciscan Nuns who were bequeathed a warehouse, a store, and the dock on the island. They turned the warehouse into a chapel, but the dock is still operating. They meet the ferries on every arrival, see that the bridge and apron of the vessels are properly set for the crew, and inform the pilots of traffic conditions. "They're all-round good people to work with," says a ferry captain.

Some of the Washington ferries date back to 1927, and originally operated in San Francisco Bay before the Golden Gate and San Francisco Bay Bridges were completed in 1930, making the ferries "obsolete." But Washington people have no desire to build any more bridges between their islands, and want to preserve an element of isolation and their ferries.

The Transportation Authority intends to refurbish its fifty-year-old ferries, and expects they'll be good for at least another twenty-five years. The Authority will also launch six new 100-car ferries over the next three years.

Puget Sound is so beautiful, and the ferries are so leisurely, that the experience seems more like a guided tour than commuter transit. As one captain, who regularly spots harbor seals, sea lions, sharks, and killer whales during his run, says, "It's not your typical Greyhound bus."

America's Best! FLAMING SOURDOUGHS

Ruth C. Allman

House of Wickersham
213 7th Street
Juneau, Alaska 99801

907-586-1251

May–September: 1:30 P.M. and
6:30 P.M.; adults, $8;
children, $6

Reservations necessary

Ruth Coffin Allman is the *Grande Dame* of sourdough, and knows more of its lore and its peculiar cuisine than anyone could imagine. In fact, she is a sourdough herself, meaning that she is a full-time resident Alaskan. During the goldrush days, prospectors and miners became so dependent on sourdough that they actually called themselves sourdoughs. Those who don't stay around to see the winter ice come in and go out again are called *cheechakos*.

Ruth's flaming sourdough dessert is a simple but elegant treat—a sourdough waffle (made from a sourdough culture over seventy years old!) topped with ice cream, wild strawberries, and a lump of sugar soaked in lemon extract that flames like a torch when ignited, served with rose syrup on the side.

The House of Wickersham, Ruth's Victorian home, was the first house built under the American flag after the purchase of Alaska from Russia. Situated on a hill overlooking Gastineau Channel, its lighted third-floor window served to guide sea captains into Juneau Dock. Ruth is the niece of Judge James Wickersham, who raised her after her father died. Wickersham was Alaska's most important statesman, having established the first courts there, and being responsible for naming Fairbanks and introducing the first bill calling for the statehood of Alaska in 1916.

He also led the first attempt to climb Mount McKinley in 1903, and initiated the building of the Alaska Railroad and the University of Alaska.

Ruth receives about 4,000 guests in her home each year. Amidst an abundance of artifacts and treasures from Russian-American days, she entertains them with a lecture on the more colorful aspects of Alaskan history, such as the Yukon Goldrush, and serves her flaming sourdough dessert. She began serving dinners in 1959. In those days her menu would include such specialties as moose sausage baked in pineapple and sourdough waffles topped with crab. It is no longer practical for her to show such extravagant generosity (the meal was free), but her gracious manner still makes a visit to the Wickersham House a very special occasion.

Sourdough is a wild yeast that feeds on flour and causes fermentation, and in the process converts the starch of the flour into protein. It became the most practical food of explorers roughing it in the Alaskan wild.

Sourdough will also come in handy as paste when you're papering your cabin with newspaper, and you can even tan hides with it after a hunt. Just rub it in with your hands until the skin is soft and dry. Sourdough beer, a favorite of Alaskan Indians, is "simple to make, but disagreeable to drink," says Ruth. "But if consumed in quantity it will produce any desired degree of intoxication." But the real glory of sourdough is sourdough hotcakes and waffles which, when properly made, are 50 percent hot air!

"There's not a man or beast who doesn't crave that wild yeast or that protein," says Ruth, whose dog and two Siamese cats always beg for hotcakes when she's cooking them. "If you got a bear in your cookshack, he wouldn't go after meat, he'd go after that sourdough pot and come out with a white face. I've seen 'em!"

Prospectors on the trail have been known to take their pot of sourdough culture to bed with them to protect it from the cold, so important was it to their survival. "If you went on the trail and took 100 pounds of flour along with your sourdough, you'd always have food," explains Ruth. "If you took 100 pounds of potatoes, they'd freeze—it gets to thirty, forty, fifty degrees below zero in the interior."

Ruth has written a cookbook, *Alaska Sourdough*, which deals entirely with sourdough. It comes with a package of dehydrated sourdough starter. Included are the recipes for the classical sourdough bread, hotcakes, waffles and biscuits, as well as sourdough beer and Baked Alaska. The book is also filled with lots of stories deriving from the long history of this pioneer delicacy. For instance, ex-Supreme Court Justice William O. Douglas's hotcakes were so light that occasionally on fishing trips they would be carried away by gnats and mosquitos—so he weighted them down with blueberries and other fruits.

America's Best! FLUTES

Wm. S. Haynes Company

12 Piedmont Street
Boston, Massachusetts 02116

617-482-7456

Lewis Deveau, President

Flutists can either wait five years for a flute from the Wm. S. Haynes Company in Boston or settle for second-hand versions, which cost $1,000 to $3,000.

The main reason for the long wait is the painstaking process in which the 350-piece flute is assembled. The coined-silver tubes, seventeen tone holes, hand-filed keys, and pads are hand-wrought. Each part is soldered on individually. It takes thirty hours to put on one set of keys, and five hours just to polish the finished product. Every key is custom-fitted to its own tone hole. Precision must be maintained. For each twenty-eight-inch-long silver tube, accuracy within ¼ of 1,000th of an inch is absolutely essential.

Standard silver flutes start at $1,700 (the leather and velvet-lined case alone costs $90), while solid-gold models sell for $13,000. The gold flutes sound mellow like their wooden predecessors, yet may be played louder than their silver counterparts. Haynes also made the first gold alto flute (bigger, and thus an octave lower, than the normal flute). It costs $16,000. A platinum flute with gold keys also costs $16,000.

Haynes' insurmountable quality may have evolved as a result of the Haynes "headjoint" structure (the part which is blown into). The headjoint-making process involves the tapering of a straight tube. It is done with a steel mandrel that has specifications so secret that they are locked in the safe-deposit box of a nearby bank. Whenever visitors tour the factory, all work on headjoint structures is halted. Only the president knows the specifications, and only he and four other workers know the 3½-hour process for making one. Many companies spend only a few minutes of time working on this very critical structure.

Lewis Deveau, president and owner of the company, employs only forty-two flutemakers. Under his constant supervision, two men laboring for 130 hours finally produce a suitable flute. A five-year apprenticeship is required of each employee and some have been working for as long as sixty years. One expert is over eighty years old and on his third pacemaker. The flute-tester has been testing Haynes flutes for twenty-five years, playing the same song on each group of flutes in order to detect the minute differences. When air escapes through a misplaced pad, his keen ears pick it up. In fact, only one in three flutes passes the test the first time. He was once a member of the Boston Symphony Orchestra.

All Haynes workmanship is guaranteed for life; indeed, workers are still repairing flutes made as early as 1900. Haynes will do a complete twelve-to-fifteen-hour overhaul on a flute for $260. Some flutes, particularly those played by people with minimal amounts of acid in their systems, can go for as long as ten years without being overhauled. Others, though, have their keys and pads eaten away within two years by a musician's acidic breath.

Each Haynes flute is registered with a serial number and placed in a vault when it is completed. In order to purchase a flute, you must send full payment one month before the date of shipping. Haynes has never had a bad debt. Most well known flutists prefer Haynes finely hewed instruments over all others. Perhaps the most famous of all flutists, Jean-Pierre Rampal, compares his fourteen-carat gold flute to a beautiful woman. But, he adds, "The flute is not like a woman. You can be at ease with a woman after five minutes, but not with the flute." Other renowned flutists who perform with Haynes instruments are Julius Baker of the New York Philharmonic and jazz flutist Yusef Lateef.

Haynes makes approximately 750 flutes a year, a sharp contrast to the 250 a year its nearest quality competitor makes, and to the

750 flutes less quality-conscious firms produce each week. Haynes makes piccolos, too, and they're harder to acquire than flutes, available only after an eight-year wait. The standard silver piccolo is $1,500, while the wood version sells for $1,900.

Haynes' tradition of excellence has progressed from the day William and George Haynes created the company in 1888. Quality remains preeminent for Lewis Deveau, a man who started out by sweeping floors, then learned how to form every one of the flute's 350 parts, to become president. "I just want to make the finest flute in the world," he says.

America's Best! FRENCH QUARTER INN

The St. Louis Hotel   *504-581-7300*

730 Rue Bienville   *Carolyn L. Hughes, General*
New Orleans, Louisiana 70130   *Manager*

The St. Louis Hotel opened its doors only six years ago, yet it has already played host to some of the world's most discriminating diplomats and celebrities. The hotel's most famous guest to date has been Giscard d'Estaing, President of France, who stayed there during his Bicentennial visit. Monsieur le President felt quite at home there, as the hotel, built on the site of an old brewery warehouse, is patterned after one in France.

The Presidential Suite is a spacious apartment with living room, dining room, kitchen, and a covered balcony overlooking Rue Bienville. It is decorated with antiques, highlighted by Oriental plates, a French Provincial desk with leather chair, a drop-leaf table, and a beautiful marble-mantled fireplace. Another set of rooms, the Patio Suite, features a Plexiglas-covered courtyard.

The hotel's room-service waiter, Bert Butler, has been there since the hotel opened. When you order room service, he will call just before serving to tell you it's ready. Then he'll arrive in thirty seconds flat. Bert efficiently substituted for Giscard d'Estaing's personal butler, and some guests won't check in if he's not there.

Visions of Old New Orleans: All rooms at the St. Louis face the courtyard.

The building is painted a charming mixture of peach and white with green shutters. All the rooms exit onto a corridor that faces a central courtyard, which conjures up visions of old New Orleans. The focal point is the fountain, designed after one in the French countryside. The courtyard is landscaped with lush Southern vegetation including plum trees, banana trees, camellias, and azaleas. The patio is appointed with used-brick flooring, ceiling fans under the balconies, and gas lanterns.

One of the hotel's innovations is a string quartet that performs at cocktail hour on Thursday and at Sunday brunch. The concerts are unusual for the French Quarter, but very much in keeping with the atmosphere of the hotel.

The lobby is beautifully decorated in green and black with a marble front desk, imported French parquet floors, Oriental carpets, Italian chandeliers, and original art. The appointments in the public areas are brass. The entire hotel, which cost $3.5 million, is decorated with French Provincial furniture (Louis XV and XVI).

There are seventy-seven rooms on five floors with king, queen, double, and twin-sized beds. All the rooms are equipped with the latest conveniences. Bathrooms are supplied with heat lamps, deluxe sewing kits, shoehorns, shower caps, a clothesline, a telephone extension, and a shoeshine machine. The hotel even offers the *Wall Street Journal* and the New Orleans papers free of charge.

There's an excellent Creole gumbo on the menu in Le Petit dining room, which seats forty-five. You'll find America's best fresh fruit daiquiris at Le Petit Bar (see below). The Herbsaint Suisse, a Southern imitation of absinthe, is a Sunday-morning treat at Le Jardin bar.

Rates at the St. Louis are $69 to $84 for singles, $79 to $94 for doubles, and $115 to $250 for suites. (New Orleans's most exclusive hotel, but not the most expensive.) Rates do not vary with the seasons. The occupancy rate is 90 percent, and prepaid reservations for Mardi Gras and the Sugar Bowl flow in as early as a year in advance.

America's Best! FRESH FRUIT FROZEN DAIQUIRIS

Le Petit Bar   *504-581-7300*

The St. Louis Hotel   *Skip Wyatt, Bar Manager*
730 Rue Bienville
New Orleans, Louisiana 70130   *Open every day: 10:00 A.M.–*
                                           midnight

The closest thing to ambrosia on earth could very well be the Fresh Fruit Frozen Daiquiris at Le Petit Bar of the St. Louis Hotel. Among Le Petit's unique creations are the watermelon, honeydew, banana, strawberry, and canteloupe daiquiris. Bar Manager Skip Wyatt's secret for these divine cocktails is to use the freshest fruits in season in the most imaginative way possible.

To make the watermelon daiquiri, Skip takes the meat of the watermelon, removes the seeds, blends it with Amaretto, adds crushed ice, reblends, and adds fresh lemon and lime juice. He adds a garnish of fresh watermelon and serves it in a thirty-two-ounce brandy snifter. Amaretto is the key to Le Petit's secret recipe for this drink, which is served from late spring to early fall.

Other daiquiris at Le Petit are rum-based and most are available year-round. One exception is the strawberry daiquiri, which is served in all but the winter months. It's made with fresh strawberries and strawberry liqueur.

Le Petit Bar is located in the St. Louis's magnificent courtyard. Here, amidst the lush native foliage, you will be serenaded by the birds and a string quartet—the perfect setting in which to enjoy a daiquiri.

America's Best! FRIED CHICKEN

Popeyes Famous Fried Chicken

1333 S. Clearview Parkway
Jefferson, Louisiana 70123

504-733-4300

Al Copeland, President

237 outlets in 18 states (37 in greater New Orleans)

11:00 A.M.–10:00 P.M.; some stores open 24 hours on weekends

N.B.: *Quality can vary from franchise to franchise.*

Popeye is not just the title of a famous comic strip; it is also the name of America's fastest-growing, highest-quality chain of fried-chicken outlets.

President Al Copeland perfected his recipe over a period of ten years and began operations in 1971 with Chicken On The Run in Arabi, Louisiana, a New Orleans suburb. His spicy chicken became so popular he changed the name to Popeyes Famous Fried Chicken a year later.

Popeyes uses only Grade A frying chicken—the juiciest fresh chicken available, always under 2¼ pounds. The secret to the spicy chicken is that it is dry-marinated for twelve hours in secret seasonings. These secret blends of fresh spices are prepared in Popeyes commissaries and delivered to the franchises. Once seasoned, the chicken is dipped in a special batter, fried in a blend of animal fat and vegetable oil, and cooled for eleven minutes in fryers tied into a computer which regulates temperatures.

Unseasoned chicken is also available. The basic order of two pieces of chicken, French fries or rice dressing, commonly known as "dirty rice" (rice cooked with gizzards, ground meat, and spices), and a roll comes to $1.39. A box of chicken with twenty-four pieces sells for $9.99. Popeyes also sells barbecued beans, corn on the cob, *jalapeños* (hot peppers), and some franchises have been experimenting with fried oysters.

Popeyes on Canal Street in New Orleans is probably the highest-volume fried-chicken operation in the U.S. The store is open twenty-four hours a day during Mardi Gras, serves 40,000 customers, and grosses over $55,000 in that one week.

Popeyes continues to center its operations in New Orleans because the city is known for good food. However, the company has over 200 outlets in eighteen states and is the third largest fried chicken franchise in the U.S. (Kentucky Fried Chicken and Church's are bigger). The chain has recently started operations in Michigan, North Dakota, Oregon, Chicago, and New York, and 800 units are under option to open in the next five years. Yearly sales exceed $50 million.

America's Best! GROCERY STORE

Jim Jamail and Sons Food Market

713-523-5535

Albert Jamail, President

314 *Kirby Drive*
Houston, Texas 77098

Albert Jamail or another member of the family might just greet you at the door with an oversized grocery cart. "One must maintain a small-store atmosphere within a complete food market," says Albert. So the 150 employees of Jim Jamail and Sons continue to serve customers in the style of an old-fashioned market, while providing them with the biggest selection of gastronomical delights in the U.S.

The eighteen butchers know their customers' preferences and special requirements—who's on a diet, who likes his sirloin strips cut exactly three-inches thick. Arnold Kitzwiller, who's been behind the counter for twenty-seven years, says "My first business is meat, the second is names." Standard stock includes Minnesota baby veal, Colorado lamb, and fresh fish from the Gulf Coast and New England. What the butchers don't have in stock, they order, even elephant meat.

Chef Rolf Meitler, German-born and Swiss-trained, oversees the preparation of some twelve different entrées, twenty-four salads, cold cuts, vegetables, appetizers, and ambrosial desserts each day. With his crew of sixteen, Meitler creates such dishes as his own famous chicken and dumplings, Boeuf Bourguinon, Oysters Rockefeller, Saltimbocca Florentine, calf's liver in Madeira sauce, Paella Valencia, shrimp gumbo, and a magnificent creamed Grand Marnier with strawberries. These delicacies are also available in Rolf's frozen-food locker.

Harry Jamail chooses the freshest produce at the market in Houston three mornings a week, and he has had a man in California selecting the best produce there for more than twenty-seven years. The store's sixteen produce people are carefully trained to arrange different fruits and vegetables for color, texture, and compatibility of taste.

You can buy eighteen kinds of strawberry preserves at Jamail's, jams from France, snail bisque, bacon, lettuce, and tomato soup, every kind of pasta, juices from all over the world, 300 varieties of cheese, chocolate tea, Hungarian coffee cake, spumoni from New Orleans, bloc de foie gras, thirty-five varieties of whole coffee beans, angel food cakes baked and delivered by a lady in La Grange, Texas, eau de fleur d'orange, baklava, six kinds of caviar, and over 200 varieties of breads, including four types of sourdough from San Francisco. The reason for the abundance of choice is that Jamail's tries to accommodate the immigrants from all parts of the country who have come to Houston. The store also stocks freeze-dried foods for backpackers.

Prices on regular items are competitive with other stores, but the Jamails never advertise or run specials. Along with wine vinegar from France at $9.50 a bottle, you can still find the 34¢ variety.

People buy much more than they normally would because they are overwhelmed by the unprecedented selection.

Jamail's has 4,000 credit cards in circulation, but trying to get one is like trying to get listed in the Social Register. As a special treat, the very oldest customers are presented with Christmas trees. It was one way Jim Jamail, the founder, felt he could thank his loyal patrons. Today this custom costs the Jamails over $10,000 a year.

"People are starved for service and quality these days," Albert says. It was with this philosophy that Nageeb "Jim" Jamail began his business in 1905. Jim, a Lebanese immigrant, opened a small fruit and vegetable stand and sold the "best quality at a fair price with the best of service." In 1946, he opened a store on Montrose Avenue with his sons, and with Houston's boom, the shop grew. A new highway forced Jamail's to move to its present location, where today it occupies over 128,000 feet of uncramped space.

America's Best! HERBAL MEDICINE MAN

Catfish Man of the Woods

Glenwood, West Virginia 25520

*Visiting hours: Thursday–
Saturday, 8:00 A.M.–9:00 P.M.*

*Catfish can't be reached by
telephone. "I half (sic) to go
miles to get to one."*

Suffer from arthritis, impotency, pimples, gallstones, obesity, or freckles? America's best herbal medicine man can help you with his unique cures for these and a multitude of other annoying conditions. In the mountains of southwest West Virginia, he's known as "Catfish Man of the Woods." He spends most of his time collecting and preparing his "bitters," the special herb remedy he prescribes for everything from cancer to black-lung disease. With merely a glance, he can recognize thousands of varieties of Appalachian plants.

Before his bitters can go to work, he believes that certain "poison" foods and drinks must be omitted from the diet. These forbidden substances are pork, vinegar, cabbage, graham crackers, salt, saccharine artificial sweeteners, grapefruit, cherries, plums, tomatoes, cranberries, fish that "don't wear scales," ducks and other web-footed fowl, round-hoofed animals, and oysters.

Why avoid these? "Your stomach cannot digest them. And it will find your weak spot (to cause tumors, gallstones, diabetes, and even pimples) and go to work on you." Surprisingly, white sugar doesn't make the list. He doesn't condemn sugar, except when used with bad food. "Sugar can't hurt you in any way if you use all good foods and drinks. In fact, your body needs sugar, but it must be allowed to do its good work and then pass through the kidneys." Otherwise, sluggishness in sex and other activities occurs. In fact, Twinkies rate as a staple in Catfish's personal diet.

Catfish—nicknamed by his fishing success but legally known as Clarence Frederick Gray—certainly doesn't lack believers who swear by his natural cures. He has received 18,000 letters seeking his advice and concoction of bitters. He makes these bitters out of bloodroot, wild cherry bark, and eighteen other dried herbs, and they're sold by mail order for only 20¢ a bag.

No matter how much the medical profession disagrees (some physicians are angry), Catfish has lectured at nearby Marshall University, conducted herb hunts, seminars, and appeared in films and on radio and television. People find him, despite his lack of access to telephone service. Each week during his "vistin' " hours, travelers manage to locate his small shack along a gravel road outside the tiny Ohio River town of Glenwood.

Catfish isn't a guru, mystic, or even an Indian steeped in herbal lore. But he does credit a mysterious Indian who cured his heart trouble with herbs as the inspiration to follow a family tradition— his great-great-grandmother was an herbal doctor. He's certain herbal knowledge helped his grandmother live to be 103. On the threshold of senior citizenhood himself, the former night watchman swears to be much more fit now that he follows his own advice than he was in his careless, younger days.

He doesn't permit alcohol, tobacco, and illegal drugs on his premises. He also abstains from prescription drugs and warns that no one should take birth control pills. Some unexpected items appear on his inventory of body, health, sex, and kidney strengtheners. That household item, Arm and Hammer Baking "Sody," is a wonder product for improving sex, according to Catfish. He also suggests ingesting a quarter teaspoon of it in water every day to help prevent any ailment except cancer. Other strengtheners include dill pickles and dill tea, olives, ginseng tea, lemonade, and lots of fresh carrots, celery, beets, peas, green beans, asparagus, and head lettuce. He prescribes a daily dose of his bitters made into tea to cure tuberculosis, emphysema, cancer, and black lung disease. It's also supposed to help arthritis.

Along with his bitters, Catfish dishes out gospel advice. He habitually quotes from the Bible, and he has decorated the walls of his shack with Biblical sayings.

America's Best! HOT-AIR BALLOON FIESTA

Albuquerque International Balloon Fiesta, Incorporated	*505-243-3245*
	Sheri Bachtell, President
401 Second North West *Albuquerque, New Mexico 87103*	*Begins 1st Saturday in October*
	Entry fee: $50, subject to change

In 1971, Sid Cutter, who is now the U.S. balloon champion, bought a hot-air balloon to use as a centerpiece at his mother's birthday party. While he was giving tethered balloon rides, pranksters cut the ropes, and Sid went up, up, and away on his first free flight. He managed to avoid rooftops and telephone lines and put down safely, and from that day on he has been Albuquerque's leading hot-air balloon enthusiast. He helped organize Albuquerque's first Balloon Fiesta that same year. Since then, Albuquerque has become America's hot-air balloon capital.

Sid now owns World Balloon, Inc., where he sells and repairs balloons and gives flying instructions. There are two other balloon shops in Albuquerque, and more than 100 balloons and 300 pilots. The Fiesta is now an annual, nonprofit event sponsored by the Chamber of Commerce, and more than 400 pilots come to Albuquerque each October to participate. It is the biggest ballooning event in the world. Albuquerque also hosted the 1973 and

99

These soon-to-be-airborne balloons will dot the Albuquerque sky for nine days during the Balloon Fiesta.

1975 World Championships, which it held in conjunction with the Fiesta.

The Fiesta begins the first Saturday of October at Simm's Launch Site, five miles north of Albuquerque. The land is flat and open, and the winds at the site are usually ideal for ballooning. In fact, winds in Albuquerque are rarely over ten miles per hour, the maximum safe velocity for operating a hot-air balloon. These winds also come from all directions, creating an "air box." A balloon is blown in one direction and, when it rises a little higher, it catches a wind blowing in another direction. It can drop and catch a wind which takes it in yet another direction. This air box functions in spring, summer, and autumn, and is one of the elements that make balloon flying in Albuquerque more fun than anywhere else.

The main event of the Fiesta is the Coyote-Road Runner Race. A lead balloon (the Road Runner) is released and after fifteen minutes a pack of balloons (Coyotes) sets out. The pilot of the Road Runner uses different winds and strategies to lead the other balloons on a chase. After forty-five minutes, the Road Runner puts down and the Coyote pilot who lands nearest wins the competition.

The emphasis of the Albuquerque Fiesta is on fun events and a relaxed atmosphere—not hard-driving competition. As a matter of fact, the National Championship held in Indianola, Iowa, was offered to Albuquerque, but Albuquerque didn't want the frayed nerves and hard feelings that result from intensely competitive flying. Local merchants donate the prizes, which have included trips, jewelry, and savings bonds. There are, however, no titles or big-money prizes awarded at the Fiesta. But that doesn't stop balloonists from England, France, Canada, Ireland, and other countries from participating. The competitors pay a $50 entry fee, and must rent a service to transport their equipment to and from the launch site.

Publisher Malcolm Forbes travels to Albuquerque as often as possible to fly his own balloon. International balloon celebrities and Albuquerqueans Maxie Anderson and Ben Abruzzo, who sailed across the Atlantic in a balloon in 1978, can be seen flying in the Fiesta from time to time, and the convention department of the Chamber of Commerce now uses a balloon design as its trademark, evidence of the pride Albuquerque feels for the sport and its Fiesta.

America's Best! HOT DOGS

Nathan's Famous, Inc.

1515 Broadway
New York, New York 10036

212-869-0600

Murray Handwerker, President

Coney Island, and 48 other locations

N.B.: Nathan's has now gone "skinless" in 80 percent of its locations. Therefore, America's best can only be found at stores in Coney Island, Livingston, New Jersey, and selected Florida locations.

Franklin Delano Roosevelt served Nathan's Hot Dogs to the King and Queen of England in 1937. Barbra Streisand's guests dined on them at a cast party for *Funny Girl* in London.

Nathan Handwerker's fortune seems to have been governed by the stars. In 1916, he and his steady girl friend Ida were working

101

for the man who invented hot dogs at Feltman's German Beer Garden, Coney Island, New York. Nathan was a roll slicer at $10 a week and Ida was a dog dispenser at $7 a week. Regular customers Eddie Cantor and Jimmy Durante, singing waiters at the time, suggested that Nathan and Ida open their own stand and sell 5¢ hot dogs instead of the 10¢ ones at Feltman's. So they pooled their life savings, which came to $300 between them, and began making hot dogs according to Ida's personal recipe. French fries were 5¢, drinks 3¢. It was only a summer operation then, but the stand was open twenty-four hours a day. Customers would knock on the counter to wake up Nathan for service.

The store measured ten by twenty-five feet and didn't even have a sign (paint was too expensive). But when Sophie Tucker's hit, "Nathan, Nathan, For What Are You Waitin'?" came out, Nathan's friends ran to him and said, "Nathan, you're famous!" So he put up a sign, "Nathan's Famous."

Today, Nathan's Famous, Inc., run by Nathan's son Murray, is a $34-million-a-year empire of thirty-one company-owned restaurants with 1,500 workers, eighteen franchises, a catering service, and a marketing distribution service. At many Nathan's locations, the menu comprises more than eighty items, but the Coney Island stand sells the most hot dogs, as many as 38,000 on a good, hot summer Sunday. All told, Nathan's sells fifteen million hot dogs a year—a big bite of the forty billion Americans eat each year.

Nathan's hot dogs are still made according to Ida's original recipe of 100 percent highest-grade beef (not jowls or necks, as in other brands). No fillers such as veal, pork, chicken, or cereals are included. The spices and condiments that go into Nathan's hot dogs include paprika, salt, pepper, garlic, nutmeg, and sugar, but the proportions are a closely guarded secret—the formula, which only three people know, is actually kept in a vault. The workers in the two manufacturing plants in New York and New Jersey, where the spice is made, as well as all workers involved in making Nathan's hot dogs, must sign an affidavit to the effect that they will never disclose the recipe.

One of the most important features of a Nathan's hot dog is its natural sheep's casing, which seals in juices that evaporate in skinless hot dogs. Nathan's hot dogs are stuffed, and put in a gas-fired, hickory-based smokehouse for thirty-six minutes, timed by computer. Then they're washed in cold water and refrigerated.

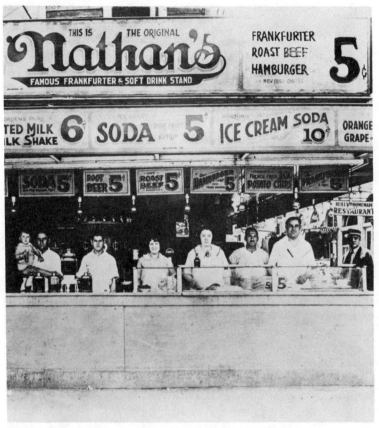

Nathan Handwerker turned his Coney Island hot-dog stand into a million-dollar-a-year business.

The hot dogs are best when grilled or broiled. Boiling is less favorable, because the flavor leaches out into the water. You should never cut a hot dog's casing before cooking—this would make the hot dog cook faster, but the juices would be lost. The hot dog is well done just when the casing splits. Customers at Nathan's get their hot dogs done to order—rare, medium, well done, etc.—just as if they were ordering steak. Nathan's hot dogs can be eaten without cooking because they're smoked, but eating them cold out of the refrigerator is not recommended. Let them warm up first.

In the 1920s, Cary Grant (his name was Archie Leach then)

worked as a stiltwalker advertising the Coney Island rides, and depended upon Nathan's for his meals. Nathan once told him to abandon his hopes of a show biz career, and offered him a job at the counter. Clara Bow, the IT girl of the silents, once worked the counter at Nathan's.

During the Depression, hot dogs were about all people could afford, so Nathan's business prospered. By 1932, the store was open year-round, twenty-four hours a day. The menu expanded to include pizza, chicken, roast beef sandwiches, corn on the cob, "Coney Island Clam Chowder," hamburgers, lobster on a bun, chow mein on a bun (because some of the workers were Chinese), and even frog's legs, which are currently a bestseller.

The Coney Island stand, known as "the Taj Mahal of the Hot Dog World," has been visited by such celebrities as Jacqueline Onassis, Rose Kennedy, Mike Nichols, Milton Berle, Governor Carey of New York, Red Buttons, Grace Kelly, Elaine May, Joey Bishop, and the Lodges. Nelson Rockefeller, who occasionally dropped in by helicopter, once said that no New York politician could be elected without being photographed at Nathan's. In fact, since it was founded in 1916, every U.S. President has either visited the Coney Island stand or enjoyed Nathan's hot dogs in the privacy of the White House. When the Fords returned from their historic trip to China in 1975, a case of Nathan's franks with all the trimmings awaited them. During New York's Operation Sail (1976), a case of franks was delivered to Queen Elizabeth and Prince Philip aboard the Royal yacht *Britannia*. Although Nathan's does not have a regular mail-order service, they do mail orders (packed in dry ice) to Steve Lawrence and Eydie Gorme, who periodically send a blank check for Nathan's Famous.

Most of Nathan's stores are in the metropolitan New York area, but there are several in Florida and California, and Nathan's products are also sold in supermarkets. Nathan's restaurant managers go through a six-week training program at "Frankie University," Nathan's own Management Training Center, where the original Nathan's motto is still kept in mind—"Give 'em and let 'em eat!" Almost all Nathan's stores are open seven days a week and twenty hours a day. The worldwide acclaim for Nathan's hot dogs fully justifies the company's proud logo, "From a hot dog to an international habit!"

America's Best! HOTEL BUTLERS

Hyatt on Union Square

Penthouse Suites
345 Stockton Street
San Francisco, California 94108

415-398-1234

John Dixon, General Manager
Sandie Wernick, Public Relations
*   Director*

When's the last time you checked into your hotel and had a penthouse suite with a butler to:

> Unpack your bags, clean and press clothes, shine shoes, wash undies, and fetch shoe trees?
>
> Leave a small gold box of Godiva Chocolates on each pillow with a note on pink paper saying "Sweet Dreams"?
>
> Have the elevator ready and hold the doors open for you when you depart?
>
> Draw your bath?
>
> Serve cocktails from the suite's pre-stocked bar, chilled Perrier water before you retire, and breakfast in bed?
>
> Announce your guests upon arrival? Bring messages?
>
> Deliver the local newspapers and the *Wall Street Journal?*
>
> Make all dinner reservations, locate theatre tickets, and handle all tipping?
>
> Be at your beck and call from 7:00 A.M. to 11:00 P.M. seven days a week?

These are just some of the duties of the butlers at San Francisco's Hyatt Hotel on Union Square. The butlers and this luxurious service come with any of the five penthouse suites on the thirty-fourth floor.

Dwain Nix, the primary daytime butler, wears a black morning suit, white round-collared shirt, and a fawn-colored waistcoat and tie. His main evening counterpart, *Jacques Plaisant*, is dressed appropriately in a tailored tuxedo. A third butler, *Brian Lane*, works alternate evenings and some days. Personalized service is their specialty, whether it be overseeing a cocktail party or serving dinner on a table in your suite—complete with candelabrum. "We'll do anything we can to make a guest happy," Jacques explains. That includes providing a piano for guest Neil Diamond (who claims to have composed a song on it), and bringing food from other restaurants for Jackie Gleason during a lengthy stay.

The list of celebrity guests includes Liza Minnelli, Warren Beatty, Hugh Downs, corporate presidents, Arab sheiks, Walter Mondale, and Chip Carter.

"Everybody's different and so are their requests," says Jacques. "Most American guests don't know what duties to assign a butler." Not many take him up on the offer of unpacking, and teenage fans of old British films are the main customers for having baths drawn.

Jacques has worked for the hotel since it opened in 1973, and he loves it. He estimates that with tips, he makes the same as a first-class waiter in San Francisco. Both butlers call the subject of tips "a delicate issue." Jacques does acknowledge, however, that sales executives tip the most, while the "average" guest (but guests here aren't average, he insists) tips approximately $10 a day per butler.

Good hotel butlers are hard to find, for there's no real training available in the U.S. Dwain is a former dining-room manager and bartender. Jacques started out as a bellhop in France. Through subsequent jobs—with the strictest dress codes and training—he learned what constitutes the very finest French service and the special skills involved. Friends helped him come to the U.S., where he worked in, directed, and owned a variety of French and international restaurants. Brian worked as a waiter at the original Hyatt in Dallas before joining the penthouse staff.

Edward G. Sullivan, presently vice-president and managing director of the Hyatt at Waikiki in Hawaii, developed the idea for the butlers in 1973. He hoped they would enable the newly opened Hyatt on Union Square to compete with the longer-established luxury hotels of San Francisco. A linen closet was converted to a pantry and Jacques was hired as one of the first butlers.

Mr. Sullivan originally intended for the butlers to serve the guests breakfast in the morning and appetizers in the evening. The butlers would discuss the food selection with the guests, rather than have them choose from an impersonal printed list of available dishes. Little did the Hyatt management anticipate the enthusiasm of Jacques and his colleagues. Through little touches, such as greeting the guests at the elevator with "Welcome home," the concept has grown far beyond the basic breakfast-and-appetizers idea.

The suites are individually and expensively decorated. Each has a dramatic view of San Francisco, and all provide extras such as designer linens, towels, and bath sheets. The bathrooms come complete with scales, plants, television sets, strawberry-scented shampoo, and bubble-bath soap, and three of them have sunken tubs and separate round showers. Prices run from $400 to $550 a day, depending on whether the suite has one bedroom or two.

Suites like this aren't unusual in luxury hotels, and other hotels have tried butler service. But the Hyatt on Union Square is the only hotel where it all comes together so nicely.

America's Best! HOTEL CONCIERGE

André de Beauharnais   *212-755-5900*

The Barclay, An Inter-   *Charles E. Guffrey, Manager*
Continental Hotel
111 East 48th Street
New York, New York 10017

"The concierge is the man who does the impossible in the shortest amount of time," explains André de Beauharnais, who graces New York's posh Barclay Hotel with his amazing services. "And I have never failed," he boasts politely in his refined accent.

André can use his extensive New York contacts to get you restaurant reservations or find a babysitter or a dog-walker within the hour. On a grander scale, he can use his international contacts to simplify problems regarding visas. "My contacts here and overseas are fabulous," he says. "I can get you anything!" Once, at The Pierre Hotel, where he worked before going to The Barclay in December, 1979, André arranged an audience with the Pope for a guest.

Americans are not accustomed to the unconditional service of a hotel concierge because this European tradition never took hold in the States. In fact, André is one of the few hotel concierges in New York. The Barclay and The Pierre have concierges because their clientele consists largely of service-oriented Europeans and South Americans.

Once André had to arrange the entire funeral of a European guest who underwent unsuccessful surgery in New York. Another time he found a magician to entertain the three children of a South American woman in their Pierre suite. It's André's business to know everyone in New York, and especially everyone in the hotel. He says it takes "a lot of observation to know what everyone needs—what drinks they like, whether they prefer white roses or red. I fulfill these small desires to make The Barclay a second home for the guests." Guests at The Pierre and The Barclay have included members of the best families of Europe, heads of state, and stars such as Sophia Loren and André's personal favorite, Jean Paul Belmondo.

Once the presidents of France, Cyprus, and Canada were all staying at The Pierre at once. For reasons of protocol, André had to make sure none of them received preferential treatment. For a particular party, he had to coordinate their elevators so they would all arrive simultaneously.

If you need a ticket for a sold-out Broadway show, reservations in a hot night spot in New York or Paris, or someone to press your suit at the last moment, André can easily take care of it. His most difficult task involved a millionaire who wanted the best cabin on the *Queen Elizabeth II*. The cabin had already been booked, however, and it seemed that none of André's influence could help him. As a last resort, he asked Cunard for the name of the man who had reserved the desired cabin. By chance, he was acquainted with that man's girlfriend. Needless to say, André got the cabin.

Another time, an Arab sheik asked André to order a brand-new Rolls Royce for him. When the car arrived from London, the sheik was "displeased with the color," so André sent it right back to London and had another shipped. The sheik gifted him with a $1,000 check.

When it comes to gratuities, André refuses to state an appropriate minimum, saying that it is entirely up to the guest. However, his tips range everywhere between $20 and infinity. One guest gave him a three-day boat trip near Cannes, France.

Because his opinion is so highly respected, André is a great favorite of the businessmen of New York. The proprietors of the exclusive disco Studio 54 will admit anyone with André's recommendation, because it's the people that André sends that make Studio 54 such an exciting place. He claims that he could dine in any restaurant in New York for nothing, but he makes a point of always paying to preserve his objectivity and his independence from unfair allegiances.

André was born in Paris in 1940. He was always fascinated by the work of the concierges, but his formal education led him to study law for four years at the University of Paris. At the age of twenty-one, André began to acquire his extensive gambling experience, working in the big casinos of the French Riviera. He also acquired fluency in English, German, and Russian. Before coming to the Pierre, André was concierge in the Hotel Ruhl in Nice.

America's Best! HOTEL SUITE

The Royal Suite (42-R) *212-355-3100*

The Waldorf Towers
301 Park Avenue
New York, New York 10022

Frank G. Wangeman,
 Executive Vice-President
Peter Zlatar,
 Towers Manager

Not long ago, a sheik who was staying in the Royal Suite at The Waldorf Towers called room service and ordered a Cadillac limousine, to be put on his tab. The car arrived promptly, and, as should be expected, it came regally gift-wrapped. What's more, the request came as no surprise to the staff. For $1,100 a day, any request should be taken for granted.

The Royal Suite is immaculately appointed to meet the tastes and needs of the most demanding king, sheik, or tycoon. This 42nd-story mansion-in-the-sky contains enormous, party-sized rooms, and spectacular unobstructed views of New York.

Pianist Van Cliburn, a permanent guest, kept three pianos in the suite—two grands in the living room and an upright in his bedroom. He chose the suite for its privacy and quiet. There are no floors above, and only two other nonadjacent apartments on the floor, including the one kept for the Permanent United States Mission to the U.N.

The apartment was totally renovated in 1977 at the cost of $100,000 and again in September 1979 by designer David T. Williams. Renovation included complete redecoration, new air-conditioning units, and new panoramic windows that can be opened—a rare treat for New York tower residents. Williams chose French Regency Period furniture for the suite to combine with the Waldorf's reproductions of antique furniture already in the apartment.

You enter the suite through an elegant, symmetrical foyer, decorated with silver gold-flocked wallpaper, mirrors, antique tables, stands and vases. The eclectic living room, measuring thirty-nine by twenty-four feet, is carpeted with a $25,000 Persian rug, and has velvet couches, an 18th-century French marquetry table, a red velvet ottoman, and a mirrored blue-and-white marble fireplace imported from an English mansion. Chinese porcelain accessories embellish the room, which can accommodate 55 people for a sit-down dinner or 100 for a reception.

The dining room, twenty-four feet by thirty-six feet, overlooks Park Avenue and nearby St. Patrick's Cathedral. It seats twenty-four guests comfortably. The colors here are apricot, beige, and celadon. The focal point is a highly polished Louis XIV-style oval mahogany dining table and Chippendale-style chairs. An 18th-century Hepplewhite sideboard, oval floral oil paintings, lavish chandeliers, and a display of fine Lenox china and Chinese porcelain complete the decor. Off of the dining room, there is a small kitchen. Many of the Arabian visitors buy their meat from the hotel and cook it themselves.

The small bedroom (thirteen feet by twenty feet) continues the color scheme of the dining room. It is decorated in Oriental-patterned wallpaper, and the Oriental motif is continued in the prints. Tufted headboards and a magnificent Biedermeier armoire

The living room of Suite 42-R is eclectically luxurious.

continue the eclectic theme of the main salon. A roomy marbled bath includes a separate shower and tub, a French Regency dressing table, and two large windows for natural light.

In the master bedroom (twenty-seven feet by twenty feet) an airy, feminine ambience is created by flocked celadon wallpaper and highlighted by apricot carpets and furniture. A springy apricot, beige, and celadon striped satin covers selected pieces of furniture. There's an expansive king-sized bed, and an adjacent dressing room. Striped material also highlights the three-room boudoir-bath, but here the designer opted for a lively flocked paper. There are ample closets, a shower and toilet room, and an outer chamber containing the tub and vanity, with floor-to-ceiling mirrors. All three rooms are lavishly appointed with imported marble.

The Towers have their own entry where Peter Zlatar, the Towers manager, will personally greet all guests of Suite 42-R. Mr. Zlatar is a perfectionist. He keeps a file of the special needs of all his special guests and a private phone line for all Towers guests. The Towers also feature elevators with operators and private service elevators. Telephone messages are printed and slipped under the door, fresh flowers appear with breakfast, and baths are supplied with exotic soaps and special towels.

America's Best! JELLY BEANS

The Jelly Belly

David Klein, President

9533 East Garvey
South El Monte, California 91733

$3.50 per lb.

213-442-6494

America's best jelly beans come in twenty-five flavors, such as watermelon (green on the outside and pink on the inside), cotton candy, green apple, baked apple (cinnamon on the outside and apple flavor inside), lemon/lime (the Uncola), tangerine, cream soda, and even chocolate banana. David Klein, president of The Jelly Belly, is so confident that his jelly beans are the best he plans to challenge other manufacturers to a jelly bean taste-off, with each company putting up a $100,000 ante.

The secret to Jelly Belly perfection is that the flavor is soaked inside out. Most companies only flavor the outside, which leaves the telltale sign of white, tasteless centers.

The process for making jelly beans is quite complicated. First, corn syrup, sugar, and flavorings are stirred at the proper temperature and put into molds. Then, these are stored in 120-pound trays that hold 600,000 beans. The trays are left in a starch room for four days at 110 degrees F., then transferred to a pan room. Here, the mixture (which is the center of the jelly bean) is put into a machine resembling a cement mixer and the outer layer is sprayed on. The beans are then dried for two to three days.

Dave began Jelly Belly in 1976. He found a food chemist to create initial flavors, and rented a store. Soon afterwards, an Associated Press feature on "the only store in the world to exclusively sell jelly beans" swamped him with orders. Dave has since become known as "Mr. Jelly Belly" and has appeared on TV shows across the country, making Jelly Belly milk shakes, doing a dance called "The Jelly Belly," and always reminding children not to forget Mr. Toothbrush.

Dave is turning down hundreds of orders, and estimates that he could be doing 40 percent more business if he had more plant capacity. He already produces over a million pounds of beans per year, and has recently added the Gum Drop Kids, twelve flavors of gumdrops, to his line.

All of his sales are made through candy distributors for worldwide distribution to gourmet candy stores. One man displays 150 pounds of Jelly Belly Beans in an elegant swan. Some people collect the beans just to make multicolored displays in their homes.

Jelly Belly jelly beans can be found at only the best stores, including America's best department store, Marshall Field (see p. 77), and throughout the U.S., Canada, Europe, and Japan. Jelly Belly does not advertise.

America's Best! JET

Boeing 747

Boeing Commercial Airplane
Company
Seattle, Washington 98124

206-237-1710

Gordon S. Williams, Manager,
Public Relations, 747 Division

Tour Center
Final Assembly Plant
Everett, Washington

206-342-4801

Tours: Monday–Friday, 1:00 P.M.;
also at 9:00 A.M., June–August;
no children under 12

Weighing in at almost one million pounds, with a wingspan of 195 feet and a length of 231 feet, the Boeing 747 is the largest commercial airplane in the world. Because of its luxurious double-decker architecture, it can carry up to 500 passengers in living room-like comfort. The main deck cabin is 185-feet long and

113

20-feet wide, allowing for well spaced seating with two service aisles, and establishing a new standard of passenger comfort.

The 747 is also the fastest wide-body airplane in the world. The 747 SP (Special Performance) can cruise comfortably at mach .86, or almost the speed of sound. With the exception of the SST, it is certified to fly higher than any other airplane—45,000 feet, although usually it flies at only 37,000 feet (that's still 4,000 feet higher than other commercial airplanes).

The 747 is the most economic plane in terms of fuel consumption per passenger, and consequently the most profitable airplane for those airlines that own them. Because it can carry so much fuel (51,000 gallons), the 747 has an extraordinary flight range—over 6,000 nautical miles, even when heavily loaded. A 747 once flew over 12,000 miles from the final assembly plant in Everett, Washington, to Capetown, South Africa, without refueling.

Best of all, the Boeing 747 is an unusually safe airplane. It has an unprecedented number of redundant systems. In the unlikely event that one system fails, there will be another (sometimes several) to take its place. For example, the 747 has four hydraulically controlled sets of wheels (called trucks), but it needs only two of these to land. Boeing built an entire airplane solely for the purpose of testing it far beyond normal operational limits. The wing tips were bent upwards twenty-nine feet before showing strain. Other fatigue tests involved simulating the effects of take-off, flight, pressurizing, cruising, rough air, landing, and taxiing. The testers even sawed through more than twenty critical points in the structure, and the craft was still capable of flying. In the "refuse takeoff" test, the plane was brought to takeoff speed, then braked to a stop. The wheels caught fire, but there was no damage to the craft.

The 747 is a highly stable aircraft, with no tendency to roll from side to side. It can land at an extreme angle in high winds, and still straighten itself out. In fact, it can land under even more adverse conditions, including abnormally high speeds or the buildup of ice on the wings and tail. Besides all this, the 747 is an easy plane to fly. The pilot has advance warning gear that monitors all systems of the craft, and, in the event of a mishap, gives him time to recover.

The 747 was originally designed for freight. To build an airplane that could be loaded through the nose, it was necessary to place the cockpit on top of the main body of the plane. This also

Shiny giants near completion in the world's largest building.

created lots of new space behind the cockpit. Most airlines used this extra space as a first-class lounge, connected to the main cabin by a spiral staircase. It took four years to build the original 747, which was finished in September, 1968, at a cost of $1½ billion, an expenditure that nearly sank the company. Since then, over 500 have been built, at $50 million apiece.

In order to build the 747, the Boeing Company had to build its own special railroad and the world's largest building. The Final Assembly Plant at Everett, Washington, is the workplace of 7,000 mechanics. It sprawls over forty-three acres of land, and encloses 200 million cubic feet. It is kept absolutely spotless and is well lit, to create a pleasant atmosphere for the workers. Boeing has also provided indoor and outdoor tracks so that the workers can exercise and keep themselves in shape.

Parts come to the Final Assembly Plant from 1,500 subcontractors all over America and are integrated into the Boeing giants. It takes eighteen months to build a 747. The planes are green when their assembly is complete, before they are painted the colors of the airline that has bought them. All of the 4½ million parts are carefully inspected before the plane is flown. After a trial flight of three hours, during which every system is tested, the craft is delivered to the buyer, who tests it himself. If you're interested in buying a 747, the Boeing Company will give you (without charge) the use of an office from which you can supervise the construction of your plane and see that everything is done according to your wishes.

The Boeing Company was founded at the turn of the century by W. E. Boeing, a wealthy timber trader. When Boeing's personal airplane was disabled in an accident, he was unable to get the parts to fix it. So, with the help of a friend who was a naval engineering captain, he decided to build a better airplane himself, and he succeeded in 1916. Two of his biplanes ended up flying mail in New Zealand. During slow times, the young Boeing Company made furniture and "sea sleds" (similar to speed boats) to stay in business. Today Boeing is a public company, traded on the New York Stock Exchange at about $50 a share.

America's Best! JIGSAW PUZZLES

Stave Puzzles

Main Street
Norwich, Vermont 05055

802-649-1450

Steve Richardson, Proprietor

Steve Richardson's jigsaw puzzles are the most sophisticated, insidious, and deceptive in the world, and guaranteed to drive you out of your mind. In fact, when Steve sells a super-difficult puzzle, he'll even throw in a special bonus bottle of Bufferin.

Two special features qualify Stave Puzzles as America's best. These are *silhouette interaction* and the exclusive *sculptured effect*.

Silhouette interaction means that many of the pieces of the puzzle are cut in the shape of animals, people, or objects that are related to each other and to the theme of the puzzle. Other puzzle makers have done this, but they have not made the silhouette pieces interact as extensively as Richardson has. In one heart-shaped Stave Puzzle, a piece in the shape of a boy "kisses" a piece in the shape of a girl.

In a puzzle depicting Arthur Fiedler and the Boston Pops, two pieces in the shape of kettle drums interlock with a piece shaped like the Pops' tympanist. Included somewhere in every puzzle is Richardson's trademark—a piece in the shape of a clown, signed and dated by Richardson.

To achieve the sculptured effect (the advance that sets him far ahead of all other puzzle makers), Richardson artfully removes thin slivers of wood from the puzzle so that the empty spaces form a design, representing some central theme. The top of the Pops Puzzle is dominated by a sculptured "bust" of Arthur Fiedler, hovering over the photograph of the orchestra like a guiding spirit.

Puzzles with the sculptured effect are especially difficult to solve becasue the empty spaces cause some of the pieces to fit loosely, and nowhere is there a picture of the completed work. To make matters worse, Stave Puzzles come with deceptive titles. For example, a puzzle named "Hole in One" shows a whale that has been harpooned, not a golf course.

Every Stave Puzzle is a unique creation, made of five-ply wood, and backed with beautiful African ribbon-striped mahogany—they are exceptionally strong and durable. They are cut on a jigsaw, and are sanded, finished, polished, and counted by hand. The name Stave is a contraction of Steve and Dave, the names of the two founders (Dave is no longer a partner). Stave also means "to break into pieces."

Stave Puzzles cost 50¢ per piece, and range in price from $75 to $1,520. There is no extra charge for special requests (except the sculptured effect). Richardson will make a puzzle of any photograph or art print you like, including special silhouettes, or sculpt your initials or your name into the puzzle. He has even made puzzles with limericks cut into them, so you have to solve two puzzles at once.

Stave Puzzle pieces are cut in three basic styles: *The Classic*, a "tastefully restrained" style that most people are familiar with; *The Fantasy*, with graceful but unusual pieces full of cloverleaf and arrowhead interlocks; and *The Nightmare*, the most difficult style, because the interlocks all look very much alike. "It's designed to bring out the masochist in you," Steve says.

Stave Puzzles climbed to new peaks with the introduction of the innovative *Winter Fantasy* puzzle, first marketed for Christmas of 1978. Richardson collaborated with local artist Jim Schubert to produce what he describes as "a puzzle spectacular—a super-deluxe, no-holds-barred, extra-difficult, super-fun puzzle." Each puzzle of this "limited edition" is hand-colored, signed, and numbered by Schubert.

Winter Fantasy incorporates all twenty-five of Richardson's puzzle tricks. The dirtiest of them all is the inclusion of extra pieces. Richardson also builds hidden images into the puzzle. They do not become apparent until you are almost done.

Available in both a 900-piece size ($500 per puzzle) and a 500-piece size ($250 per puzzle), *Winter Fantasy* is chock-full of silhouettes especially designed for the puzzle—seventy in the large one, forty in the smaller.

Added to the twenty-five tricks, silhouettes, and the hidden images are all the usual Stave features, such as the sculptured effect and the Stave clown silhouette. Another clever way that Stave Puzzles mislead their avid enthusiasts is with the occasional "irregular-edged" puzzle (not bounded with the usual straight edges) and the "crooked corners," straight edges that do not form part of the border, but are part of the interior.

"The World's First Modular Puzzle" was introduced in February, 1979, with the unveiling of the *Dollhouse*. The puzzle is designed with five separate sections that can be put together side-by-side in any order. The house has an "open room" effect showing a view of each room inside. To make things a little more difficult, Richardson decided to make the frame and roof of the house separate puzzles. And, of course, the edges are irregularly shaped. It sells for $1,520.

For pure difficulty, however, *Snowflake* is the ultimate. It features irregular edges, all white with empty spaces conforming to the internal geometry of a snowflake. Though the puzzle is listed in three sizes, Richardson says that he'll make it in any size. Stave also makes a limited set of *New Yorker* cover designs (by

By no means the most difficult of the collection, the 560-piece *Tristram Coffin Mansion* includes all the usual Stave tricks.

special permission) in puzzle form. They sell for $100 each, and have complex silhouettes.

The earliest jigsaw puzzles were created in a London printshop in the 1760s by John Spilsbury. His "dissected maps" were meant to instruct young people in geography and history. Stave also produces similar didactic puzzles, including an unmarked map of the U.S. "It's amazing how many people don't know the shapes of the states," says Richardson. He also makes an American flag puzzle that can be put together only by matching the names of the states with their nicknames, or with items of trivial information.

One of Richardson's favorite puzzles is *Ludwig's Ladies*—an irregular-edged cartoon portrait of Ludwig van Beethoven, with a voluptuous Muse (source of artistic inspiration) tangled in his unkempt hair. And, as a last refinement, he decided to sculpt into the hair two nudes flanking a G-clef.

Richardson has a degree in mathematics and worked in the think tank of a computer company before he started making puzzles. He was approached by a number of puzzle lovers who were patrons of Par Puzzles in New York, which was near dissolution because the sole surviving puzzle maker wanted to retire. Richardson began studying examples of virtuoso puzzle making in 1970, and opened Stave Puzzles in 1974.

Stave Puzzles are unavailable at stores and must be ordered directly from the company in Vermont. There is a great demand for the puzzles throughout the year, but especially at Christmas time, when people looking for unusual gifts inundate Richardson and his two assistants with requests. Special orders come from all over the world, and there is usually a healthy three to four weeks backlog of orders, six weeks at Christmas. Eighty percent of Stave's customers are regulars.

Richardson exercises all his diabolical cunning only on those special customers who request it. He adamantly refuses to reveal the names of his famous customers, but he does say that his most regular business comes from one of the wealthiest families in the world. He sends them a new and more difficult puzzle every two weeks. How chic—a puzzle budget of $6,000 a year.

America's Best! JOGGING ROLLER SKATES

**RC Sports, Inc., Division
Medalist Industries, Inc.**

*315 North Lindenwood
Olathe, Kansas 66061*

913-782-5277

Ronald J. Creten, President

Since May, 1978, RC Sports of Olathe, Kansas, has been combining the best of jogging and athletic footwear with roller-skate technology to make America's best jogging roller skates.

As outdoor skating takes on all the proportions of a national fad, RC President Ronald J. Creten can't keep up with the orders for his skates that flow in from 3,000 rinks, pro shops, and specialty footwear stores all over the country. He's sold 140,000 pairs—$12 million worth—since he began marketing them. One concession in New York's Central Park rents 800 pairs of the joggers on an average weekend.

RC was the first company to contract with a major athletic footwear manufacturer to design an athletic shoe exclusively for outdoor skating. Hyde Spot-Bilt of Cambridge, Massachusetts, designs an all-leather-and-suede shoe with nylon stitching for strength and special cushioning inside. The heel and insole are reinforced to withstand the special pressures of skating—combining comfort, appearance, and strength. ETI of Boulder, Colorado, makes the bright yellow, "high rebound" wheels with a special polyurethane, not soft enough to drag, but resilient so your teeth won't rattle when you hit a bump or obstinate rock.

The double-seal precision steel bearings (as opposed to the single-seal variety that gets dirty and slows down after only a few outings) are manufactured by Hartford Bearing Company, and General Bearing Company, Hartford, Connecticut. And to bring it all together, RC utilizes a specially designed Sure-Grip plate chassis for the skate, made with "356" sand-cast aluminum instead of the weaker, less precise "380" sand-cast aluminum used by competitors.

"This is sporting equipment that has rejuvenated the young adult market for roller skating—people in their thirties who skated when they were little but gave it up," says Creten. "Now they can skate outside, away from crowds, and exercise. The skates are no longer a toy." In fact, the RC Joggers have been most popular with people in the twenty-five-to-forty age group.

Dr. Max Novich, U.S. Olympic Team physician, says that skating is better than jogging for keeping fit. In fact, two worldwide athletic shoemakers, Hyde and Puma, believe so much in the future of skating that they will soon put their specially designed shoes on RC Jogger skates and market them as their only non-track shoe products.

With normal maintenance, like a quick wipe-down of the wheels and axles after use, the jogger skates should last ten years with ten to fifteen hours of use per week. The unisex sizes (three to thirteen) run in whole numbers only. Women need only subtract

1½ from their normal size to order the correct size jogger skates. (If you're in between, go for the looser fit.) That means a store, pro shop, or rental concession does not need a separate inventory for both men and women, saving money and space and encouraging many outlets to sell roller skates for the first time.

With its full line of skate products, RC Sports, Inc., offers a total of twenty-two million custom combinations of indoor and outdoor skates, which the assembling plant in Olathe, Kansas, will make up within twenty-four hours of receiving your order. The models include:

> *Riedell Shoes*—highest quality competition-type boots, traditional black and white color, $90;
>
> *Rexor Shoes*—initially for outdoor use, designed by Riedell, now for outdoor or indoor use on quality chassis assemblies, "Disco" boot in brown, suede exterior, complete with disco laces and leather lining, $94.95;
>
> *All-Star*—traditional unlined outdoor skate boot with same undercarriage as Jogger Skate (Sure-Grip plate), $79.95;
>
> *The Celebrity*—lined version of the All-Star, $89.95.

Only outdoor skates are assembled before being ordered. RC Sports will custom-make any indoor skate to order, using one of twenty-two million possible combinations of its full line of components (5,600 styles of shoes in all major brands). One of the largest orders to date was for 2,000 jogging skates in red and gold for the University of Southern California.

RC also makes the *Roller Ski*, used by the U.S. Olympic Team to condition skiers before they go into competitive training. It utilizes a wider "offset truck" with the cushion, axles, and wheels of a regular skate, but the wheels are farther apart so you can distribute your weight and handle turns like you would on skis.

Creten also designs roller rinks. He will put down a plastic Rollerglide floor (for about $18,000 for the average 12,000-square-foot rink) or install lighting and sound systems. Lighting for a rink ranges from $5,000 to $50,000, and a sound system costs between $12,000 and $15,000. He recently supervised the installation of an $80,000 light system in a Quebec rink.

For old buildings like supermarkets and storage houses converted to rinks, where a plastic floor isn't feasible because the base isn't level concrete, Creten has an exclusive arrangement with the California-based Rollerboard Company to factory-install a special tongue-groove construction flake-wood floor with a wax no-skid finish on an asphalt base.

The ultimate, of course, is to have RC Sports custom-build a rink from the ground up with its exclusive designs and equipment. For a 22,000-square-foot building, housing an average 12,000-square-foot rink, Creten estimates total costs with land, building, rink, and equipment at $750,000 to $1,000,000. The company built three rinks in the Milwaukee area between 1976 and 1978.

The son of a roller-rink owner, Creten has been skating since he was six. As a high-school champion he placed in the Nationals and won two regional titles for dance. In 1972, he went into partnership with his father and soon began acquiring equipment and accessory distributorships. Medalist Industries, Inc., acquired RC Sports and its subsidiaries in 1979, and Creten has stayed on as president.

America's Best! JONNYCAKES

The Dovecrest Restaurant

Summit Road
Arcadia Village
Exeter, Rhode Island 02822

401-539-7795

Eleanor and Ferris Dove,
Owners

7 days a week: 11:30 A.M.–9:00
P.M., closed Christmas Day

Visa, Master Charge

Society for the Propagation of
the Jonnycake Tradition in
Rhode Island
Box 433
Rumford, Rhode Island 02916
Helene Tessler, First Vice-
President and Jonnycake
Journal editor

401-253-5705

The first governor of the Plymouth Colony said the new settlers wouldn't have survived in the New World without jonnycakes. Thomas Robinson Hazard, the Rhode Island humorist, called them "the best article of farinaceous food . . . ever partaken of by mortal man." For 400 years they were a staple of the Rhode Island Narragansett Indian diet. Roger Williams said a serving of them could sustain a man for a full-day's trek through the wilderness.

Eleanor (Pretty Flower) and Ferris (Roaring Bull) Dove, both Narragansett Indians, still serve jonnycakes at the Dovecrest Indian Trading Post and Restaurant in Exeter, Rhode Island. They make them to order at $1.95 a serving, $2.95 with sausage and $2.95 with bacon. They also serve them as a side dish.

Eleanor mixes seven cups of meal with four teaspoons of salt and ½ cup of sugar, then adds boiling water. She thins the mixture with milk, lets it sit for a few minutes, then pours 2½-inch-wide patties on a hot iron griddle, and cooks them ten to fifteen minutes on each side. The Doves mix fifty pounds of batter to make approximately 1,500 jonnycakes a week. They use only corn meal ground on fine-grain Rhode Island granite. The meal must be ground slowly in the right part of the recessed bottom stone lest it get mushy or too hot, spoiling the flavor, as some claim happens when metal is used to grind the corn.

Dovecrest's jonnycakes are the "South County" variety, thicker and mushier in the center than their "Newport" counterparts. Both types have a golden, crispy exterior. The crêpe-like "Newport" jonnycake cooks faster and is darker. The Doves' jonnycakes are not the jonnycakes in cookbooks, the popular New England cornbread made with egg and leavening. They are most akin to the Southern corn meal "hoe cakes," so-named because they used to be cooked on hoes over fires.

The Doves say purists only eat their jonnycakes with butter, although they do serve syrup on the side. The cakes go well with buffalo- and venison-meat entrées on the Dovecrest menu.

Dick Donnelly, a Saunderstown, Rhode Island, school teacher who writes jonnycake recipes for a Rhode Island corn mill, cooked 6,000 jonnycakes at the 1979 jonnycake festival in Usquepaugh, Rhode Island. He also makes a gourmet jonnycake, with orange rind, Grand Marnier, and Triple Sec.

Donnelly uses corn-meal batter ground on Westerly (western Rhode Island) granite, and mixes it with dry milk, salt, sugar, and some boiling water. On a dry griddle (he uses just a drop of corn oil), he cooks each side of the two-inch-wide patties about five to seven minutes or until the edges are golden brown. He breaks the air pockets on the undersides of the jonnycakes against the griddle, leaving only a small void on each side when they are cooked.

A 1940 Rhode Island law declares that genuine Rhode Island jonnycakes can be made only with meal from Rhode Island White Cap Flint corn, grown nowhere else. But variations of the jonnycake are now more commonly made with other types of corn meal, since the Flint Corn is hard to grow, frail, and cross-pollinates easily with other corn.

Rhode Islanders adhere vehemently to their spelling of jonnycake without an "h." No one is sure how the spelling originated, but this distinguishes the Rhode Island jonnycake from any other. Some etymologists say jonnycakes have also been called "journeycakes," popular with wagon travelers of the 18th and 19th centuries. Others say white trappers learned to make these cakes from the Shawnee Indians and soon corrupted "shawnee-cakes" into "johnnycakes."

The Society for the Propagation of the Jonnycake Tradition in Rhode Island (SPJTRI) was founded in Bristol, Rhode Island, in 1971. Anyone interested can join. For annual dues of $3.50, members receive four issues of the *Jonnycake Journal*, which documents the activities of the group and jonnycake events, advises where to get the precious White Cap Flint corn meal, and gives special recipes for jonnycake batter.

Helene Tessler, the Society's vice-president, says there is great controversy over how to make a genuine jonnycake, even in the State House. One session convened with a legislator cooking jonnycakes on a grill inside the chamber to prove a case for his jonnycake recipe. There is even disagreement over the type of barrel lid on which settlers cooked their jonnycakes. The dispute has narrowed the possibilities to oak or red cedar.

For those who can't come to the Dovecrest in Exeter, Rhode Island, the Doves sell Palmer's Yawgoog Johnnycake Mix for 90¢ per pound box plus postage.

America's Best! KING SALMON FISHING

Bell Island Hot Springs Resort

Bell Island, Alaska 99950

Mailing Address:
131 3rd Avenue North
Edmonds, Washington 98020

206-776-7100

Donald S. Peterson, President
Julie Charrington, Reservations
*   Manager*

License fee: $15

3 nights: 2-person occupancy,
* $607–$666; 4-person*
*   occupancy, $516–$565*
6 nights: 2-person occupancy,
* $1,044–$1,147; 4-person*
*   occupancy, $957–$1,051*
Additional nights: $136–$186
*   per person*

$150 deposit by January 1,
*   balance due 60 days prior to*
*   arrival*

Rates include lodging, meals, boat,
*   motor, rod, reel, bait, cleaning*
*   and packaging of fish. Leader,*
*   sinkers, lures, gratuities extra*

At Bell Island Hot Springs Resort, forty-five miles north of Ketchikan, Alaska, more King Salmon are caught (per licensee) than anywhere else in Alaska, a state renowned for its salmon runs.

Bell Island King Salmon weigh between thirty-five and fifty-five pounds and run so close to the shore that you catch them with ease from the two-man boat the resort provides at no extra charge. The resort also gives you a rod and reel, furnishes instructions on how to properly use herring bait for life-like action in the water, and provides a guide to acquaint first-timers with the rivers, inlets, and the best fishing areas. After your day on the sparkling waters, the resort will even wrap and pack your fish.

Coho, or silver, salmon (twelve to twenty pounds) begin their runs in July. You can also fish for cod, red snapper, and halibut, and you will even find crab and shrimp in these fertile waters. There's also trout fishing a few minutes away by air taxi.

All meals are included in your stay. The resort packs a lunch for you so you can fish without being interrupted. Rates include luxurious lodging in cabins with twin beds and private bathrooms.

Opened in 1902 as a health spa amidst natural hot springs, Bell Island Hot Springs Resort didn't become a fishing resort until the 1950s. It soon became the favorite spot for many fishermen celebrities, including John Wayne. The 125 to 184 degree springs are used to heat the fourteen cabins and supply naturally invigorating water to the huge bathtubs inside. The outdoor pool is maintained at a steady eighty-four degrees.

The fifty accommodations are usually taken a year in advance of the summer fishing season, so make your reservations early. Air service is easily arranged from any part of the U.S.—Bell Island is only two air hours away from Seattle via Ketchikan. There's a surcharge for baggage weighing more than forty pounds, so leave your fishing gear at home.

America's Best! KITES

Nantucket Kiteman and Lady

41 Main Street
Nantucket Island, Massachusetts
  02554

617-228-2297

Al and Betty Hartig

Open year round: Monday–
  Saturday, 10:00 A.M.–4:00 P.M.

Self-addressed, stamped envelopes
  required for all mail orders and
  inquiries

Jaws, a 10½-foot shark kite, has menacing teeth that stand out against a jet-black dorsal. Eagles have mistaken *The National Eagle* kite as one of their own.

These and other specialty kites, "the Rolls Royces of Kitedom," are constructed on Nantucket Island, thirty miles off the coast of Massachusetts. The Nantucket Kiteman's and Lady's kites defy all laws of aerodynamics. There is no need to run to get them aloft. One Brooklyn, New York, man watches his friends run themselves ragged trying to get their kites in the air while he sits in a beach chair between two tall buildings. Within minutes, the funnel-like draft sweeps his Nantucket kite into the sky.

Al Hartig is president, production manager, and chief test pilot, and Betty Hartig is secretary, treasurer, bookkeeper, and chief seamstress. They make America's first repairable-fabric, replaceable-dowel, center-keel kites. The main difference between a

Kiteman and a run-of-the-mill kite is the Hartig's center keel. This unique piece of cloth hangs down from the center of the kite, provides a point to which the string is attached, and keeps the kite stable. According to Al, the difference between a kite with a keel and a kite with a tail is as great as the difference between a jet and a biplane.

Al says that a seven-to-ten-mile-per-hour wind is ideal for kite-flying, although a four-mile-per-hour wind will do. At four miles per hour it takes some running to attain lift-off, but at 150 feet air thermals take over and the kite zooms. Nantucket Kiteman kites will climb faster than nine out of ten competitors, usually in about twenty seconds. In fact, it takes Al only ten minutes to reach a height of 3,000 feet (the highest he has flown). The highest one of Kiteman's kites has gone is 14,000 feet. Not bad, considering the highest a single kite has ever flown is 18,500 feet. Two kites in tandem (necessary once the string gets too heavy) have approached the 39,000-foot mark! Not surprisingly, permission from the Federal Aviation Administration is needed for high flying.

During the year Kiteman and his Lady construct about 5,000 kites. They sell some through mail orders, and others to selected retail outlets across the country. The kites are available year-round at the shop on Nantucket Island. The Hartigs make five models:

> The Ace, with a fifty-two-inch wingspan, for children, printed cotton, $11; The Valkyrie (named for the Norse goddesses who carried the souls of the heroes off to Paradise), with a seventy-two-inch wingspan, for adults, printed cotton, $18; The Flying Fox, with a fifty-eight-inch wingspan, for teens or adults, black, $20; The Snowy Owl, with a fifty-two-inch wingspan, for adults, silkscreened on rip-stop nylon, $25; The National Eagle, with sixty-five-inch wingspan, silkscreened on rip-stop nylon, for adults, $35.

The Hartigs, who hold a patent on their kites, use a unique crossbar held in place with drapery hooks and grommets attached to the wings. Al says that sewing is the single most critical part of kitemaking, and Betty does nearly all the sewing before the dowels are set. Every seam must be balanced or even. Otherwise, air will not flow evenly over the surface and the kite will not fly smoothly. Al can determine whether or not a kite will fly just by feeling the dowels, and he throws out at least one-third of all the dowels he buys because they are not springy or strong enough.

When they aren't making kites, the Hartigs are flying them.

Every piece of fabric must also pass a detailed inspection. If it is too light, it will be torn to shreds by high winds. If it is too heavy, it will pull too hard. Even the color makes a difference. Black dye is heavier (and thus less suitable) than yellow dye.

The Nantucket kites have been flown all over the world. For one friend, the Hartigs designed a red-white-and-blue kite with "détente" (in Russian) emblazoned across its midsection. He flew it in Moscow's Red Square, where kites are unknown, and to his surprise, no one said a word. Later, though, the Russian Government sent to the Kiteman for information about his kites.

The Hartigs began making kites in 1963. Their original kite, The Red Baron (which cost them $1 to make), has been retired after 870 hours of flying time, although it is still operable. One tattered and faded kite of theirs has logged 1,382 hours of air-time.

The Smithsonian Institution recently acquired one of the Hartigs' first kites, *The Warlock*.

The Hartigs made their first sale in New York's Central Park. A well dressed elderly woman ran up to Betty, grabbed the orange kite she was holding, slapped a $10 bill into her hand, and "took off like the dickens." Betty realized then that their product had some appeal.

By 1968, the Hartigs' avocation had blossomed into a thriving cottage industry. So Betty quit her New York office position and Al left his nine-to-five ceramics-factory job. On Nantucket, a toy store offered them a home in exchange for kites. The toy store folded, but the Kiteman and Lady continued to make kites on Old South Wharf. Kiteman and Lady now grosses $50,000 a year. Along with success have come demands for mass production, but the Hartigs are too quality-conscious for that. Betty painstakingly produces twenty-two delta-wing kites a day, and needs two full hours just to sew a bird kite together. Al test-flies every bat and eagle kite before it is sold. They have politely turned down offers for 5,000 and 10,000 eagle kites and for other mass orders. Says Al, "It's a cottage trade. And, besides, we wouldn't want to do anything that doesn't benefit the island."

America's Best! LOBSTER

Maine Lobster

Homarus americanus

For information on lobster legislation:
  Wayne C. Gray,
  State Representative
  67 Lawn Avenue
  Rockland, Maine 04841

They're omnivorous, cannibalistic, and look like giant beetles. Once these "scavengers of the sea" crawled along the beaches in great numbers, and were the food of peasants. But now, lobsters are the most coveted delicacy of all sea creatures. Lobster meat currently sells for an average of $15 to $20 a pound.

The best, and the most, lobsters can be found off the rock-bound coast of Maine. Lobsters spend their adult lives on the bottom of the sea, and prefer rocky terrain because it offers them innumerable places to hide during their vulnerable moulting periods. The Maine (or American) Lobster can be found only in the Atlantic from Labrador to North Carolina, and is one of only three true species of lobster in the world, the other two being *Homarus vulgarus* and *Nephrops norvegicus*, European varieties. True lobsters have two pairs of antennae, twenty pairs of gills, five pairs of swimmerets, and five pairs of legs. Male lobsters are usually heavier and have bigger claws, but the main difference between male and female lobsters is that where the tail meets the central body is a pair of swimmerets—two protrusions that are larger and harder in the male, smaller and softer in the female. Those *soi-disant* "rock lobsters," which can be caught in the warm Florida or California waters, are imposters. They have no claws, and should properly be referred to as crawfish.

There are only about 4,500 full-time lobstermen in Maine (10 percent of them are over sixty-five years old) and each year they land nearly twenty million pounds of lobster. Because of extensive fishing, and a recent drop in water temperature off Maine, lobsters have become somewhat rarer than previously, when they were plentiful enough to be used for fertilizer. So the state protects the lobster with a number of regulations that are strictly enforced by coastal wardens.

It is illegal in Maine to keep a lobster that is shorter than 3⅛ inches from the eye to the end of the back, or longer than five inches. Egg-bearing females are also prohibited, and before they are set free, their tails are notched, protecting them forever as productive females.

Fishermen must display their assigned buoy colors on the top of their smacks (boats) so wardens can tell at a distance if they are hauling their own traps. But lobstermen police themselves and usually resist the temptation to keep short lobsters or wash the eggs off large females. The real problem has been with unlicensed weekend fishermen, who don't have to deal regularly with the wardens and have been known to steal lobsters out of other folks' traps.

Lobstermen lay their pots (traps) on the sea floor at depths ranging from only a few feet to nearly 100 fathoms (600 feet). They resemble wooden cages which are entered through net passageways. The lobsters, attracted by bait, walk backwards into the trap (lobsters seldom swim, but when they do they do that backwards, too). Once inside, they are not clever enough to figure a way out.

If you ever wonder why lobster is so expensive, consider that a thirty-six-foot boat equipped with depth-finders, radar, a hydraulic hauler, VHF and CB radios, a diesel engine, and miles of pot warp (line) can bring a lobsterman's initial investment to over $50,000. Bait, fuel, and crew cost at least $100 a day.

Lobster is very high in protein. Virtually all of it is edible, with the exception of the skeletal shell, the craw in the head, and the dark vein running down the back of the body. Still, some of the best parts of the lobster are often neglected by the unadventurous—the tomalley (liver), the legs, and the body are often left unexplored by those who prefer to tackle only the claws and the tail.

Downeasters generally agree that the best way to prepare a lobster is to boil it in no more than three inches of salted water (as one lobsterman explains, "You only want to cook 'em, not drown 'em!") for seventeen to twenty minutes, depending upon the size, and to serve it with drawn butter. Of course, the lobster is also suitable for broiling and baking, and can be made into stews, casseroles, cocktails, and salads.

Lobsters mate shortly after the female has shed her shell, usually in the summer, and before her new shell has had a chance to harden. She carries 9,000 to 100,000 eggs inside her body for a year, and then carries them under the curl of her tail for another year before they hatch. The young lobsters are no bigger than insects and entirely helpless. They float on the surface of the water for two to eight weeks, and are defenseless prey to dozens of natural enemies. They will even eat each other. The mortality rate at this stage of their development may be as high as 99 percent. But lobsters have one thing going for them—the power of regeneration. If they lose a claw or other limb in the course of battle or escape, it will grow back. It takes six or seven years for a lobster to reach legal size.

Some people think that eating lobster is good for your love life. "But don't you believe it," one Downeaster warns, "'cause I tried ten, and only nine worked!"

America's Best! LUAU

Germaine's Luau

1451 South King, Suite 508
Honolulu, Hawaii 96814

Reservations: 808-949-6626,
941-3338
Executive Office: 808-947-1244

Marcia M. Germaine, President
Kim Higa, Vice-President

6 nights a week: adults, $27, tax
included; children, $18.20, tax
included

Cash, traveler's checks; major
credit cards when used at tour
desks in Waikiki

Casual dress

Luau means "feast" in Hawaiian and feast is what you do at Germaine's Luau in Honolulu. A whole kalua pig, mahi mahi fish, teriyaki, fried chicken, pipikaula, lomi salmon, sweet potato, macaroni potato salad, boiled rice, chicken long rice, poi, plus special desserts including banana-nut bread, haupia, and chocolate and vanilla cake, followed by bananas, pineapple, watermelon, and other tropical fresh fruits—you get this, sixteen courses in all, washed down with all the beverages (alcoholic and nonalcoholic) you can consume for $27. That includes round-trip transportation.

Luau Queen Marcia M. Germaine (originally from Chicago) has been preparing luaus in Hawaii since 1972 and welcomes 600 to 675 feasters each night. Kim Higa, second in command, is a dietician and supervises the feasts nightly.

Buses pick up guests for the luau between 4:30 and 5:00 P.M. at various locations in Waikiki. Hostesses and hula dancers greet guests upon arrival at Ewa Beach with kisses and a gift of a shell *lei* (necklace). Bartenders serve tropical drinks such as the mai tai, and the less familiar "blue Hawaii" (rum, fruit juice, coconut milk, and ginger ale). Beer, wine, standard hard liquor, and soft drinks are also available.

First, the kalua pig is brought forth in the *imu* ceremony. Two kalua pigs are usually prepared for each luau. Early in the morning, kindling wood topped with green *kiawe* wood and green ironwood is placed in a two-feet-deep pit and lighted. Porous rocks are placed on the wood and heated for about two hours. (The stones must be porous because solid ones would explode from the heat.)

When the rocks are white-hot, some are placed in the cavity of the 150-pound pig to ensure that it will cook on the inside as well.

The pig is placed on the rocks and covered with leaves of the banana and ti plants, with wet burlap bags on top to make more steam. Canvas seals the pit tightly and sand is placed on top to prevent any steam from escaping.

The kalua pigs are left to roast for nine hours until the *imu* ceremony at 6:00 P.M. The sand is removed very carefully, and

After the luau, you'll see hulas and other Pacific dances.

the canvas is peeled back from the pit to prevent sand dropping onto the pig. After the leaves are removed, the pig is hauled up by a wire underneath. It's placed in a pan and the bones are removed, leaving the succulent pork falling into chunks.

The guests sit on the ground or at communal tables. The pork, the only food prepared on the premises, is served immediately along with fifteen other courses. Other dishes include deep-fried mahi mahi, a fish indigenous to Hawaiian waters, teriyaki, a Japanese dish of beef marinated in soy sauce, ginger, sugar, and garlic, raw lomi salmon cut into cubes and mixed with cubes of raw tomato and onion, spicy pipikaula, a highly seasoned dried beef, and chicken long rice, transparent noodles made of mung bean flour.

134

Several vegetable courses are served, including sweet potato, steamed rice, and poi, the staple food of Hawaii made from the root of the taro plant. For dessert there is chocolate and vanilla cake, banana-nut bread baked by Kim Higa's son, and haupia, a pudding of coconut milk, cornstarch, and sugar. Seasonal fresh fruits such as pineapple, banana, and watermelon are also served.

After the feast, John Piilani Watkins and twenty-six other dancers perform hulas and Samoan, Maori, Tahitian, and Philippine dances. The show changes every three months. John's grandmother, who was 102 when she died, was a dancer for the Hawaiian Queen. Before a Hawaiian dies, he must pass on his talents to a younger person who will perpetuate them. John is the only child who became a dancer like his grandmother, and he considers his talents to be a gift from the old people and from God.

Many guests at Germaine's are native Hawaiians, not tourists, who come for the colorful and authentic flavor of the luau. Years ago, Hawaiians thought nothing of spending three to four days at a luau, eating, drinking, and enjoying themselves while celebrating a wedding, birth of a child, or a holiday. Guests at a Germaine's Luau are taken back to their hotels at 10:30 P.M. Maybe the present-day feast isn't as long as an old-fashioned luau, but the *aloha* spirit and the food are just as good.

America's Best! LUMINARIAS

Albuquerque, New Mexico	Mary Kay Cline Albuquerque Convention and Visitors Bureau 401 Second Street, North West Albuquerque, New Mexico 87102
	505-842-0220

One of New Mexico's oldest traditions, the luminaria displays on Christmas Eve attract thousands of visitors to Albuquerque each year. A lighted candle set in sand inside a paper bag doesn't sound exotic, but the spectacular sight of thousands of them leaves you breathless.

Luminarias, which symbolically light the way for the Christ child, are easily made with a brown-paper bag and a ten-to-fifteen-hour votive candle planted in two inches of sand. The total cost is only about 7¢ each! No wonder Albuquerqueans line their streets, driveways, and even the flat rooftops of their adobe homes with them. The top of each bag is turned down to form a cuff for extra stability, and the sand will extinguish any fire.

Some controversy has arisen as to what a luminaria really is. Residents of Santa Fe call small bonfires of piñon wood *luminarias*, and refer to the paper-bag lanterns as *farolitos*. In Albuquerque, the bonfires are not seen very often, and the lanterns take on the name *luminarias*. This confusion came to the attention of the state legislature, but the lawmakers decided New Mexicans could "call them by either name."

Luminarias are a long-standing New Mexican custom. In 1534, a Franciscan *padre* described a village in New Spain illuminated by small bonfires as "resembling the starry skies." Then, in the 1820s, brown-paper sacks were brought down the Santa Fe Trail by Yankee traders.

A Christmas Eve contest in Santa Fe, sponsored by the Historic Foundation there, sparks lavish displays of the small lanterns. But Albuquerqueans go one step further. Since 1953, The Albuquerque Chamber of Commerce has operated a no-charge Luminaria Tour for guests registered in hotels and motels that are members of the Chamber. Various Albuquerqueans volunteer to serve as tour guides, and the Chamber arranges for buses to pick up 600 or more hotel guests and return them one and a half hours later. Phillip W. McCollum (Mr. Burger King of Albuquerque) loans two double-decker London-style buses for the tour—complete with complimentary bar service.

The buses wind through three areas of Albuquerque along a prearranged route. The highlight of the first area, a residential neighborhood, is the Hebenstreit estate, which is always decorated with luminarias and blue electric lights. The tour continues into Old Town, developed in 1706, where the Plaza glows with the light of 5,000 luminarias. Later in the evening, at 11:30, the traditional Spanish pageant, *Las Posadas*, takes place there. A young man and woman, representing Joseph and Mary, reenact the search of the Holy Family for shelter on the eve of Christ's birth. Followed by a crowd carrying candles, they go from doorway to doorway and are always turned away. The procession ends at

Albuquerque becomes the "City of Little Lights."

midnight at the church of San Felipe de Neri, the first structure built in Old Town, where a midnight mass is celebrated.

Los Altos, a chic residential neighborhood of adobe homes, is the last leg of the tour. As a community effort, the residents have decorated their homes each year since 1952 with 10,000 luminarias.

The city offers another tour through the same areas for $2. Convoys of buses for this tour leave the downtown area every fifteen minutes from 6:00 P.M. to 9:00 P.M. You must have a ticket to board the bus, and tickets go on sale the second week of December and sell out the first day. (Mail reservations are not accepted.) There are usually more than 2,500 people on this tour.

The luminaria tradition spreads widely over New Mexico, but Albuquerque is the only city that offers special tours to see them. And the luminarias in Albuquerque generate not only a soft light, but also a healthy increase in the revenues of the hotel and restaurant trade there. The Chamber of Commerce estimates that the Luminaria Tours attract just under $1 million worth of business during the Christmas season.

America's Best! LUXURY SPORTS AUTOMOBILE

✉

The Excalibur Automobile Company

1735 South 106 Street
Milwaukee, Wisconsin 53214

David B. Stevens, President
Nancy von Grossmann, Director
of Communications

414-771-7171

*$28,000, plus options; $2,800
down payment, balance on
delivery; 12 month/ 12,000 mile
warranty*

Sweeping fenders, louvered hood, gleaming grille and gratework, shining steel exhaust pipes swooping out from under the hood, and side-mounted spare tires immediately place the Excalibur in the Great Gatsby era.

Modeled after the Mercedes Benz SS of 1934 to 36, the 4,350-pound Excalibur Series III (two-seat roadster or four-seat Phaeton has the suspension, low center of gravity, handling, and power of a sports car. Yet it has the weight, stability, and comforts of only the most expensive luxury cars.

Standard equipment on the Excalibur includes air conditioning, a heating system with three heaters (one each under the dash and the front and back seats), three-speed turbohydramatic transmission, telescopic and adjustable steering wheel, fully adjustable leather bucket seats, removable hard top that can be replaced with a canvas top for summer driving, AM/FM radio, and choice of tape deck or CB radio.

Dual air horns, self-leveling rear suspension, aluminum (no rust) bar bumpers, steel door panels, power-assisted steering and brakes, double-pin aluminum alloy locks, latches, and Lucas Chromium headlights guarantee safety. The shock absorbers are air-adjustable.

The engineering is that of a fine sports car and includes: disc brakes on all four wheels; a slinky five-inch ground clearance; independent suspension on all four wheels based on the Corvette suspension; 454-cubic inch, 215-horsepower Chevy engine; a steel exhaust system that works so efficiently a catalytic converter is not needed to fulfill EPA regulations; a fiberglass body enforced for

The Excalibur is a sports car with all the comforts of a luxury car.

safety by a steel frame that is light and rust-resistant; and a unique 1,100-pound steel chassis that is bolted, instead of welded.

Al Hoelzer, plant supervisor, stresses that there are no unnecessary "frills" in the design of the car. For example, the attractive louvers facilitate cooling of the disc brakes, and the side-mounted spare tires can act as a cushion in a side impact, reducing injury and damage. Hoelzer also insists that the car is "built like a tank," citing a recent head-on collision in which there was no engine damage to the Excalibur but the "engine of the other car wound up in the back seat."

Interiors are installed by hand, and the grille work and acrylic paint job are hand-polished. The Excalibur plant designs its own body molds and makes its own fiberglass. However, of the 2,750 parts in the car, 750 are standard GM components and another 1,000 are ordered from standard suppliers. This means easy servicing, a problem with other limited-production cars. In fact, virtually all parts of the drive train, transmission included, are readily available at any of 6,000 Chevrolet dealers across the country. Tires are standard size, too.

The warranty covers the first year or 12,000 miles. It's basically the same as the standard GM warranty, with a more personal touch—any work under $100 can be done (fully reimbursed by Excalibur) by the mechanic without consulting the Excalibur Company. Above that amount, Excalibur requests owners to contact them so that a company mechanic can help them troubleshoot the problem (usually over the phone), and discover the exact cost of the repair, and the amount of work to be done.

The plant's 106 workers turn out one Excalibur Series III every 6½ hours, exactly 300 per year. Each car takes fifteen days to build, then it is given a thorough check, including a minimum 100-mile road test.

The care of making the Excalibur is reflected in its value. An Excalibur that sold for $17,000 four or five years ago is worth at least that now—a well maintained Excalibur will sell for a higher price than new.

The story of the Excalibur begins with Brooks Stevens, an auto designer who was commissioned in 1964 to design a "show car" for Studebaker to be exhibited in the New York Automobile Show that year. As the car was being readied, Studebaker announced the termination of its auto production. Brooks's son David nevertheless got show space and exhibited the car under the banner of Brooks Stevens Associates.

Called the Studebaker SS (nicknamed the "Mercebaker" because it was modeled on a 20s Mercedes roadster), the car generated an overwhelming response. Features included aluminum bodywork, a Studebaker Lark Chassis, and a supercharged Avanti 2 engine. The prototype was also shown in Los Angeles and Chicago, and a single ad in the *Wall Street Journal* resulted in 300 inquiries and over a dozen firm offers to buy.

Nearly 2,000 Excaliburs have been produced since 1964, and the company keeps careful track of where they are with pins and flags on a map in the main office. In 1979, there were twenty-eight Excaliburs in the Broward County, Florida (Fort Lauderdale area), alone. This tracking is simplified by the fact that 30 to 40 percent of Excalibur's orders come from previously satisfied Excalibur owners. People buying the Excalibur today are looking for luxury and elegance as well as pure speed and power, which explains the large number of accessories on the cars.

Since 1973, Excalibur has hosted a mid-August rally weekend for Excalibur owners. A newsletter, the *Circle and Sword*, keeps owners informed about each other, innovations on the Excalibur, tips on maintenance, and driving and interest stories involving the Excalibur.

The Excalibur Company is the sixth largest manufacturer of automobiles in the U.S. and the oldest maker of limited edition automobiles in the country. There are only six exclusive Excalibur car dealers in the U.S.:

Vintage Car Store, Inc., 93 S. Broadway, Nyack, New York 10960, 914-358-3800

Excalibur Motorcars Ltd., 3160 Skokie Valley Road, Highland Park, Illinois 60035, 312-433-4400

Excalibur West, Inc., 3764-66 Mill St., Reno, Nevada 89502, 702-323-2758

Excalibur Southwest, Inc., 5900 North Freeway, Suite 113, Houston, Texas 77076, 713-691-1703

Allen Motorcar Corporation, 1612 E. Sunrise Blvd., Ft. Lauderdale, Florida 33304, 305-763-5010

Excalibur Sales Incorporated, 1735 S. 106 St., Milwaukee, Wisconsin 53214, 414-771-8240.

America's Best! MELODRAMA

The Imperial Players

The Imperial Hotel
Cripple Creek, Colorado 80813

303-689-2922

Wayne & Dorothy Mackin,
Proprietors

June–mid-September: Tuesday–
Saturday, 2:15 P.M. and
8:30 P.M.; Sunday, 1:00 P.M.
and 4:30 P.M.; closed Monday;
$3–$5

In a dimly lit basement theatre filled with hundreds of black top hats, amidst a cacophony of boos, hisses, wild cheers, and the crashing chords of a piano, The Imperial Players carry on the Victorian tradition of the melodrama. These quaint plays bear such provocative titles as "Rogue's Revenge, or A Fox In Petticoats" and "Flying Scud, or A Four-Legged Fortune." The plots are often highly complex, but they always involve clear-cut heroes, heroines, and villains, and there is always a love interest.

On a show night, pianist and musical director Danny Griffith (also called "King of Melodrama Pianists") starts playing at 7:30 and doesn't stop until after midnight. And he has played more than 2,500 melodrama performances in his fifteen-year career with The Imperial Players. He has also cut twelve albums of his melodrama music.

After each of the three acts of the Imperial Melodrama, there is a short vaudeville-type act. This keeps the audience entertained during set changes and gives the actors a chance to rest (Danny never rests). This tradition, called the olio, meaning a hodgepodge, is the American version of the French *entr'acte* and the Italian *intermezzo*.

Cripple Creek was once known as "the world's greatest gold camp." This patch of volcanic terrain, about five miles square, produced more gold than anywhere else in the world in the late 19th century, and it was during this period of prosperity that the Imperial Hotel was built. Those days passed, and Cripple Creek became a virtual ghost town. But the renovation of the Imperial and the establishment of the summer melodrama season have effected a small renaissance for the old gold camp. Even the gold seekers are coming back.

The Imperial Players perform in the Imperial Hotel's Gold Bar Room, converted from a basement gambling hall. The room seats 285 at tables, which come right up to the stage, creating a very intimate ambience. Guests may enjoy drinks along with the show, but they are served only during intermission so as not to disrupt the play.

Since the melodrama was established at the Imperial in 1948, almost a million guests from all over the world have come to the Gold Bar Room. The actors are mostly the top students from college drama departments. Each year, over 100 actors apply for only ten or eleven roles. Eighteen are invited to audition, and if they don't make the play, they are offered alternative jobs at the theatre as ushers, waiters, or box office clerks. Many of The Imperial Players have gone on to careers in television, often in the soap operas, and have included singer Tom Paxton and pianist Max Morath.

The Imperial Players perform only one show each season, chosen from the hundreds that the Mackins have reviewed in the

The Imperial was built during Cripple Creek's gold rush days.

course of their library research. One of the Mackins' favorite playwrights is Dion Boucicault, the Irish author of "After Dark" and "Flying Scud." Dorothy edits the plays to make them more suitable to the Imperial's purposes. Many of these works would run upwards of three hours, so Dorothy cuts them down to about an hour and a half. The Mackins are also careful to choose a play that will have a good role for every actor, so that discord won't set in during the 2½-month summer season.

The Imperial Hotel, which opens for the summer season in mid-May, is full of antique Victorian furnishings and paintings, and offers beautiful accommodations at unusually reasonable rates. A double room with a private bath is $25 a day. Many of the rooms are appointed with big brass beds. There are four bars where you can slake your thirst, and three dining rooms where a generous buffet is available, featuring twenty to thirty selections, including at least three meat dishes. Lunch is $4.50 and dinner is $7.50.

143

America's Best! MOROCCAN FEAST

Dar Maghreb Restaurant

7651 Sunset Boulevard
Hollywood, California 90046

213-876-7651

Pierre Dupart, Owner

7 days a week: 6:00 P.M.–
11:00 P.M.; closed Thanks-
giving and Christmas

Visa, Master Charge

The façade resembles a plain, white, Moroccan building; the interior is an exact replica of a lavish Moroccan home, complete with high-vaulted ceilings, elaborate tapestries, and intricate tile work; every evening, owner Pierre Dupart tastes each dish to make sure it matches his high standards. It's no wonder diners at Dar Maghreb feel more like guests in a private home than customers in a restaurant.

You enter Dar Maghreb through huge brass doors into a patio leading to two large rooms, where diners relax on Moroccan couches. One room duplicates the interior of a palace chamber with high-vaulted ceilings and rich brocades. The second room is reminiscent of an elaborate southern Moroccan home, with rich carpets, brass tables, and low ceilings. These two rooms seat about 200 people. A small private dining room, seating fourteen to twenty guests, is decorated with tapestries.

The heritage of Moroccan hospitality is to serve guests extremely generous portions of food. Dar Maghreb duplicates this aspect so accurately that it is suggested diners come in groups of at least four. After you settle on low, soft, comfortable couches, a waiter describes the evening's menu. The elimination of a printed menu is another detail that makes you feel more like a guest in a private home than a restaurant.

The waiter appears with a basin, a jug of hot water, soap, and towels so you can wash your hands. This is more than a mere formality, as Moroccan custom requires that you eat only with the fingers of your right hand. No silverware is used, not even for serving. Because wealthy Arabs of the 12th century would not condescend to eat from plain, local pottery, great quantities of dishes were brought from China. So, in keeping with Moroccan tradition, the plates at Dar Maghreb are all Chinese in decoration.

All Dar Maghreb feasts begin with a Moroccan salad of raw or cooked vegetables mixed with oil, vinegar, coriander, onions, parsley, and paprika. The second course is B'stilla, a cross between a meat pie and a sweet cake made from paper-thin strudel dough stuffed with shredded pigeon or chicken, ground almonds, sugar, egg curd, onions, coriander, parsley, saffron, and cinnamon. It is topped with powdered sugar and cinnamon and served immediately while very hot.

Diners choose two entrées from a selection of at least eight for their third course. The two most popular entrées are Lahm Mrouzia, braised lamb with honey, sesame seeds, and prunes, and Tajine de Poulet aux Citrons, braised chicken with pickled lemon peel and pink olives. Pink olives are very difficult to find in the U.S., but Pierre Dupart manges to get them from a ranch in California's San Bernardino Valley—at triple the price of regular olives.

Other main dishes at Dar Maghreb include braised chicken cooked with a mixture of scrambled egg and coriander, marinated lamb on a skewer, braised squab stuffed with rice and almonds, braised rabbit cooked with pepper, and Brochette de Kefta, freshly ground lamb seasoned with fresh mint, parsley, and onion. It is shaped like a sausage and cooked on a skewer over a grill. Couscous, coarsely ground and steamed semolina, accompanies all entrées.

As a last course, dried dates and figs are served with almonds, and then the traditional Moroccan mint tea with almond cookies, fried and dipped in honey.

A Dar Maghreb dinner costs $13 to $14.50 per person; the higher price is charged for dishes made with squab rather than chicken. A couscous dinner, served with lamb and cooked vegetables, is available for $10, but it is not considered a Moroccan feast and is rarely ordered.

Although Moroccans traditionally do not drink much wine, fifty years of French influence have left their mark. Pierre Dupart offers a full selection of both red and white Moroccan wines, and he considers a Moroccan Cabernet to be particularly exceptional.

Pierre is originally from the Bordeaux region of France. After receiving hotel training there, he worked in Portugal and then in San Franscisco, where he ran his own restaurant from 1963 until 1970. After selling the San Francisco restaurant, he travelled in Morocco for nine months, where he researched Moroccan architecture and engaged a Moroccan chef. Dar Maghreb opened to the public in 1974.

Actress Jacqueline Bisset was one of Dar Maghreb's first regulars. She passed the word around Hollywood, and the restaurant now attracts a celebrated clientele, including Rod Steiger, Diana Ross, Raquel Welch, and Richard Chamberlain. High-ranking Moroccan officials stop in for dinner whenever they are in Los Angeles.

Dar Maghreb will also cater a five-course Moroccan feast in your home for $25 a person—you must invite at least fifteen feasters. You can rent all the couches, tables, and cushions you need for $150. Dar Maghreb does not supply the dancers, but there is no shortage of talent in Hollywood.

America's Best! MULES

Missouri Mules

Superintendent of Mules
Missouri State Fair
Missouri Farmers' Association
201 South 7th Street
Columbia, Missouri 65201

314-874-5111

America's best mules are from Missouri, where this stubborn creature's wayward habits are as much appreciated as its peerless quality. Missourians who know mules from long experience will say, "You must not think hard of a mule if it kicks you—that's how it shows that it likes you." No wonder Missourians can make yet another proud claim: "In mules, Missouri stands at the head—the only safe place!"

The product of selective breeding for over 300 years, the ungainly mule is the most successful hybrid ever developed by man. The sturdiest and most dependable beasts of burden, mules can survive heat, poor food, and heavy loads as no horse or ox could, and have proven themselves in coal mines and wars, on farms and mountain trails, and everywhere else men have worked under difficult conditions.

A mule is neither here nor there. Its mother is a horse and its father is a jackass. Because of its unusual parentage, the mule is sterile and can only be bred one generation at a time. But it also inherits the best qualities of both its parents, being a large-boned, shambling animal of 1,100 to 1,200 pounds, with limbs of iron and a stomach to match. Missouri mules are bred from Belgian mares, who impart their beautiful sorrel (light brown) color to their offspring, and Spanish jackasses, who give them strength and size.

The first American breeder of mules was George Washington. In 1785, he wanted to import "a good jackass from Spain to breed from," but he couldn't afford one. Learning of his interest in breeding mules, King Charles IV shipped him two jackasses as a gift, and General Lafayette sent him one from Malta. But George's mules weren't as big as modern Missouri mules because he bred them from military horses. Alexander Hamilton also bred mules.

The mule trade began in Missouri on the Santa Fe Trail in 1822, when Missouri traders discovered that oxen were incapable of the long haul required of them. Nor could they be induced to eat the buffalo grass, which was the only forage available beyond the Arkansas River. Spanish jackasses from New Mexico were first crossed with heavy workhorses, then with lighter-spirited thoroughbreds that were not so heavy. After long experimentation, the Belgian mare was determined to be the best mate for the Spanish jacks.

Today, there are more mules bred in Kentucky and Tennessee than in Missouri, but Missouri mules are better. Having bred mules for so long, Missouri has developed the finest breeds of mares and jacks, and this well established breeding stock makes for the best mules. The Missourians have also developed the mules that are easiest to handle.

147

Handling a mule is no easy business. It's been said that the best way to put a mule in its stall is to hire someone else to do it. The famous kick of the Missouri mule is also something to deal with. Mule buyers learned early on to take the shoes off the hind feet of the mules they purchased, and even to this day, railroads refuse to carry a Missouri mule with its shoes on. But Missouri mules make up for their nasty personalities with their Spartan eating habits. They will eat almost anything rather than go without—straw, pine boards, tree bark, leather, anything. There is even a Civil War story about a team of mules that ate a government wagon.

Mules have been involved in many of the processes that have made America great—the building of railroads, plowing and harvesting, coal mining, logging, and more. Yet, they are too seldom the object of admiration and praise, and too often the butt of jokes and nasty remarks. Nevertheless, they received their greatest tribute on the inauguration day of President Truman, when four special Missouri mules with white tails and manes were brought from the President's birthplace, Lamar, Missouri, and given a place of distinction in the inaugural parade.

America's Best! MUSHROOMS

Moonlight Mushrooms   *412-297-3402*

Butler County Mushroom Farm   Elmer Bennitt, Chairman of
Worthington, Pennsylvania 16262   the Board

Mushrooms have been recorded as far back as Egyptian hieroglyphics. The Greeks called them *bromo theo*, food of the gods. The ancients bestowed upon them the power to cure disease, prolong life, and send the soul into the realms of the gods. The Roman writer Martial said this of the mushroom's delectable flavor: "Gold and silver dresses may be trusted to a messenger, but not a mushroom, because he would eat it on the way." Julius

Caesar once decreed that anyone caught eating mushrooms would be condemned to death. Why this harsh edict? He simply wanted them all to himself.

Centuries later they became popular in the courts of Europe. Louis XIV encouraged citizens to grow them for him in caves around Paris. It was about 100 years ago that they became popular in America, where now the best to be had are Moonlight Mushrooms.

The limestone caves at the Butler County Mushroom Farm in Worthington, Pennsylvania, have proven to be the perfect breeding ground for Moonlight Mushrooms. They have a uniformity of temperature, the correct darkness, and the proper moisture.

Mushrooms are unlike any other vegetable. They have no leaves to make food from sunlight: their nourishment must come from specially prepared organic compost. Life for Moonlight Mushrooms begins in a sterilized laboratory. Scientists grow microscopic spores in test tubes, where they grow into vigorous spawn. The spawn is next innoculated into large containers of sterilized rye grain and left to multiply in an air-conditioned growing room for two weeks. Hundreds of tons of compost are prepared each day. This substance is placed in large trays, which are stacked twelve high and pasteurized for several days. The spawn is then mixed with the prepared medium and delivered underground, where the growing cycle of about ninety-six days will be completed.

A ripe mushroom is not determined by size. The key factor is the cap; the mushroom is "ready" when the veil breaks. When this occurs, the spores drop and the mushroom turns color. All 550 pickers at the Farm are well trained in knowing just when the mushroom is ready. Their highly specialized job is complicated by the conditions in which they work. They work in the dark, in low-ceilinged caves, with only miner's lights to guide them.

Mushrooms contain some protein, vitamin A, vitamin B, and vitamin C. But a whole pound of mushrooms contains only 125 calories. The versatile mushroom can be used in everything from a salad to a surrogate for the olive in a martini.

Greenhouse operators Ira and Johannes Yoder began the Butler County Mushroom Farm in 1937. They found the limestone caves in Worthington, Pennsylvania, the perfect place to grow their mushrooms underground, as they are grown in France. Fortunately, these mines did not have the ninety-foot ceilings that are common where limestone has been removed. Mushrooms need low ceilings, as they must have five changes of air per hour or they will die of their own carbon dioxide wastes.

The Yoders use the two-zone system of growing mushrooms. They grow them in trays, not in the usual ground beds. Mushrooms thrive in the caves because of the natural temperature of 46.8 degrees F. The heat of the mushrooms growing actually raises this figure to about 56 degrees.

In 1939, the Yoder Brothers produced 100 pounds of mushrooms a day. Today, the Butlers produce 120,000 pounds of mushrooms per day, or about 12 percent of the nation's 398.7-million-pound yearly mushroom crop. Within the past decade, annual per capita consumption of mushrooms in the U.S. has more than doubled to 2.5 pounds. Moonlight Mushrooms are packed in eight-, twelve-, and sixteen-ounce packages and ten-pound baskets, and are available in most cities within a 500-mile radius of the Farm.

America's Best! MUSICAL THEATRE

The Goodspeed Opera House

East Haddam, Connecticut 06423

Michael Price, Executive Director
Kay McGrath, Publicity Director

Box Office: 203-873-8668
Main Number: 203-873-8664

"The first exclamation of every lady entering the hall was, 'Splendid!!!!' (with at least four notes of admiration) and that of the male bipeds was 'Gorgeous,' but neither adjective fits the case exactly. It is simply perfect."—Review of the Goodspeed Opera House, *The Deep River New Era*, October 24, 1877

Today, the Goodspeed Opera House, situated on the banks of the Connecticut River, is the only theatre in America dedicated to the preservation of the American musical. Since Michael Price, executive director, assumed the reins in 1968, membership has increased from 4,000 to 6,600. Performances, which are held from

The Goodspeed: Dedicated to the preservation of the American musical.

April through November, are always sold out, and many of the shows, including *Annie, Man of La Mancha, Shenandoah,* and *Whoopee,* have gone on to Broadway.

Despite these successes, Price insists that the Goodspeed is not a tryout house for Broadway. "We remain true to our original purpose. We preserve the musical heritage by reviving two shows a year, and we add to that heritage with one totally original production. But," says Price with a grin, "if a play goes to Broadway, we're happy and excited about it." Royalties from these shows are a healthy boost to the Goodspeed coffers, since box-office sales (tickets sell for $7.50 to $12 and the annual gross is just under $1 million), endowments from arts foundations, and donations are not enough to cover all the costs of producing the shows and maintaining the building.

The Goodspeed's orchestra is culled from the New Haven and Hartford Symphonies, and actors and actresses (all unknowns) are recruited in New York. Casts were formerly arranged repertory-style, but with the increasing frequency of shows being sent to New York, companies of about twenty are selected for each show.

The six-story building, which recently celebrated its 101st birthday, was built in 1876 by William Goodspeed, a shipping magnate, who docked in East Haddam on his New York-Hartford run. The Opera House was on the top two floors under the mansard roof. Goodspeed brought troupes of actors from New York on his own steamlines, and East Haddam became known as a musical summer resort. The Victorian cottages from that period are still standing.

The operation declined with Goodspeed's death and the building was used as a railroad warehouse and eventually as a highway garage. In 1959, the Goodspeed Opera House Foundation was formed to save the building from demolition. This nonprofit organization reopened the 375-seat auditorium in the summer of 1963 with revivals such as *Oh Lady Lady* and *Gaslight Flickers*.

The theatre is a museum of the best of American Victoriana. No detail has been overlooked, from the gilt and red-carpeted stairway to the Ladies' Drinking Bar, which is decorated in antique French murals. (Until recently it was illegal in Connecticut for a woman to stand at a bar, and thirsty ladies at the Goodspeed had to sit at tables in this room.)

The building's other unusual features include the Green Room, which is filled with rare Victorian antiques, the Peacock Bar, which has served passers-by for over a hundred years, a sweet shop offering ornate arrangements of confections, and an old popcorn wagon, which pops before every performance.

The unique feature of the Goodspeed Opera House is the feeling it generates. Every Saturday, the ladies of the town prepare dinner for the cast and crew between shows. And Michael Price stands at the foot of the grand staircase bidding his guests good night after every performance.

America's Best! MYSTERY BOOKSTORE

✉ ———————————————————————————

Scene of the Crime   *Ruth and Al Windfeldt, Owners*

13636 Ventura Boulevard   *Tuesday–Saturday: 10 A.M.–*
Sherman Oaks, California 91423   *5:30 P.M.; Fridays till 8:00 P.M.*

213-981-CLUE   *Master Charge, Visa*

———————————————————————————————

Red-flocked wallpaper, Victorian bookcases, blood-red carpeting, and a Sherlock Holmes "deerstalker" hat on a nearby rack greet the unsuspecting visitor. Flowers, dolls, roll-top desks, graduates and beakers incarnate Christie, Doyle, Chandler, Hammett,

Sayers, and Simenon mysteries at Scene of the Crime in Sherman Oaks, California. Even Hercule Poirot, Sherlock Holmes, and Philip Marlowe would be at home with owner Ruth Windfeldt.

Each September 15th, Agatha Christie's birthday, Scene of the Crime has a special séance in which Ms. Windfeldt says an "audioclairvoyant" has successfully communicated with Agatha Christie. Ruth says the psychic has seen Agatha hiding the key

Ruth Windfeldt relaxes at the Scene of the Crime.

that opens a locked diary describing her well known eleven-day disappearance.

The front door creaks and bells ring softly as you enter the bookstore amidst the suspended bones of a left leg and foot. An antique Victrola plays reprints of old Sherlock Holmes radio shows with Basil Rathbone. A skeletal hand is perched atop one of the nearby bookshelves and a crystal ball entombs a bat in flight. The bat is her maternal grandfather, Ms. Windfeldt says, who was so much of a nuisance that her husband had to "bottle him up."

Wild Turkey, Anchor Steam beer, cherry Grand Marnier, and

gimlets (Philip Marlowe's favorite) facilitate relaxed conversation between readers and writers. Although many celebrities frequent Scene of the Crime, Ruth insists only writers get special treatment.

Many of the 15,000 volumes are second-hand copies or later editions of out-of-print books. Agatha Christie, Sir Arthur Conan Doyle, Dorothy Sayers, Georges Simenon, Raymond Chandler, and Dashiell Hammett are perennial bestsellers. A first-edition quality work sells for $150. Ms. Windfeldt has first editions of Sherlock Holmes's *The Hound of the Baskervilles* and works by Hammett, Chandler, and Simenon that are so rare she will not display them until she obtains a locking glass case.

The Windfeldts coordinate "mystery" tours each year to San Francisco, Scotland and England, Los Angeles, and Egypt. The one-day Los Angeles tour ($50), which the Windfeldts conduct twice a year, goes back fifty years. Musicians play tunes from the '20s and '30s, accompanying a reading from Chandler's works, which immortalized 1920's Los Angeles. Chandler's detective, Philip Marlowe, visited real places in the stories, and many of them are still there.

The weekend San Francisco tour ($375) retraces scenes from the works of Dashiell Hammett, with a stop at John's Grill, focal point of *The Maltese Falcon*. On the second night, a Victorian house is the scene of a party and séance. The Windfeldts offer an England and Scotland tour ($1,795) every summer. Famous writers lecture, and lectures literally resurrect the Scotland and England of old. The *Death on the Nile* ($2,895) tour is a week-long boat trip inspired by Agatha Christie's book.

"Just Desserts" is the collective name for the special services and meetings offered by the Scene of the Crime. In 1979, authors Nicholas Meyer (*Seven Percent Solution, West End Horror*) and Frank Thomas gave a talk on Sherlock Holmes. The Windfeldts also hold special autographing parties when famous writers visit.

Ruth Windfeldt procures one-of-a-kind mystery items for film and television studios, and even recommends mystery writers to Hollywood studios. They, in turn, show screenings to the store's customers who scrutinize the latest mystery thrillers.

Ruth gets to know her regular customers and offers suggestions on what to read, based on their experience and taste. She also orders books specially for her clientele, some of whom read as many as three mysteries a day.

Scene of the Crime also prepares special gift baskets containing mystery paraphernalia. Tea cups, a bottle of special liqueur, a statue of the Maltese Falcon (wrapped only in Oriental newspaper), a model gun, shortbread, bookmarks, or a tin of tea might be included with a book.

America's Best! OCTOPUS-INK PAINTINGS

Diana Tillion

Halibut Cove
Homer, Alaska 99603

907-235-8000

Tours held June–September: adults, $20; *children under 12,* $10

Diana Tillion loves her art, even if it means she has to catch her own octopuses. "They really are just as ucky and slimy and scary and offensive as you think they are. I've handled a thousand and I still want to give them a toss as soon as I feel that cold, slimy, slithery skin!"

During the Middle Ages and Renaissance, when artists prepared their own natural colors, the secretions of octopuses and cuttlefish were used to create the distinctive reddish-brown color known as sepia (from the Latin for cuttlefish). Now, with the availability of synthetic colors, the use of these natural pigments has totally disappeared.

Octopus ink is a thick, dark fluid that the octopus uses to confuse his attackers. When the ink is ejected, it hangs in the water like a dark image of an octopus, and obscures the water so that he can escape. The ink is accompanied by a nerve poison, so that if the enemy attacks the ink cloud his taste and smell will be impaired.

One of the virtues of octopus ink is its color density. To do a twenty-two-by-thirty-inch painting, Diana uses only four drops of ink, which she dilutes with water. A typical octopus yields only about one cubic centimeter of ink. The largest octopus Diana has ever caught weighed forty-seven pounds and measured twelve feet from the tip of the head to the end of the tentacles. She got five centimeters of ink from it, probably enough for 100 paintings.

Octopus ink is indelible. "Once a mark is made, you have to live with it. The ink won't cover up any mistakes. In fact, it carries forward any mark made previously," explains Diana. While this "unforgiving" feature of the medium makes painting more difficult, Diana considers it one of the beauties of octopus ink, which she has been using since 1950. You can't achieve the effect of "carrying forward" with watercolors or acrylics, because watercolor will smear and acrylic will cover up. "Octopus ink is very flexible," says Diana. "It lets me wash a mood tone over the top of something I've already painted, which you can't do with other paints."

Most of Diana's paintings portray various aspects of Eskimo life. She travels extensively, sketching things that excite her. Then at home she paints from the sketches. Her technique is a variant of watercolor technique. She lays clean water on 300-pound watercolor paper, and as the water soaks in, she introduces the color. The effect varies, depending upon how completely the water has been absorbed, so absolute water control is necessary.

Diana completes about eighty paintings each year, and sells virtually all of them, priced between $250 and $700. She also gives about three one-woman-shows each year. She has exhibited in San Francisco, Lenox and Amherst, Massachusetts, at the World Congress of Poets in Baltimore, and in many locations in Alaska. She also maintains a gallery in a thirty-nine-foot geodesic dome (half of the dome is actually her sister's home). Diana also works in sculpture, pastels, oils, watercolors, and printmaking.

Diana never has to go more than half a mile from her door to get an octopus. When the tide is out, she catches them under the rocks along the beach where they live. The octopus never ejects ink in his own den because the nerve poison would make his home unlivable. He will only resort to this method of self-defense when he is free-swimming. He can bite, however (he has a beak very much like a parrot's), so Diana wears heavy gloves when she's

(Top) Diana Tillion and her husband, Clem, came to Ismailof Island in 1952. (Right) Diana combs the beach at low tide for octopuses.

hunting. As she finds octopuses very unpleasant company, Diana doesn't go after them very often—she only uses three or four a year. She removes the ink from the ink gland with a hypodermic syringe, and she and her husband Clem eat the octopus. The meat is tough, but can be ground up for a delicious chowder.

Between Memorial Day and Labor Day, you can visit Diana's home and gallery to browse, buy, or just chat. A ferry, piloted by Diana's daughter Marion Beck, leaves Homer Spit daily at 1:00 P.M., tours the beautiful Gull Islands, and arrives at Halibut Cove, Ismailof Island, at 2:15. Guests are greeted by Diana's pet seal Scrape, devoted to her since she found him abandoned in the wild and nursed him back to health (he just scraped through). After a visit to the gallery with Diana, guests are treated to a hot drink at the Tillions' *kashim* (beach house), and the return ferry leaves at 4:00.

Diana was born in Paradise, California, and came to Alaska in 1939 when she was eleven. She and Clem, who is now a state senator, moved into a two-room log house on Ismailof Island in 1952, when there were only two women and six bachelors living there. Now they own seventy-two acres of the island, and have two sons and two daughters.

America's Best! OYSTERS

The Olympia Oyster Company   *206-426-3354*

Route 1, Box 500   *David C. McMillin, Vice-*
Shelton, Washington 98584   *President*

Don't look for pearls in Olympia oysters. Just savor them. These dime-sized mollusks are so delectable they caused their own boom during the San Francisco gold rush, plus brought the capital of Washington to the town of Olympia so that legislators could dine on them. The late Bing Crosby, a native of the area, savored them.

Olympia oysters are rare, growing nowhere else in the world but in the salt-water inlets off Puget Sound in Mason and Thurston counties. Their extraordinary taste has won them so many fans that the major producer, the Olympia Oyster Company, tries to reserve them for VIPs and the best customers of its "bread and butter" products, clams and large Pacific oysters.

Three-fourths of all Olympia oysters that the company sells are served in the state's best restaurants, while most of the remainder make their way to fine eateries in San Francisco. Olympia Oyster Company produces 250 bushels a year, and a handful of small competitors contribute a total of another 500. Years ago, before pollution intervened and most of the delicate Olympia oyster population died, 100 shipments were made to New York each week.

Olympia oysters are so tiny it takes 2,200 of them with the shells removed to make up a gallon (selling for $140 wholesale), compared to 200 to 300 East Coast oysters and 120 Pacific oysters. Unlike other oysters, Olympia oysters are never served on the half shell. Instead, they arrive already immersed in cocktail sauce in a small cup. Otherwise, it would be too much work for the diner.

For that reason, Olympia oysters are always shucked before being sold and are only sold fresh. There is a Japanese woman, Akiko Smith, whose sole duty is to shuck every single Olympia oyster by hand. These oysters are then packaged naturally, minus additives and preservatives, and delivered on dry ice or in a refrigerated truck.

The Indians were the first to harvest and eat these succulent oysters, but it didn't take settlers long to follow suit. Olympia oysters rapidly grew into a boom item for the state's economy. Unfortunately, Olympia oysters take two to four years to mature. Too many people overharvested, and there were hardly any Olympia oysters left by 1910.

Oyster farms then sprang up to increase supply and create better growing conditions. Concrete dikes were built to create artificial tide pools so that oyster beds could always be covered with a beneficial layer of water. "The entire bottom of this bay has been terraced," explains David McMillin, a shellfish biologist and vice-president and manager of the Olympia Oyster Company on Totten Inlet. The harvesting itself must still be done by hand.

Farming proved quite successful, and industry-wide production climbed to 50,000 bushels a year. But in 1927 a large pulp mill, with political clout behind it, was built and began discharging its wastes into the bay. Olympia oysters sickened and died, and production plummeted to 1,000 bushels annually. Oyster farmers tried repeatedly to dispose of the mill through the legal process, but the courts ruled otherwise. Finally, in 1957 the mill shut down for economic reasons and the water situation started to improve.

In the meantime, however, producers had imported heartier Japanese oysters and clams. These oysters and clams thrived in their new setting, but so did the pests that accompanied them—Japanese Oyster Drills (snails that feast on oysters) and flat-worms, which go after baby oysters. These pests are now the industry's biggest handicap. "That's the sad story of the Olympia oyster," says McMillin. Producers have declared war on the drills and flatworms. For example, they are installing sprinklers in the bay to create artificial rain to thwart flatworms.

McMillin is confident that science can help the Olympia oyster's tale achieve a happy ending and that this delicacy won't be relegated to that of only a scarce cocktail item. Besides being served raw in cocktails, Olympia oysters are delicious roasted and in stews and dressing. In fact, he prefers them fried, dipped in egg and cracker crumbs, and pan-fried in bacon grease. The Olympia Oyster Company will send you brochures featuring recipes that local restaurants developed just for Olympia oysters.

America's Best! PERSONAL SUBMARINES

Kittredge Industries, Inc.

Route 1
Warren, Maine 04864

207-273-2626

George Kittredge, President

Terms: 25% down with order,
25% down when framed, 25%
when all systems are installed,
balance due when submarine is
completed, depth-tested and
ready to dive

Over 300 years ago, Mother Shipton, a famous English prophetess, predicted the coming of the submarine: "Under water man shall walk, shall ride, shall sleep, shall talk." Certainly, man's desire to include the underwater world in his dominion was greatly enhanced in 1620 by a Dutchman, Cornelius Van Drebbel, who is thought to have developed the first navigable underwater boat, with chemical purification of the air permitting a passing acquaintance with the depths.

It is doubtful, however, that even Russian Emperor Alexander II, who enlivened his 1855 coronation with an audible concert given by musicians submerged in Kronstadt Harbor, could have foreseen an era in which Kittredge Industries, Inc., of Warren, Maine, would be producing America's best personal submarines.

Since 1967, retired Navy Captain George Kittredge, a World War II submariner, has been constructing one-man subs. He recently developed a newer two-man model that was tested successfully at a simulated depth pressure of 900 feet. A scientist saw Kittredge's plans for a small sub in a magazine and commissioned him to build one. Kittredge Industries was formed from the proceeds, and Kittredge has since built thirty-six subs.

The subs are built for maximum visibility. Transparent acrylic hatches and optional acrylic portholes on the bottom facilitate oceanographic research, scavenging, and simple underwater touring.

The K-250 model ($16,000), Kittredge's basic one-man sub after which the other three versions were designed, is eleven feet, eight inches long and three feet in diameter. The K-250 can remain submerged for an hour and a half, which is plenty of time to go to the maximum depth of 250 feet and then surface to replenish air. There are two independently movable external engines for maximum maneuverability. Maximum speed with "full steam" from the batteries is 2½ knots.

The K-350 (one-man model, $34,000) is twelve-feet long, and is basically the same as the K-250 except for its maximum operating depth of 350 feet and maximum speed of three knots with a little more horsepower from a stern motor. Its operating time underwater without optional air-revitalization equipment is also a little longer, one hour, forty-five minutes.

The K-600 ($125,000) is the new two-man sub capable of submerging to a standard maximum depth of 600 feet. Its technological advances include a maximum submerged operating time of one hour, forty-five minutes with the inclusion of an emergency seventy-two-hour life-support system. The maximum speed is a nifty seven knots with three motors, two of which are external and can be fully rotated independently for maximum maneuverability. Maximum thrust is achieved with a three horsepower internal motor utilizing an external, center-line propellor. The sub can also go in reverse. The K-600 is eleven-feet, five-inches long and three feet in diameter, and features the acrylic viewing port built into the earlier models.

Kittredge is planning a larger sub which will carry as many as six people! It will be a major development, paving the way for group research, eliminating the problems of claustrophobia, and opening new transportation possibilities.

Kittredge options now include a mechanical claw for an additional $350, an underwater telephone (many customers have this

George Kittredge makes America's best and most affordable personal subs.

installed for safety) for $1,200 ($600 per terminal, two terminals needed), a floodlight operable to 500 feet for $150, and a digital directional depth sounder and search sonar for $500, with installation. For the more sophisticated and versatile K-350 and K-600 series, an underwater television, an underwater metal detector, a directional gyro for navigation, and air-revitalization equipment are available. A tandem trailer ($2,200) is available with all the subs.

The subs are equipped with scuba gear to expedite a safe escape in the event of an entanglement or another emergency thwarting resurfacing. Also, emergency drop lead weights, adding stability to the sub during normal operation, may be dropped to lighten the sub by over a hundred pounds. Kittredge personally tests all the subs he builds. They have a perfect safety record.

Kittredge retired from the Navy in 1962, prior to running unsuccessfully for a seat in the Maine congressional delegation. He began to draw and sell (for $2) submarine plans based on his knowledge of World War II submarines, and constructed his first personal submarine in 1967. He sold his company in 1969 to a fast-diversifying Connecticut sports firm, but bought it back in 1972 when the firm fell on hard times.

Kittredge keeps a relatively low price tag on his subs and rarely makes a profit. He and his wife "make do" on his military pension and do not need much money from submarine sales. This allows him to maintain a unique, soft-sell approach to his business. He'll even host potential buyers for a couple of days to "explain everything" about the subs.

The price range eliminates potential competition. A Florida-based firm also manufactures small subs, for three or four people, at a price of $350,000 to $1,500,000, not quite as affordable to most would-be submariners.

America's Best! PIZZA

The European Restaurant

218 Hanover Street
Boston, Massachusetts 02113

617-523-5694

Albert (Nick) Maiocco &
Gaetano (Gus) Aprile, Owners
Michael Jannini, General
Manager

7 days a week: 11:00 A.M.–
1:00 A.M.; closed Thanksgiving
and Christmas

Master Charge, American
Express, Diner's Club, Visa

One bite of a deluxe extra-large pizza from the European Restaurant in Boston's North End will convince anyone that it is America's best. Layered with special tomato sauce, sizzling cheese, mushrooms, peppers, sausage, salami, pepperoni, onions, and anchovies, this $6.75 pizza will easily satisfy at least six hungry Italians.

The first secret to creating such a masterpiece lies in the dough. At the European, only unbleached white flour is used. It is mixed with water, yeast, salt, and oil for twenty minutes in a special machine. Then *panini* (round portions of dough) are formed and weighed to determine the various sizes of pizza. A small pizza, for

163

instance, requires a twelve-ounce portion, while the extra large requires thirty ounces of dough. Once they are properly formed, the *panini* are placed in special drawers and allowed to rise for three to four hours. If permitted to sit longer, the dough rises too much and must be discarded. Those passing inspection are then hand-kneaded, placed on the "peel," a flat baking board, and covered with tomato sauce and ingredients of your choice.

Then, they're slid right onto the hot oven bricks for a twelve- to fifteen-minute bake (as opposed to cooking them on the traditional pizza pan). Because of this special touch, every European pizza is more crispy, light, and airy than any other pizza in America.

The second secret of these pizzas lies in the ingredients, all of which are bought fresh daily from local vendors in Boston's North End. Benny Penta, the European "pizza man" since 1948, proportions all of the ingredients by sight. Only the best full-cream mozzarella is used, and the tomato sauce is carefully concocted with crushed whole Italian plum tomatoes, salt, pepper, oregano, and garlic. The vegetables, cheese, and meat (or fish) are then spread evenly over the sauce in order to insure uniform baking of the pizza. These ingredients do not form one amorphous mass of flavor. Each fresh ingredient stands out by itself before mixing subtly with the others. A European deluxe extra-large pizza includes three of the most expensive ingredients—anchovies, pepperoni, and salami. In just one normal week, the European uses 180 pounds of pepperoni, 250 pounds of sausage, 1,000 pounds of mushrooms, and 1,000 pounds of flour! (One 100-pound bag of flour makes 250 pizzas.)

The origins of pizza are shrouded in legend. Some people claim it dates back to Ancient Rome and a cook named Pompeius Pizius, circa 80 B.C. Others claim that it was created in modern Naples. (In Italy, where there are many different kinds of pizza, the style familiar to us is called *pizza napoletana*.) One thing's for sure: no matter where pizzas come from, the whole world loves them.

A Gallup Poll has found that pizza is the favorite food of 42 percent of U.S. teenagers—with the hamburger showing a poor 10 percent. Americans spend more than $1.6 billion on pizza in restaurants each year. Santo Forcone, president of International Pizza Exchange, Inc., in New York, thinks that figure is conservative, and that it's closer to $4 billion.

There are as many pizza recipes in the world as there are pizza chefs, and each has his own secret to "the perfect pizza." Every possible combination of garnishes has been tried at least once, but the most unusual has got to be the creation of Deanna Ellis of Runnells, Iowa. Her Pizza aux Vers de Terre Extraordinaire, or pizza with earthworms, is "just a pizza with the works. You boil the worms, mix with sausage, fry real crisp and sprinkle on." Deanna says the crunchy worms taste "kind of like dirt" and have a "mildew smell." The European doesn't make Deanna's exotic treat, but they do make many variations on America's best. One prominent Boston celebrity enjoys his pizza *without cheese*, so he can savor the rich taste of mushrooms, peppers, and anchovies atop a delectable tomato sauce.

In a 1976 *Boston Globe* poll, Bostonians chose the European as their favorite pizza parlor by a five-to-one margin over its nearest competitor. Co-owners Nick Maiocco and Gus Aprile normally serve 5,000 pizzas to between 15,000 and 20,000 customers each week, and sell more than $1 million worth of pizza each year.

Chuck, the maitre d' who has been at the European since 1948, says that the true intent of the restaurant is to provide good eating rather than fine dining. Seating capacity in the three rooms (the Main Dining Room, the Roman Room, and the Venetian Room) is about 520 and the usual turnover is one table per hour. Chuck recommends informal attire—the more informal the better —for this rather messy meal.

Owner Nick Maiocco's father opened the restaurant in 1917 after emigrating from Italy. In those days not many Italians went out to eat, and the Maioccos were lucky to pull in 100 people a week. Pizza was not even on the menu then, although other Italian specialties were served. According to Nick, a dish of spaghetti could be had for 15¢. "You could get a complete steak dinner with antipasto, soup, steak, spaghetti, and beverage for 45¢." Co-owner Gus Aprile entered the restaurant as a pizza man in 1946, about ten years after pizza was introduced to the U.S. The pizza recipe now used by the European came directly from Gus's mother.

Some people claim that the European Restaurant can satiate any voracious appetite and pizza epicure. Indeed, Gus says that some of the heftier young people in the North End can eat a whole extra-large deluxe—a pretty amazing feat, considering it will barely fit on the table.

America's Best! PORTRAIT PHOTOGRAPHERS

Bachrach, Inc.

44 Hunt Street
Watertown, Massachusetts 02172

617-924-6200

Fabian Bachrach, President

Branches:
647 Boylston Street, Boston,
Massachusetts 02116

48 East 50th Street, New York,
New York 10022

1611 Walnut Street,
Philadelphia, Pennsylvania
19103

Short Hills Mall, Short
Hills, New Jersey 07078

104 South Michigan Avenue,
Chicago, Illinois 60603

Every U.S. President since Lincoln (as well as several important First Ladies) has been photographed by Bachrach. David Bachrach, who formed the company in 1868, was but an apprentice when he first happened upon Lincoln delivering the Gettysburg Address. He had no idea what a momentous event he was capturing. Nor did Louis Bachrach expect Eleanor Roosevelt to order hundreds of copies of her portrait over the years. Perhaps the most famous presidential portrait was John F. Kennedy's, which has been reprinted thousands of times and is probably the picture of him you most remember seeing.

The presidential mystique affects even the best photographer, and Fabian describes restless, tension-filled nights on the eve of presidential sittings. "You realize," he says, "these men have so

A 1902 Alexander Graham Bell family group.

little time that each shot has got to count. And, with the other officials present and watching you (they've seen the President before), you can't help but feel the tremendous power this man wields."

Bachrach, Inc., has also photographed a host of prominent world figures, people such as Thomas Alva Edison; Henry Ford I (whose picture Bachrach copyrighted immediately for fear that Mr. Ford would reproduce it himself more cheaply); Robert Frost

(Fabian's favorite photograph, taken in Cambridge just two years before Frost died); Prince Don Carlos and Princess Sophia of Spain; the Duchess of Windsor; Jacques Cousteau; and John Kenneth Galbraith.

The bridal business comprises half of all Bachrach's work and is Bradford Bachrach's specialty. For most photographers, wedding assignments are clustered around the month of June. For Bachrach, however, August, September, and October are equally as hectic. The price of a Bachrach wedding is $295 for a minimum of five hours time, and includes 100 to 150 proofs (often of as good a quality as the finished prints), as well as forty prints displayed in two leather-bound books.

Another special feature of Bachrach, Inc., is its specialization. Recognizing the important differences between male and female sittings, Bradford has come to specialize in female photography. Women are more difficult to photograph, as hair, coloring, and personality take considerable time to coordinate. Of particular challenge are older women, many of whom feel as if they are getting less attractive as they age. Talking fast and confidently, Bradford reassures them, tells them when they look their best, and eases their camera shyness. These skills are particularly important since the current trend at Bachrach is toward informality. Bradford's ultimate goal is to photograph Queen Elizabeth, a handsome woman whose portraits have been all too formal, he says. "So far the photographers have done her usually in an evening dress. I'd like to do something a little less formal."

Children sometimes create presidential-level problems for the portrait photographer. "You get the feeling that you have no control over the situation," Bradford says. "In order to win their confidence you have to show you like them. Lollipops and jumping through hoops won't do."

According to Fabian, the secret to good portrait photography is its realism and its ability to endure. "Portrait photography is an attempt to capture the romantic moments in life. There are no special techniques or processes; rather it's all a matter of the photographer's concept of what he's trying to do. He must be empathetic and he must get to know his subject on a very individual basis in a short time."

At the Boston studio alone, eight photographers usually do five one-hour sittings every day. They try a variety of views, poses, and lighting effects to get ten or fifteen good proofs. Though all work is done in color, the technique is perfected to produce excellent black-and-white prints as well.

The minimum price for a black-and-white sitting is $77.50. That includes a one-hour sitting, ten to fifteen proofs, and up to six glossy prints from one negative. A color portrait, carefully mounted, retouched, and embellished, is $118. But, adds Fabian, most customers spend between $100 and $300. If the president of General Motors happened to want his portrait taken in his office, Bachrach would gladly oblige, for maybe $500 plus expenses.

Although such prices may seem high, Fabian is quick to assert, "I think people of discrimination find you. If you don't think enough of your own work to charge good prices, no one else is going to either." He must be right, as more than 6,000 people have their pictures taken by Bachrach each year.

When Muhammad Ali visited Bachrach, he insisted on being photographed in a red sports shirt. "It's unusual," says Bradford, "but you don't tell Muhammad what to do." (That's what happens when The Greatest meets The Best.)

America's Best! POTATO CHIPS

Maui Potato Chip Company	*Dewey Kobayashi, President*
Kahalui, Maui, Hawaii 96732	*Only available in 7-oz. twin package; $1.45–$2 at major*
808-877-3652	*hotels and grocery stores on Maui only*

"No more orders, please!" pleads Dewey Kobayashi. But the orders keep pouring in from all over the U.S. to the town of Kahalui, Maui. To date, there is a six-month backlog of orders for Kobayashi's scrumptious potato chips.

Little wonder that the Maui Potato Chip Company sells $600,000 of Kitch'n Cook'd (available in seven-ounce packages only) potato chips per year. Ever since national media coverage lauded Kobayashi's product, including a front-page article in the *Wall Street Journal* in 1975, offers have poured in begging him to expand the business on an international scale. Kobayashi has already turned down offers of over $5 million to franchise the business; he simply has no desire to change his way of life.

The secret to the potato chip, according to Kobayashi, is the potatoes. Not just any potato goes into Kitch'n Cook'd chips. Kobayashi selects only Burbank russet potatoes from the Tule Lake area of northern California, which are known for their high sugar content. After thorough cleaning, the potatoes are sliced fairly thick and fried in cotton-seed oil. The salting and drying processes are a family secret, but the result is the crunchiest, tastiest chips in America. They contain no preservatives.

Kobayashi's parents learned about cooking potatoes when they were interned in New Mexico and Montana during World War II. Then, in 1957, the family bought a small potato chip business from a friend for $500. The Maui Potato Chip Company is still basically a family business, although Kobayashi now has sixteen people working for him. With all his success, he still puts in a twelve-hour day. "It's not like the old days when we used to soak our potatoes in the bathtub, but I still could use some modern equipment," he says.

Potato chips are an American invention. They originated in 1853 at Saratoga Lake, in New York, when Commodore Cornelius Vanderbilt sent some fried potatoes back to the chef at Moon's Lake House Restaurant complaining that they were too thick. This time the chef sliced them as thin as he possibly could, fried and salted them, and sent them back to Vanderbilt. Within a year, the "Saratoga Chips" were being introduced worldwide. The average American now eats an average of four pounds of potato chips a year. The potato-chip-eating capital of America is Detroit, Michigan, where residents eat seven pounds of them a year per capita.

Connoisseurs claim Kobayashi's potato chips are the most flavorful, crunchiest, and just plain delectable potato chips available. The chips are so popular, it's difficult to find the cheery red-and-yellow packages on supermarket shelves. Knowledgeable tourists snatch them up from the hotels and grocery stores—that is, what's left of them after the natives' appetites are sated. In Honolulu, lines form on delivery day, and a customer can purchase only one twinpack bag at a time. A piqued Bloomingdale's buyer wanting 10,000 bags of Kitch'n Cook'd potato chips once had to return to New York empty-handed.

So, mail no orders to the people at the Maui Potato Chip Company. They can't fill them. But, if you're passing through Kahalui, stop into a store and try a sample of America's best potato chips.

America's Best! POUSSE CAFÉ

Pat O'Brien's

718 St. Peter
New Orleans, Louisiana 70116

504-525-4823

Drew the Bartender

10:00 A.M.–4:00 A.M.; *till*
5:00 A.M. *Friday and Saturday*

At Pat O'Brien's, head straight for the young mustachioed bartender named Drew for his Pousse Café. You'll find him in the smaller of the two bars, the one on the left just after the main entrance. This rather plain room is patronized by New Orleans locals, who go there for the best and cheapest drinks in town.

Drew's Pousse Café is an exotic concoction of ten liqueurs poured separately into an elongated liqueur glass, according to weight. The final effect is a beautiful rainbow of colors, which remain distinct without blending. The order in which he pours is:

Jero's Passion Mix (green or yellow)
Grenadine
Kahlua
White Crème de Menthe
Blue Curaçao
Galliano
Meyer's Rum (dark)
Green Chartreuse
Southern Comfort
Club 190 or Evenclear, with strawberry liqueur.

Drew pours only ⅛th of a shot glass of each ingredient, which represents about ¼ inch of a band of color in each glass. Watch out, though. Club 190 and Evenclear, which are mixed with strawberry liqueur, are 190 Proof Grain Alcohol. The Pousse Café costs

$1.50, and Pat O'Brien's collects another $1.50 as a refundable deposit for the glass.

Pat O'Brien's is crowded 365 days a year, including Christmas. There are always people queued up waiting to get in on weekends. Established in 1943, this popular "joint" currently sells more liquor than any other bar in America ($50 million a year). There is a variety of atmospheres, including a huge entertainment room with sing-alongs, two crowded bars, and a secluded courtyard with lush vegetation and fountains.

Ignore the crowds, and by all means single out Drew, *who is only there in the evenings*. He is quite shy, but he is always willing to make that rainbow-colored drink that is in itself a pot of gold.

America's Best! PUEBLO TOURS

Piper Tour and Travel	Indian Pueblo Cultural Center
P.O. Box 14266 Albuquerque, New Mexico 87191	2401 Twelfth Street, North West Albuquerque, New Mexico 87102
505-293-2880	505-843-7270
Shelly Kurdi, Director	Jim Trujillo, Director
	7 days a week: 9:00 A.M.– 6:00 P.M.; admission free

All nineteen of New Mexico's Indian pueblos are still inhabited. The best place for a formal introduction to Pueblo culture is in downtown Albuquerque, however, at the Indian Pueblo Cultural Center. There you'll be introduced to a culture that, through more than 400 years of continuous contact with people alien to its traditions, has maintained its religion, style of living, and identity.

Next, you should visit a pueblo on a tour arranged by Piper Tour. Acoma Pueblo, called "City in the Sky" because of its location atop a 365-foot sandstone mesa, is the most popular.

Acoma's San Estevan Mission has been in use since 1629.

Each pueblo has its own governor and is a member of the All Indian Pueblo Council, which sponsors the Indian Pueblo Cultural Center. The purpose of the Center is to acquaint non-Indians with the Pueblo people and to supply Pueblo children with information about their background. Completed in 1976, the Center houses a museum, an arts and crafts exhibit, a marketing area, and an Indian restaurant. Stone bowls, mallets, storage jars, fragments of baskets, pottery, drums, woven sash belts, and arrowheads are on permanent display, and an arts-and-crafts exhibit features work made in all nineteen pueblos since 1900. San Ildefonso Pueblo is represented by the work Maria Martinez, a world-famous potter. Also on display is lapidary work of San Felipe, drums, sash belts, and pottery of Cochiti, red pottery of Tesuque, black pottery of Santa Clara, and the micaceous pottery of Picuris.

The gift shop sells jewelry, rugs, stone sculptures, pottery, moccasins, silver bridles, and other objects made by the Indians. The Indian Arts and Crafts Association guarantees the authenticity of each object, and the selection at the Center is bigger than that at the individual pueblos.

The restaurant serves typical Indian food, including pinto beans, fry bread, sandia salad, which is made with fresh vegetables, cheese, and sunflower seeds, and posole, a dish made with dried corn and beef and served with red or green chili. Open seven days a week in the summer and five days a week in the winter, the restaurant serves breakfast and lunch. Hours are 7:00 A.M. to 3:30 P.M.

Piper Tour and Travel schedules a five-hour tour to Acoma Pueblo for $13.50 on Tuesdays and Thursdays, and will take you to any of the other pueblos on a charter.

The fee includes transportation between Albuquerque and Acoma, a tour of Acoma guided by a native escort, and a tour of nearby sights. There is an additional $2.50 camera fee.

Shelly Kurdi, director of Piper Tour and Travel, has established a good relationship with the pueblo governors. As a matter of fact, the Acoma Indians have shown her a special and little-known back way up the 365-foot sandstone mesa to "Sky City."

An especially good time to visit the pueblos is during the *Fiesta Encantada*. From December 15 to January 7, the Indians celebrate their feast days with dances and other activities.

Indian law is in effect at the pueblos, and offenses committed by non-Indians, such as visiting the *kiva* (sacred ceremonial area) are decided by an Indian court. Restrictions on recording or photographing special ceremonies must be strictly observed. The regulations are posted at the governor's office of each pueblo. If a visitor plans to go alone to a pueblo, he is urged to phone ahead for information on special events, and especially to make sure the pueblo is open to the public at that time.

New Mexico's pueblos are:

North of Santa Fe:
Tesuque
San Ildefonso
Santa Clara
San Juan
Pojoaque
Nambe
Picuris
Taos

West of Albuquerque:
Acoma
Laguna
Zuni

South of Albuquerque:
Isleta

North of Albuquerque:
Sandia
Santa Ana
San Felipe
Zia
Jemez
Santo Domingo
Cochiti

America's Best! Resort Hotel

Mauna Kea Beach Hotel

Kamuela, Hawaii 96743

808-882-7222

Robert H. Butterfield, General Manager

N.B.: *"This is not a 'swinging singles' resort; don't come alone!"*

"The leaders of society are the forgotten people. They must be revitalized. This is the kind of place they can come to for that," says Laurance Rockefeller, developer of luxurious resorts around the world. The "place" he speaks of is Mauna Kea Beach Hotel on the big island of Hawaii.

The luxuries provided by the Mauna Kea are enough to relax any harried key government official (Henry Kissinger, Gerald Ford), foreign dignitary (Emperor of Japan), top executive (David Rockefeller, Stavros Niarchos), or show business celebrity (Lucille Ball, Alfred Hitchcock) and give them privacy away from the limelight.

Vacation benefits at the Mauna Kea Beach Hotel include:

A year-round temperature of seventy-two to eighty-nine degrees and annual rainfall of seven inches;

An eighteen-hole golf course ranked among the top fifty courses in the world;

Nine championship tennis courts;

Horseback riding, swimming (ocean or fresh-water pool), sailing in a catamaran, hunting (sheep, boar, birds), deep-sea fishing, surfing, waterskiing, snow skiing, skin diving, snorkeling, helicopter flights over the island;

A special luau on Tuesday;

Day camp for children during the peak children seasons— summer, Christmas, Easter;

Thirty acres of gardens;

Nightly entertainment by three musical groups;

Over 1,000 Oriental and Pacific Basin art objects.

In 1960, leaders of the newly admitted state of Hawaii asked Laurance Rockefeller to create new vacation areas. After considerable research, he decided to build a luxury hotel on the Kohala coast of Hawaii, at the foot of the highest peak in the Pacific, Mauna Kea.

You approach the hotel through a remarkable lunar terrain formed from *a'a'* lava, which covered the land in the early 1800s and cooled very slowly. Out of this lava, golf architect Robert Trent Jones sculpted a lush, eighteen-hole golf course. He covered it with soil and planted grass, and every night the hotel pumps one-million gallons of water onto the fairways and greens to keep them green.

Golf Digest lists the course as among the top fifty in the world, and the third hole is renowned for the 120 yards of Pacific Ocean a golfer must tee across.

Nine championship all-weather tennis courts are available, as well as a tennis hostess who will arrange instruction or matches. For hunters, the Mauna Kea has exclusive hunting privileges on the Parker Ranch, which abounds with wild boar, big-horn sheep, and wild birds. The Kohala Coast is world-renowned for deep-sea fishing. The International Marlin Competition is held there, and the waters abound with mahimahi, tuna, bonito, and opakapaka. The hotel will arrange full- and half-day fishing trips for six, and the chef will prepare the fish you catch. You can also rent a small sailboat or a fifty-eight-foot catamaran. There is even a ski club atop Mauna Kea.

Meals at Mauna Kea are a gourmet treat. The hotel operates on a "modified American plan," and two meals a day are included with the price of the room.

The hotel has separate china for each of the three dining rooms, and each dining room uses different china for breakfast, lunch, and dinner. Most guests eat breakfast, which often includes an omelet and a steak, in the Dining Pavillion, although many choose to eat on their balconies and enjoy the view. The Cafe Terrace's buffet lunch, which includes fifty or sixty items, from Korean chicken to ono fish, is legendary throughout the islands. Most of the lunch guests are sightseers or local islanders, since people staying at the hotel usually make do with a light lunch at the Hau Tree Terrace on the beach or do without in preparation for the Mauna Kea dinners.

The dinner menu is the same in the Dining Pavillion and the Garden Pavillion, and rotates on a ten-day cycle. A typical dinner includes pâté of pheasant, coulibiac of mahimahi, and macadamia-nut ice cream. Guests must dress for dinner—a jacket for gentle-

Informal elegance is the hallmark of Mauna Kea.

men and a dress or pants suit for ladies. An orchestra plays in the Garden Pavillion until 9:30.

Dinner is also served on the Batik Terrace. The menu is even more extensive than in the other dining rooms, and the service is more lavish. The tables are used only once an evening, so guests are required to make reservations and pay an extra charge. An indoor-outdoor cocktail lounge adjacent to the Batik Terrace provides a dance band until 1:00 A.M.

Every Thursday evening, the Mauna Kea stages a luau, complete with leis and Polynesian entertainment. ($4.50 surcharge). It is scheduled early so guests can watch the sunset. During the walk back to the hotel, a show is provided by manta rays, who come to the shoreline to feed on plankton.

Built at a cost of $20 million, the award-winning hotel has 310 guest rooms and can accommodate 700 guests. Rates are $155 to $200 per night for two, including breakfast and dinner. All of the rooms at the hotel are the same; only the views are different. The Mauna Kea suites (rates available on request) each have a bedroom with connecting sitting room, two dressing rooms, and a wet bar, as well as a corner location, which affords the most breathtaking view of the ocean. The hotel can accommodate 700 guests, and is usually 92 percent occupied.

The guest who comes most often and stays the longest, sometimes two months at a time, is a very wealthy retired gentleman who has a beautiful home in Kona, only twenty-five miles away. He has found that he can relax at the Mauna Kea, so why should he go "around the world" when such luxury is so near?

America's Best! RESTAURANT GAME PRESERVES

Rosellini's Other Place

4th and Union
Seattle, Washington 98101

206-623-7340

Robert Rosellini, Owner

Robert Rosellini believes in fine dining in the extravagant tradition of post-revolutionary France—courses by the tens, each richer and more scrumptious than the last, one wine after another to suit the variety of courses, and lots of time to enjoy it all. In fact, two or three times a year, Robert throws a *grande bouffe* for his friends—a gourmet meal that goes on (and on) for nearly a full day.

Needless to say, Rosellini is a fussy man, both for himself and for the guests in his restaurants (he owns two, Rosellini's Other Place, which serves continental cuisine, and Rosellini's 610, which serves seafood). Unable to obtain game of the quality he felt was necessary for his *haute cuisine*, Rosellini created his own game preserves. This way, he'll always have game that's fresh, tender, and flavorful enough to please even the most finicky gourmand.

On his four-acre game fowl preserve, Rosellini raises pheasants, ducks, quails, partridges, and guinea fowls, all of which he serves at the Other Place. Once a week, he will call Bud Bruins, his keeper, to find out which birds are ready for eating, and will adjust his menu accordingly. A typical order calls for 80 to 100 pheasants, 50 partridges, 120 quails, and 40 ducks.

Among the birds the preserve produces are wild mallards of a quality unavailable to any restaurant but Rosellini's. Other restaurants have to settle for frozen white mallards from Wisconsin and the East Coast, which are fat and very greasy (the flesh even tends to fall off as you carve). Not so with Rosellini's mallards. These small fowl (1½ to 2½ pounds) are very lean, and their meat is very dark and intensely flavored. Bud is currently trying to breed a larger duck.

In the line of pheasant, most restaurateurs have to settle for frozen Chinese ringneck pheasants, which are very bland, not un-

Robert Rosellini is famous for his *grandes bouffes*.

like domestic chicken. Rosellini's pheasants are tender, juicy, and have a "gaminess" to their taste that easily distinguishes them from domestic fowl.

"Frozen birds are grown in brooder houses on concrete floors," Bud Bruins explains. "They never get bugs or grass as they would in nature. Ours are as close to nature as they can be and still be captive."

Bud has carefully staggered the generations of his birds so that full-breasted, twenty-week-old birds are available year-round. To get the birds to lay in the winter, Bud keeps them in a controlled breeder where for thirteen weeks they are given only six hours of light a day. When they come out of there, no matter what season it is, the birds think it's spring, and they commence laying. Eggs are kept in incubators where heat and humidity are controlled, and electronic machinery turns them every two hours to keep the yolks from settling against the shells. It takes between twenty-four and twenty-eight days for the various birds to hatch, and their placement in the incubator is timed so that they all hatch on the same day.

Rosellini claims that his birds are the best-fed fowl in the nation. Their diet of fish meal, linseed, corn, and wheat is well balanced to provide sufficient protein, starch, and fiber. The result is a quick-maturing, well feathered bird that plucks well.

The game preserve is also the home of black-shouldered peacocks, pea fowl, and valley quail, but these are strictly to delight the eye—they are not good table birds. Bud also keeps a small herd of Scottish highland cows because, he says, his wife likes them. The cows are also useful, since their ominous horns help to ward off intruding dogs and children.

Rosellini also keeps a 1,000-acre fur game preserve near Redman, Washington, where he raises white and black fallow deer, red stag deer, moro deer, sylka deer, antelope, elk, moufloon sheep, and Corsican rams. However, he does not always offer fur game on his menu, because to do that he would need 2,000 animals a year, whereas he actually only butchers 300 a year. Fur game is brought in only once a month, and is aged to give it a little more flavor and a gamier nature.

Rosellini likes to structure his menu to include fish, veal, beef, lamb, game birds, and fur game. The menu changes almost daily, because a fixed menu would force Rosellini to serve frozen game or game that was not optimally ready for eating. Rosellini raises all the food for his restaurants himself or buys it fresh in the immediate area. He even serves organically grown vegetables, delivered daily from a co-op in the Kent Valley. A friend of his is trying to raise frogs for fresh cuisses de grenouille (frog's legs), and he's working on snails. Rosellini even grows his own spices hydroponically—in water rather than soil.

Rosellini is a fourth-generation restaurateur. He studied in restaurants in France and Switzerland, and under the legendary chef Jacques Lacombes. He is modest, however, saying that he is not a great chef, although he is very good at wines. He opened the Other Place in 1974, with the intention of making it the ultimate dining experience in Seattle. He eats five or six meals a day, but keeps trim by running twelve miles daily.

If you want to sample Rosellini's food in its most glorious state, try getting invited to one of his *grandes bouffes*. He held one of his more recent bashes at a lakeside home. Music was provided by seventy members of the Belleview Symphony Orchestra, and the eight guests were served thirty courses, all beautifully embellished and served on silver plates. The meal began at two o'clock in the afternoon, and didn't end until nine o'clock the next morning!

America's Best! RIDING INSTRUCTOR

George Morris

Hunterdon Riding Academy
Hunterdon Farms
R.D. 1, Box 144
Sidney Road
Pittstown, New Jersey 08867

201-782-0044

Lessons: $40–$100 for 1–1½ hour sessions with George Morris; special students only
Special Clinics: $1,500 for six hours
Group and individual lessons with Hunterdon staff: from $30 per hour

Four of George Morris's students are members of the United States Equestrian Team, and in the last ten years he has trained ten riders for the Olympics. As many as thirty-five riders from his prestigious Hunterdon Riding Academy perform in the Madison Square Garden Horse Show each year.

Hunterdon students begin training when they are as young as thirteen and spend approximately $15,000 on lessons, horse care, and show entrance fees while they are under Morris's tutelage. That doesn't include the $30,000 they spend for the horse, which Morris helps them select. He can judge a horse just by watching it go over a small jump, and prefers a thoroughbred in its prime (eight to twelve years old) for champion equestrian riding.

Training is rigorous. Even a beginner spends ten hours a week at Hunterdon classes, plus competition time, and there is always a long list of riders waiting for one of the fifty spots. Their acceptance is determined by talent and availability for competitions.

"Riding is not a great muscular sport," Morris says. "In fact, the better you ride, the less you do. You ride by balance and feel. It's a good mental exercise since you have to concentrate on your relationship with the horse."

He looks for someone who can go with the "feel" of the sport—a tall, thin, leggy type of person. "Riding is just like any other sport," he says. "A good rider has got to have an athletic sense."

The Hunterdon program also stresses appearance. "I can instantly detect things that don't appeal to me," says the meticulous Mr. Morris. He prefers plain collars to velvet, since velvet is out of place when riding. Coat sleeves should be worn to the palm of the hand, not to the fingertips. Coats are shorter than they once

George Morris goes over a jump.

were. Morris rides in a Brooks Brothers-style pinstripe jacket. He thinks breeches should be canary, beige, rust, or buff, and white breeches should be worn only with formal attire and top boots that go to the knees. Breeches should be skin-tight, never flared. He recommends E. Vogel boots because of their fit and softness, and thinks riders should always wear the protective hunting cap when they compete, not the dressier hacking cap.

Morris was raised in New Canaan, Connecticut, and began riding when he was nine years old. He studied under Gordon Wright, whom he calls "the grandfather of all modern equitation in this country." (Wright has tutored such champions as Ronnie Mutch, Victor Hugo Vidal, and Bill Steinkraus.) In 1960, Morris won a Silver Medal at the Rome Olympics.

He bought Hunterdon in 1971, and since then has added an adjacent farm and more stables. He now has 100 acres, including a full Grand Prix course. The $1.5-million farm is only seventy-five minutes from New York City and within an easy drive of the key competitions on the East Coast. Although he spends most of his time teaching, Morris competes in the Madison Square Garden Show every year and travels all over the world looking for horses for friends and clients. His horse "Jones Boy" finished second at the Gothenberg, Sweden, World Cup. If you can't afford his lessons, Morris has recently revised his book, *Hunter Seat Equitation*, a comprehensive riding guide for beginners.

America's Best! ROLLER COASTER

The Beast

Kings Island
P.O. Box 400
Kings Mills, Ohio 45034
(20 miles north of Cincinnati
on I-71)

513-241-5600

William C. Price, Vice-President
& General Manager
Ruth Voss, Manager of Public
Relations

Memorial Day weekend–Labor
Day weekend: 7 days a week,
9:00 A.M.–11:00 P.M.
Mid-April–mid-May and
mid-September–mid-October:
weekends only, 9:00 A.M.–
8:00 P.M.

$9.50 admission includes entrance
to park and all rides; children
2 and under free; senior citizens
(60 and over) $7; wheel chairs,
ramps free
Special group rates for 25 or more

Master Charge, Visa, American
Express, Shopper's Charge

Even the name is scary. "The Beast is absolutely the best coaster I've ever ridden," says Richard Rodriguez. And he knows what he's talking about, since he recently took a 128-hour spin on the Circus World, Florida, roller coaster. Paul Greenwald, vice-president of the American Coaster Enthusiasts, says, "The Beast is the first coaster since Space Mountain (Disneyworld, Florida, enclosed within a metal building looking like a mountain) that scared me. I felt out of control and that's beautiful. It blew my mind."

The Beast opened April 14, 1979. (There was a press preview the day before, Friday the 13th.) Built at a cost of $3.8 million, it has a top speed of 70 m.p.h. and a vertical drop of 141 feet. The course is 7,400 feet, or about 1¾ miles long, and a ride takes an eternal three minutes and forty seconds.

At the end of one long drop you fly into a dark passageway that twists 540 degrees on a 628-foot helix. Eight banked turns, with a few that go frighteningly near overhangs and ravines, are included just to be sure that the most diehard enthusiast wants to take another ride—to retrieve his stomach and mind.

Designer Charles Dinn studied the great coasters of the world for three years before setting to work on The Beast. Forty-three hundred hours of design work, 87,000 hours of construction work, 650,000 board feet of lumber, 5,180 washers, 37,500 pounds of nails, 82,480 various-sized bolts, and 2,432 square yards of poured concrete (enough to pave a 3.5-mile, two-lane highway) went into the coaster. On the track, 132 sensors connected by eighty-four miles of copper wire to a computer and a sixteen-foot display panel make The Beast the first fully computerized roller coaster in the U.S.

There are three other roller coasters at Kings Island, including The Racer, the first double-track coaster in any modern American park. The Racer features two sets of coasters that race each other on parallel and "mirrored" courses. It inspired the drive to build the ultimate roller coaster in America, culminating in The Beast.

Roller coasters developed over the past 300 years. In 17th-century Russia, sledding became so popular that giant ice slides were constructed in the winter months. The sleds and slides were exported to France, but since the warmer weather there made them less practical, they were replaced by small-wheeled carriages that rolled on tracks.

America's first modern-day roller coaster was built in 1886 at Coney Island by Charles Alcoke, and since then his basic design has been duplicated all over the country. As of 1979, there were about 200 coasters, down from about 900 in 1956. However, amusement parks, on the decline for the past twenty years, are becoming increasingly popular.

So hang onto your hat, because there's a roller-coaster renaissance in America. If you survive your ride on The Beast, come back in 1981. Word's afoot that Kings Island will be opening the first suspended roller coaster.

184

America's Best! SADDLERY

✉

M. J. Knoud, Inc.

212-838-1434

716 Madison Avenue
New York, New York 10021   *David H. Wright, President*

M. J. Knoud, Inc., sells the best of everything you could possibly want for your equestrian pleasures: saddles, bridles, all of the leather used on the horse, a complete line of stable supplies, even custom jodhpurs—right down to your boot hooks and jacks.

No one else in America provides the range of services available at M. J. Knoud. While the people at Knoud can make you a pair of breeches, a pair of boots, or a made-to-measure saddle, they'll also gladly show you a dozen different carriages imported from England. Need an estate appraised or a horse show judged? Again, Knoud's is the place to call.

Since horses have different backs, Knoud's will even make house calls for special saddle fittings. David H. Wright, president, flies to St. Louis regularly to fit Budweiser's Gussie Busch for his saddles.

You should budget $1,000 or so for a custom-made fox hunting outfit, which will include custom-made boots for $210 to $250, custom-made breeches for $215 to $425 or $45 to $100 for ready-made, and several coats, ranging from $160 to $450. Your riding outfit will not be complete without a velvet hunt cap ($33.50 to $125), special shirts, stock ties, and assorted horsing jewelry, all gold-mounted crystals, at $300 to $7,500. Further, Knoud will gladly outfit you with your hunt's insignia emblazoned on buttons for only $4.50 to $20 per button. A well adorned coat may cost you in excess of $400.

Knoud's handles a wide range of horse clothing also. Outfitting a horse includes a saddle ($450 to $800), a bridle ($100 to $150), a breastplate (martingale), a blanket, and a couple of sheets. To ensure a perfect fit, every customer is encouraged to try his saddle out on Knoud's block. By so doing, he simulates the way each saddle will feel on his mount. M. J. Knoud now imports the finest saddles from England, France, Italy, and Germany. "There are no quality saddles made in this country," says Wright.

Blankets, sheets, and breastplates are important items in any

185

horseman's bag of accessories. Blankets, at $50 to $150, and sheets, at $25, must always be kept on a horse, except during the summer months, when just one sheet will suffice. The wool blankets are thrown over a horse when he's hot, while the sheets are pieces of duck fabric that keep the horse's coat from becoming turned up. Breastplates ($50) are important in that they control the horse's head and keep its saddle from slipping back.

According to Mr. Wright, a well groomed pleasure rider would wear a nice tweed or Glen plaid coat. Unlike sports jackets, these riding coats come in at the waist and taper out into a skirt over the hips. They can be blended or contrasted with custom-made breeches. To add the finishing touches, you'll want to wear either black or brown dress boots, or special field boots with lace insteps.

M. J. Knoud, Inc., has been a success since opening in 1913. Knoud (Wright's uncle) was a quality-conscious saddler and craftsmen who learned the trade in Ireland and knew it well before he entered the business. Everything was, and still is, of the finest quality available, and his customers continue to recognize that.

Alice Colgate (of the original soap family) first put Knoud's name on the map. Since those days, the Mellons, the Duponts (who once ordered a $7,500 carriage), the Roosevelts, the Kennedys, and such notables as Princess Grace have been Knoud's customers.

America's Best! SALAMI AND PROSCIUTTO

Prosciutto means "ham" in Italian, and only the best ham legs are used to make this delicacy. Air curing, careful aging, hand rubbing, and even a properly aged building makes John Volpi & Company's "Splendor Brand" America's best prosciutto.

186

Prosciutto has become more popular as Americans have been acquainted with it abroad, but because of disease problems, prosciutto can't be shipped to the U.S. from San Daniele and Langhirano, Italy, where prosciutto has been a delicacy for over 800 years. Armando Pasetti, president and owner of Volpi, estimates his company sells 1.5 million pounds of prosciutto and salami per year.

Volpi dries its hams for four weeks.

The Volpi plant, used since 1905, is crucial to fine quality. Pasetti explains that yeast spores must multiply in the air and mold spores must grow on the concrete and brick walls before proper air-aging can occur. A new building, or materials other than brick and concrete, won't do. In fact, Pasetti claims that a curing building must be properly aged for five years.

No artificial process hastens the Volpi natural air-curing and drying. Volpi hams are not smoked. Instead, they are hung in carefully monitored rooms kept at sixty to sixty-five degrees F. with low humidity. The four-month drying period is twice as long as the time required by government health standards. The ham is salted by hand and hung in sacks in a special room at the Volpi plant for forty days. The ham must be rewrapped several

187

times by hand during the air-curing, which extracts moisture that might cause spoilage. The ham loses as much as 25 percent of its weight during the initial curing. Pepper, nutmeg, cloves, and more salt are hand-rubbed on the ham after the forty days, and it is then moved into the drying room for up to four months, depending on size, as the spices enliven the flavor.

The prosciutto (fourteen to sixteen pounds each, $25 wholesale, $7.50 a pound retail) is sold with the bone still in the leg and skin intact, sealing in the flavor. Pasetti says experimental boneless "prosciutello," the soft center of a prosciutto without bone or skin (six to ten pounds, $9 a pound), is sold for the convenience of those not wanting bone or larger cuts.

The same care goes into the Volpi 100 percent pork shoulder salami. Garlic, pepper, and salt are added by hand in the right proportions, and depending on size, it's aged up to 120 days in natural hog or beef casings. The Genoa salami ($4 a pound), named for the Italian city, is the largest Volpi salami (four inches in diameter, four to five pounds). It's used by restaurants and delicatessens.

The Toscano is the same as the Genoa, but coarser with larger chunks of fat. The Sopressa is coarsely ground, but more pepper is added to give a distinctive taste. It sells for 10¢ more per pound than the Genoa type. Pasetti adheres to tradition by aging the Sopressa in beef bung caps that are open at only one end. The Filsetta is a smaller section of the Genoa Salami for home use. The cacciatore links are the smallest salami, aged only twenty-five days in beef casing.

The bone, fat, and skin of prosciutto are sold separately to be boiled with beans and other vegetables or to make broth. Volpi also sells sausage and mortadellas to restaurants and delicatessens through national distributors. The Volpi store, adjacent to the plant in St. Louis, also sells select Italian delicacies.

John Volpi came to St. Louis from Milan in 1898. He was a sausage-maker by trade, and word spread of the quality of the work he did for local households. Soon, he was shipping sausage to Chicago and New York. He founded the Volpi Company in 1905 and his brother-in-law, Gino Pasetti, became his partner. Armando Pasetti immigrated to America in 1938 and inherited the company in 1957 after the elder Pasetti and Volpi died within a year of each other. There are now fifteen people working at the plant, which produces 30,000 to 40,000 prosciuttos a year.

America's Best! SCRAPPLE

Habbersett Brothers, Inc.

P.O. Box 564
42 South Knowlton Road
Media, Pennsylvania 19106

215-876-7226

E. R. Habbersett, President

89¢ per lb., 1- or 2-lb. packages

What did Benjamin Franklin and George Washington have in common with Frank Sinatra and Pearl Bailey?

Scrapple!

Scrapple is a pork product that has a 300-year-old tradition in the Philadelphia region. There are several references to it in the writings of Ben Franklin and George Washington's Pennsylvania Dutch chef. For the last 115 years, Habbersett Brothers, Inc., has been making America's best scrapple.

The name "scrapple" refers to the fact that it is made from the scraps left from parts of the hog used for other products. The thrifty and creative Dutch settlers around the Delaware River invented it. In hard times, scrapple proved the perfect "poor man's dish," as it was cheaper than other pork products. Even today, it's only 89¢ a pound.

Habbersett, unlike many of its competitors, uses only fresh meat and selects only the choicest part of the trimmings: the meat from the bones, heart, liver, and tongue—no offal or snouts.

After the hog is "broken up" for various uses, the bones are cooked to remove the meat. The liquid from this process, called the "liquor," is then thickened with a top-quality yellow corn meal. This stock is then added to the meat, and a portion of the liver, and seasoned with salt, pepper, and sage. The mixture is heated, put into one- or two-pound molds, immediately chilled, and wrapped for shipping.

Habbersett delivers all the scrapple by truck to the New Jersey, Pennsylvania, Delaware, and Florida areas. But you can also mail order Habbersett scrapple in any other part of the country. Cooking the scrapple is easy. It's even self-greased. Just cut ¼-inch slices, and fry eight minutes on one side and four on the other, until a crunchy crust forms.

Habbersett Brothers, Inc., began in 1863, when Isaac Habbersett began selling his product in the Old South Second Street Headhouse Market in Philadelphia. In those days, Isaac's son, Esmonde, ground the meat on a treadmill powered by horses who walked in circles. Isaac only made the scrapple in winter, because there was no refrigeration. In the summertime, the Habbersetts made their famous ice cream.

Today, Habbersett Brothers, Inc., produces over twelve tons of scrapple a day, four million pounds a year.

America's Best! SHOO-FLY PIE

✉ ────────────────────────────

Dutch Haven Amish Stuff, Inc.   *Bakery, restaurant, and gift shop*
open every day except
U.S. Route 30   *Christmas Day:* 7:00 A.M.–
Soudersburg, Pennsylvania 17577   9:00 P.M.

717-687-7611   *Visa, Master Charge*

Roy M. Weaver, Owner

────────────────────────────

One of America's unique desserts, first made by the nation's settlers, and later made famous in song, is still pouring out of the ovens of the Dutch Haven bakery, at the rate of 100,000 a year. Shoo-fly pie is a delicious confection whipped-up from the most ordinary kitchen ingredients—flour, vegetable shortening, brown sugar, water, molasses, and spices. Dutch Haven's secret recipe for shoo-fly pie makes it America's best.

When the early colonists were preparing for their trips to the new world, they packed staples that could survive the long sea journey. They had to live on these provisions for a long time after they landed. However, as a treat they occasionally concocted a pie from their limited pantry. Into a pie crust they put a crumb and liquid mixture and produced a three-layered pie with a gooey bottom, cake-like middle, and crumb topping. The sweet pie was baked in outdoor ovens and attracted flies, and as time passed, it became known as shoo-fly pie.

Ever since 1940, when he converted his gas station to a lunch counter, Roy Weaver has been faithfully duplicating that early recipe.

The pie filling is basically corn syrup, refiner's syrup, dark molasses, and water. These ingredients are cooked and then cooled to a temperature of between thirty to forty-five degrees F. The crumb topping is flour, brown sugar, mixed spices (salt, nutmeg, ginger, cloves, cinnamon, and mace), and shortening, which is poured on top of the pie filling seconds before it is popped into the oven.

Weaver admits there are several secrets to his recipe. "The syrup has to be the right temperature, and the way the crumbs are put on top of the pie is very important. And the pie dough has to be perfect. No cracks or holes, or the syrup will run out." He serves his pies when they are warm, and thinks a topping of whipped creams is a must. Ice cream also makes a good topping, he says.

Dutch Haven is in the heart of the Pennsylvania Amish country, and the shoo-fly pie has become popular with tourists. When visitors began asking Weaver if they could order the pie through the mail, he set to work and developed a specially reinforced carton. Since entering the mail-order business, he has shipped more than 15,000 pies, and less than 1 percent of them have arrived damaged—they usually arrive with every crumb in place. If a pie isn't perfect on arrival, Dutch Haven will mail another without charge.

Customers can carry a pie out of Dutch Haven for $2.50, or have one mailed at prices ranging from $4.90 to $7.10, depending on the distance from Soudersburg, Pennsylvania. You can pay with check or money order, or charge your pie on Master Charge or Visa.

Dutch Haven's shoo-fly pie has a shelf-life of eight days, and will last longer if it is refrigerated. The pies can be frozen for up to six months. To serve, keep the foil wrapper around the pie and place it in a preheated oven at 425 degrees F. for fifteen minutes. Slice into servings, top with whipped cream, and you'll be treated to America's best shoo-fly pie.

America's Best! SICILIAN RESTAURANT

Caffe Sport
574 Green Street
San Francisco, California 94133

415-981-1251

Tony LaTona, Delio Cuneo,
   Owners

Tuesday–Saturday: 11:00 A.M.
   – 11:30 P.M.

Cash only

Modestly named after the ubiquitous sports cafes in Italy, the Caffe Sport is the creation of chef Tony LaTona and his partner Delio Cuneo.

Tony LaTona worked as a cabinetmaker and woodcarver in his native Sicily for twenty years, then came to the U.S. in 1969. His rococo craftwork fills the restaurant. Each table, chair, and booth is fancifully and ornately carved. One table depicts the life story of the Italian hero Garibaldi, and others portray the history of Sicilian gastronomy. In fact, every table and chair is one-of-a-kind, and art flows all over the walls. Imported cheeses and rolled meats hang from the ceiling.

"I control the food every day," says LaTona in his broken English. "I am happy when the people are happy." Tony learned to cook at the elbows of his parents in Sicily, but Caffe Sport's menu is his own creation. There are twelve dishes on the menu, and quite often Tony will have unlisted specials (it's worthwhile asking the waiter for the evening's surprise feast).

Tony makes ten sauces, six red and four white, fresh daily. They contain a gentle, savory tomato base with such varied ingredients as sardines, prawns, eggplant, onions, raisins, walnuts, pine nuts, aniseed, and saffron.

Start your feast with Special Green Salad, which contains chilled green peppers, juicy and ripe tomatoes, bay shrimp, calamari (squid), and a dash of herbs. A pasta dish is a must at the Sport, but remember, the servings are over-generous and enough for two or three diners! Pasta con Pesto is made with a basil-based, olive-oil sauce that contains chopped walnuts and is topped with grated cheese. In Pasta con Sarde, the pasta is bathed in a sauce built around sardines, to which onions, raisins, aniseed, pine nuts, and saffron have been added. Pasta Rustica alla Carrettiera is a ribbon pasta with a sauce of prawns, olive oil, lemon garlic, and herbs. LaTona also makes a dish from his hometown of Palermo called Melanzane alla Palermitana—slabs of delicately flavored eggplant covered with thick, savory cheese.

The fish dishes are equally tantalizing: calamari, which can be ordered *fritti* (fried), sautéed, or in a salad; lobster, which is served in a sauce or in a salad; a huge Combination Plate (the name understates the size and variety of the dish), of calamari, prawns, and clams; and a fried combination of squid, prawns, and scallops. If you don't mind waiting twenty-four hours after you've placed the order, Chef LaTona will assemble Pizza alla Palermitana, a meal that will satisfy five hungry people, and contains, among other delicacies, clams and squid.

Caffe Sport serves only wine and beer from a small and elaborately decorated bar on one wall of the cafe. Prices range from $6 for a pasta dish to $14 for lobster. Bring cash because Caffe Sport does not take credit cards. You can make a reservation for a party of four or more, but because of the restaurant's immense popularity, there's no guarantee it will be honored. If your reservation is overlooked, wait for the next seating—the food is worth the wait. Before and after the dinner hour, Caffe Sport is an espresso, cappuccino, and sandwich shop.

America's Best! SKI HATS

Moriarty's Hat and Sweater Shop

Mt. Mansfield Road
Stowe, Vermont 05672

802-253-4052

Anabel Moriarty, Owner

September–Spring: 7 days a week,
8:00 A.M.–6:00 P.M.

Mail order brochure available
year-round

Anabel Moriarty of Stowe, Vermont, never intended to become queen of the ski-hat business. But that's what she is, and her unique caps can be seen on ski slopes all over the world.

In 1957, Ma Moriarty (as she's known in the Vermont mountains) set out to design and knit a top-quality ski hat for her son Marvin that would be snug and warm under his unlined racing helmet. The result was the "Original Moriarty," which immediately attracted the attention of other skiers. These unusual three-cornered caps, with one point at the top and another over each of the wearer's ears, have been worn by the U.S. Ski Team since 1960. (The U.S. Ski Team also wears Moriarty sweaters.) Many state teams wear Ma Moriarty's famous hats, as do some foreign teams, including the French.

Twenty-some knitters make the ski hats on hand-operated machines and finish them off by hand. They complete at least 60,000 each year. Half of these are Ma Moriarty's famous three-corner style. Older and more serious skiers tend to prefer this, while trendier, younger skiers opt for her other types, such as those with pompons. New styles come out each fall, but aren't shown until the season opens to make it harder for her many competitors to manufacture copies. "Millions are being copied," Ma says. Still, even without the ever-present Moriarty label, an "M" inside a tiny green shamrock, it's easy to distinguish a true Moriarty hat from the imitations.

The heavy, tightly knitted, fine wool caps are distinctly simple with bold and colorful patterns ranging from traditional Swiss alpine designs to modern geometric patterns. Mrs. Moriarty and her daughter-in-law do all the designing. They use only pure wool, usually in twenty standard rainbow-bright colors, although you can special order your hat in any hue. In fact, Mrs. Moriarty makes half her hats as special orders, with names and even logos knit right into the pattern.

The hats are quite modestly priced from $7 to $12. Scarves, relatively new in the product line-up, run from $8 to $10, depending upon length. Moriarty ski sweaters have been made for numerous years, although their popularity has just started to soar. They run from $42 to $60, and are so warm a ski jacket is hardly necessary. Children's sweaters are the newest addition.

Moriarty hats and sweaters are made so well they appear to last forever before wearing out. Ma says countless people bring her ten- to fifteen-year-old Moriarty hats for mending.

Mrs. Moriarty no longer knits in her spare time. She crochets. "I'm crocheting afghans for all my grandchildren," she says. Nor does she wear her own hats and sweaters. "I'm allergic to wool."

America's Best! SOPAPILLAS

Pete's	*Pete and Priscilla Jojola, Owners*
San Antonito, New Mexico	*7 days a week: lunch, 11:30–2:30; dinner, 5:00–10:00*
505-281-9969	*Master Charge and Visa*
Mailing address: P.O. Box 397 *Cedar Crest, New Mexico 87708*	

The sopapilla, a traditional food of American Indians in New Mexico, is a fried bread that is typically served on special occasions. Originally flat and unleavened, the sopapilla was used as an eating utensil to scoop up food. It was also dunked in soup, and some people believe that the origin of the word is related to *sopa*, the Spanish word for soup. The puffed sopapilla first appeared in New Mexico in the early 1950s and quickly became popular.

You'll find America's best sopapillas at Pete's in the tiny village of San Antonito, New Mexico. Pete Jojola uses the basic dough of white flour, salt, baking powder, and shortening, then adds extras such as yeast and milk to make his sopapillas as light and fluffy as possible.

After the dough has risen for twenty minutes, Pete rolls it thin and cuts it into three-inch squares. Most restaurants roll their sopapillas with a pizzza roller, but Pete prepares his by hand—he hand-kneads them, hand-rolls them, and hand-cuts them. Then he dips the squares in fat and fries them to a golden brown. They rise and puff up as they cook, and Pete serves them hot to his customers, who devour 2,000 sopapillas each week.

You get two sopapillas with each dinner at Pete's; if you're still hungry, Pete will give you one more for free, then after that he'll charge you 20¢ apiece. He also serves them stuffed, as an appetizer, and as a dessert. He invented the giant stuffed sopapilla as an inexpensive and filling meal for hungry skiers at nearby Sandia Peak. He fills it with beef, potatoes, beans, green chili, and cheese. In the dough for the dessert sopapilla, he substitutes sugar for salt. Then he dusts the finished product with sugar when it is still hot from the fire. One regular customer always orders his own version—stuffed with ice cream and topped with Kahlua. Pete stuffs his appetizer-sized sopapillas with cheese, pimentos, and other tidbits. At Christmas, he makes sopapillas in the shape of Santa Claus. For Ben Abruzzo, a regular customer who sailed across the Atlantic in a hot-air balloon, he made a balloon-shaped sopapilla. In fact, he's willing to try any design for his special customers.

San Antonito is a mountain village twenty-one miles northeast of Albuquerque and thirty-one miles north of Sante Fe on the original Turquoise Trail. Only five families live there, including Pete, his wife Priscilla, and their three sons, who help out in the kitchen and dining rooms.

America's Best! SPECIAL DINING EXPERIENCE

The Palace Restaurant

420 East 59 Street
New York, New York 10022

212-355-5150

Frank Valenza, Owner

Monday–Saturday: 7:00 P.M.–
    9:30 P.M.

All major credit cards

"An animal feeds, a man eats, a cultured man dines." That is Frank Valenza's philosophy, and that is what he had in mind when he created The Palace Restaurant.

Dinner at The Palace is a four-hour virtuoso performance, during which French Chef Claude Baills gets to show off his talents. Guests each pay a $95 prix fixe for the twelve-course meal, not including wines or liqueurs. Add to that a 23 percent suggested tip and 8 percent tax.

Dinner begins with a large assortment of hors d'oeuvres, soup, a fish course, and sherbet to cleanse the palate. Then the entrée arrives, followed by salad, fruit, cheese, and five desserts (you don't have to worry about which one to choose—you get them all).

Entrées at The Palace are made to serve two. They are roast duck with grapefruit and lime, prime rib of beef with truffles and Madeira sauce, rack of lamb in a pastry crust with bearnaise sauce, rack of veal with tarragon sauce, and capon poached in a double consommé and served with morels *á la crème*. Every other day there is something new.

Only the finest ingredients are used—veal from Wisconsin, Scotch salmon, baby chickens grown in the backyards of New York's Chinatown. Appetizers change according to availability and season, but might include caviar roulade, lobster salad, fresh goose liver, crabmeat, caviar with iced vodka, or sliced raw filet mignon, and *specialités du jour*, like quail eggs and goose liver. Soups are gazpacho, mussel soup (highly recommended), lobster soup, and deviled chicken consommé with truffles.

The desserts, in order of appearance, are frozen vanilla soufflé with pralines; cake; chocolate truffles (vanilla butter cream and *créme patissière* wrapped in wet chocolate and dusted with dry chocolate); petits fours with glazed fruits and, of course, cookies.

The best wine at The Palace, Domaine de la Romanee Conti, 1961, costs $850 a bottle. If you care for champagne, there is naturally Dom Perignon at $125 per bottle. After dinner, try some of their best brandy, Gaston Briand, le Paradis, 1880, $80 a shot.

Food critics Gael Greene (*New York* magazine) and Craig Claiborne (*The New York Times*) have praised the food at The Palace, and have said it is as good as any three-star restaurant in France. The Palace was inspired by Valenza's travels in France and the work of the great French Chef Paul Bocuse, creator of the *nouvelle cuisine* (the latest revolution in the French cooking world).

The atmosphere at The Palace is elegant, not snobbish. Mr. Valenza warmly greets all his guests, every night, and waiters address the diners by name. The tables are set with Lenox china, Gorham crystal, and very heavy silver plate. The room is full of special button roses (white with pink borders) and Russian gold chandeliers and French sconces shine overhead. There used to be music piped into The Palace, but Valenza did away with it when someone complained that he had heard *Madame Butterfly* four times during his dinner.

The kitchen crew begins making preparations at noon for a 7:00 P.M. dinner, and there is a corps of thirty waiters in the dining room to serve the ideal number of forty guests (sixty is the absolute maximum).

"Part of the art of fine dining is to revel in the presentation," says Frank Valenza. "You eat with your eyes, not just with your mouth." Fish dishes are brought to the table in a toasted-bread clipper ship, and the beautiful flowered pastry cart is made entirely of sugar. If you want to incur the wrath of Mr. Valenza, you can even eat it, for an extra charge of $200. "After all," he says, "it took an expert pastry chef twenty hours to make it!" The Palace's version of the "doggie bag" is a container fashioned out of foil in the shape of a swan.

Portions at The Palace are small, so that the diner can enjoy them all without overeating. Otherwise, how could you possibly get through? "It's better to eat one bite of something exquisite than a lot of something *ordinaire*," says Valenza. The twelve courses are arranged to provide a maximum variety of flavor, texture, aroma, and appearance. "The art of eating is tasting," says Valenza. "If you eat a steak or chicken, by the third bite the texture is the same, and you really don't have to eat the rest. When you give many different textures and tastes, the customer will enjoy it better." Also, the courses are carefully timed, at twenty-minute intervals, for proper digestion and conversation. In this way, each new course is not an intrusion, but a pleasant surprise.

When The Palace first opened in 1975 at $50 per person, Frank Valenza asked food critics to stay away and give him a chance to "warm up." So no one came for two weeks. "They either didn't know about the place, or were obviously too poor," Valenza says. He brought the media in, but they only publicized the price, not the quality of the restaurant, frightening more customers away. It was not until the critics came that the future of The Palace was launched. Now, weekends are booked two or three weeks in advance.

The Palace has served dinner parties costing between $5,000 and $10,000. Valenza refuses to reveal the names of his more famous clients, because he wants people to come to The Palace for the food, not because of the clientele. But he does have many "regulars." Ninety-five percent of his customers return within a year, and ten percent visit more than ten times a year! One Christmas, to show his appreciation to his steadiest customer, he

Putting the finishing touches on a Palace dessert; for $200 extra, you can even eat the pastry cart.

gave eighteen-carat gold credit cards to customers who had spent more than $10,000 during the year. The ten cards cost $500 each to make.

Former *New York Times* food critic John Canaday admitted that the food at The Palace was excellent, but he said it was immoral to charge such prices and gave the restaurant a no-star rating. Valenza doesn't think that a great meal is any less moral than a diamond ring or a Rolls Royce. Besides, according to Valenza, The Palace doesn't make a large profit on its dinners— preparation is too costly. In fact, Valenza has had to struggle to keep The Palace open.

Food critic Mimi Sheraton wrote in *The New York Times* that The Palace looked like a Fifth Avenue beauty parlor, but Valenza is convinced that her attitude was prejudiced from the start. "She was determined to do a number on us." Gael Green says, "The town's French restaurant Mafia would love to see The Palace fail." Mr. Valenza, a Bronx-born former actor, is Italian.

Nonetheless, the test of quality has prevailed, and now it's quite clear that an evening at The Palace is worth its price. But then, as Frank Valenza says, "I'm only providing a service for people who have already made their money."

After a meal at The Palace, the diner should feel that he has shared something with a culinary artist, because that is the way Frank Valenza envisions the dining experience he created. "Dinner at The Palace should be as exciting as a night at the theatre or as exhilarating as a home run with the bases loaded," says Valenza.

America's Best! SPECIALTY CEMENT

✉ ——————————————————————————

Sauereisen Cements Company   *412-781-2323*

RIDC Park   *Phil F. Sauereisen, President*
Pittsburgh, Pennsylvania 15238

——————————————————————————

The unique and secretly formulated cements manufactured by the Sauereisen Company in Pittsburgh is in the handle of every silverware knife used around the globe.

But silverware is not the only application of Sauereisen cements. They were also used to grout the baseplates of the Apollo launch pads at Cape Canaveral and easily withstand 7.5 million pounds of thrust and the thermal and mechanical shocks of a launch. Sauereisen cements are used in thermocouples to measure the heat of molten metal in steel mills, and to line the inside of the world's tallest chimneys.

Nuclear power plants, hair dryers, light bulbs, automobile elements, baby bottle warmers, bifocals, slide-projector bulbs, igniters for home gas dryers, curling irons, roaster and self-cleaning ovens, and candelabra bases all contain Sauereisen cements. They are able to tolerate temperatures up to 2,800 degrees F. without shrinking or corroding. One type even expands as it hardens, a claim no other cement manufacturer can make.

200

Sauereisen pioneered and developed the field of inorganic cement, which is made with materials that are taken from the earth, such as silicas, potassium, clays, and zircon. The cements are blended to resist high temperatures, to conduct electricity, and to be corrosion proof and totally weather resistant.

The company was founded in 1899 by C. Fred Sauereisen, an attic inventor with a fifth-grade education. Mr. Sauereisen's first customer was Du Pont Chemical Company. The cement worked so well, the firm ordered twice again as much the next day. The late Mr. Sauereisen was fond of saying that he had "doubled his business overnight."

Sauereisen sharpened his technical skills in plants manufacturing ceramics, pottery, and sanitary ware, and ran George Westinghouse's porcelain department. He believed there was a vast market for a specialty cement, because virtually every industry had the need, at some point in manufacturing a product, to bond one material to another.

In 1920, Sauereisen was granted a patent on a "Special Glazed Surface for Spark Plug Insulators," which was later sold to the AC Spark Plug Division of General Motors, and has been used on all spark plug insulators since. His other inventions included Sani-Feet Stove Rests, "V" Knife Sharpeners, and Sauereisen Pour-Lay Brick.

The company still mixes its materials in a dozen second-hand bread-dough mixers that Sauereisen bought when he went into business. Because the company has continually produced high-quality special cements for more than seventy years, the name Sauereisen has become so synonymous with the product that most people think it's a generic name.

The silverware industry began using Sauereisen cements in the 1940s to bond the knife blade to the handle. The bonding of the two parts with Sauereisen cement is so perfect, the knives are able to withstand a torturous test of tumbling for twenty-four hours inside a drum filled with ceramic balls. This seemingly bizarre test becomes important because many restaurants tumble-dry their silverware.

The company produces more than fifteen-million pounds of specialty cements each year, which are sold in every part of the world at prices ranging from 20¢ to $1.08 per pound. Even a Russian silverware manufacturer uses Sauereisen cement.

America's Best! SPUMONI FUDGE

Uncle Mary's

1011 Prospect Street
La Jolla, California 92037

714-454-7896

Marianna Jacobson, Owner

7 days a week: 10:00 A.M.–
10:00 P.M.; closed Thanks-
giving, Christmas, New Year's
Day

Master Charge, Visa, Diner's
Club, American Express

Westwood Store:
Villa Westwood Building
10930 Lindbrook Avenue
Westwood, California 94377

$4.50 per lb.
Half Squares (5–6 oz.): $1.50,
$1.60 with nuts
Full Squares (8–12 oz.): $2.25,
$2.50 with nuts
Snack Pack (small square with
knife, napkin): $1

Mail-order fees: $1.50 first lb.,
50¢ each additional lb.;
shipped U.P.S.

Spumoni may be great as ice cream, but it's even better as fudge—especially when it comes from Uncle Mary's.

Owner Marianna Jacobson makes the fudge in her store-window kitchen using only pure ingredients: cream, milk, butter, sugar, corn syrup, and chocolate. She makes her Spumoni Fudge with a twist of citron, fresh maraschino cherries, pistachio extract, and nuts. Fudge is best two days after it's made, she says, but you must keep it in a cool, dry place in a covered container. It should never be refrigerated, but it can be frozen.

Uncle Mary's is renowned for its innovative flavors, such as chocolate caramel almond, chocolate orange rind, vanilla cinnamon raisin, rum nut, two story (chocolate on top of vanilla), chocolate mint, walnetto, chocolate raisin, and date.

Marianna opened her first store in La Jolla, California, in 1978. She is already grossing $250,000 a year, and has just opened a second store in Westwood, California. She will ship her fudge anywhere in the country.

In case you're wondering, Uncle Mary's got its name from Marianna's three-year-old nephew, who was obviously confused about family relationships and genders.

America's Best! STEAKS (Veal and Beef)

Murray's

26 South 6th Street
Minneapolis, Minnesota 55402

612-339-0909

Patrick J. Murray, Vice-President

11:00 A.M.–midnight; closed
  Sundays and holidays

Master Charge, Visa, Diner's Club,
  Carte Blanche, American
  Express, Shopper's Charge,
  Murray's Card, Traveler's
  Checks

Steak connoisseur Maurice C. Dreicer found Murray's 4½-pound porterhouse steak so tender that he presented the restaurant with the Golden Butter Knife Award—only the nineteenth citation he had given in his worldwide quest for the perfect steak! The Golden Butter Knife Steak is still the premier specialty of the house at Murray's, and is served as a complete dinner for three with a bottle of wine (white, rosé, or burgundy), salad, choice of potato or vegetable, and rolls and butter for $59.95.

The Golden Butter Knife Steak is seasoned by hand, with special Murray's seasoning, and placed in an extremely hot broiler at 800 degrees F. so that the inside will be done before the exterior is burned. It's cooked on all sides simultaneously for forty-five to sixty minutes (the seasoning provides a crusty flavor on the outside and seals the juices inside), then put on a patented "thermoplate," a stainless-steel platter that is thoroughly heated.

Your steak sizzles when it comes to your table. Your waitress will cut into it and wait for your approval, then neatly carve and serve the portions on fine china.

Silver Butter Knife Steaks are smaller. A two-pound New York

203

strip steak for two costs $33 and the twenty-six ounce Chateau-briand tenderloin for two costs $35. Prepared like the Golden Butter Knife Steaks, they are also served with wine, salad, and all the other trimmings. They too can be cut with a butter knife, and won the Silver Butter Knife Award in 1953.

Single-serving steaks are also special. They're cut from the loin before cooking and special seasoning is hand-pounded into the meat. Then they are seared in a very hot dry pan with only seasoning to draw the juices out from the center of the meat and seal them in at the sides. The steak is placed in a broiler at 600 to 700 degrees F. and cooked uniformly on all sides with heat coming only from the top of the broiler as the steak is rotated by a special conveyor.

The single-serving steaks include the Dinner Steak Special, a ten-ounce sirloin from the butt of the full loin ($10.95); New York strip sirloin, which comes in twelve-ounce ($13.95) and sixteen-ounce ($17.50) servings; peppercorn New York steaks served in twelve-ounce ($14.95) and fourteen-ounce ($18.50) sizes; beef tenderloin in six-ounce ($9.95), eight-ounce ($11.95), and ten-ounce ($14.95) sizes; and a two-pound porterhouse steak ($23.95). All of these steaks are served on thermoplates, and come with salad, potato or vegetable, rolls and butter, and a beverage.

Murray's also serves America's best T-bone veal steak, which it purchases from the Delft Blue-Provimi Company (see p. 223). Murray's cuts the veal T-bone steaks from the loins and cooks them to order in twelve-ounce portions for $12.95. As with all single-serving steaks, you get a complete meal including a beverage.

The service is also special at Murray's. Gussie, the senior waitress, has worked at Murray's since the restaurant opened in 1933. Donna has been at Murray's since 1946. In fact, no one on the evening staff has been there less than three years.

Murray's uses only corn-fed cattle from northern Iowa and southern Minnesota for tenderness and flavor. A special distributor selects the choice beef for Murray's, over 2,500 pounds per week. Murray's serves more than $750,000 of steaks per year. Only steer beef is used with proper marbling and fat cover, not too heavy but enough to ensure the proper flavor. All meat is selected within one week after slaughter. It's fresh and not deep-frozen.

Murray's has its own aging room at the distributor's plant. At any one time, 200 loins are aging in the room for seventeen to twenty-one days. Pat Murray, vice-president, thinks that hanging the meat and letting the air do its work is preferable to chemical methods, even though his way is more expensive because of time and shrinkage. He buys the meat in forty-eight to fifty-four pound loins.

Murray's can seat 250 people in two dining rooms and another 200 in the bar. Bill and Stanley, who've been at Murray's for fourteen years, provide dinner-and-dancing music from 7:00 P.M. to 1:00 A.M. nightly.

If you can't come to Minneapolis, you can have Murray's meats shipped to you on dry ice via U.P.S. You can order a box of sixteen filet mignons, a mixture of four New York steaks and eight filet mignon cuts, or box of twelve New York steaks. Prices vary with the market.

America's Best! SUMMER HOTEL

The Grand Hotel

Mackinac Island, Michigan 49757

906-847-3331

R. D. Musser, *President-Owner*
John M. Hulett III, *Vice-President*

Mid-May–October 31

Winter Address (November 1–
April 30):
222 Wisconsin Avenue
Lake Forest, Illinois 60045

312-234-6540

No credit cards

"Full American Plan," includes
breakfast, luncheon, dinner:
$60–$100 a day per person,
double occupancy; 4% state
tax, 18% service charge, $2
baggage handling and transfer
charge additional

Summer air service from
Pellston, approximately $25;
Phillips Flying Service,
616-347-8225

The Grand Hotel, situated on 500 acres exactly 100 feet above the Straits of Mackinac, opened its doors July 10, 1887, and still reigns as America's best summer hotel.

Crimson-plumed horses—there are no automobiles on the island —pull your carriage up the 1,000-foot-long driveway lined with geraniums, alyssum, pansies, marigolds, begonias, mums, and beautifully manicured lawns. As you walk up the red-carpeted steps through the columns supporting the huge overhang, you see window boxes of geraniums and pansies extending along the front of the building more than the length of a football field in either direction. The doorman, dressed in top hat, bow tie, scarlet jacket, white shirt and trousers, and spats assists you out of your carriage. Don't worry about luggage—the dock porter sent your bags to the Grand when you stepped off the ferry. And don't tip the doorman. Tipping is not allowed at the Grand; instead, the staff is compensated from the 18 percent service charge added to your bill.

The 262-room hotel, listed in the National Archives as a historical landmark, features complete dining facilities, a nine-hole golf course, six clay tennis courts, a nightclub, complimentary feature films, live entertainment, and an assortment of reception and convention services using the vast 880-foot porch and "special function" rooms.

The large windows in the Dining Room, which is 211-feet long and 40-feet wide, afford a stunning view of the Straits of Mackinac. Three meals a day are included in the American Plan rates, and the exquisite cuisine often includes Mackinac Whitefish, a specialty of the house.

High tea is served every day between 4:00 and 5:00 P.M. in the parlor for $2.50. A pianist and violinist play popular and classical music. After dinner, a harpist plays from 8:30 to 9:00 P.M. in the main parlor on the second level.

The Grandstand, open from 10:00 A.M. to 3:00 A.M., offers a pleasant alternative to the Dining Room. You can eat breakfast, lunch on a light sandwich, or have a small steak in the evening in this pagoda-type building. (Food here is not included in the American Plan.)

While all of the rooms at the hotel are luxurious, the Presidential and Governor's Suites are extraordinarily elegant. Each suite has two bedrooms and a parlor with a large balcony overlooking the Straits. One balcony is so large that an orchestra sometimes plays on it for special receptions on the main porch below.

Dignitaries and celebrities have visited the hotel since it opened,

After almost a century, The Grand still reigns as the best.

including Teddy Roosevelt, President Cleveland, socialite Mrs. Potter Palmer, who could claim *l'haute société* of the East and Midwest within her realm, George Mortimer Pullman, the inventor and industrialist and head of the fabulous Pullman Palace Car Company, President Taft, and former President Ford. As a special service each year, the Michigan Parks and Recreation Association coordinates visits to the Grand Hotel for groups of senior citizens at reduced rates.

The story of the Grand Hotel began in 1882 when U.S. Senator Francis B. Stockbridge of Michigan purchased the land in order that Michigan could have a great hotel resort. In 1886, he approved the plans submitted by the Michigan Central Railroad, the Grand Rapids and Indiana Railroad, and the Detroit and Cleveland Navigation Company, which together formed the Mackinac Island Hotel Company and bought the land.

The limited summer season and hard economic times caused the Grand Hotel a great deal of difficulty in its early years. It was nearly razed in 1910, saved only by island cottager Frank Nagel, who bought the hotel and prolonged its shaky existence.

He was unable to turn the finances around, however, and it was not until W. Stewart Woodfill began working summers at the hotel as a college student that things changed. Mr. Woodfill worked overtime to get acquainted with the financial and business side of the hotel, and became manager in 1923, his fourth year with the Grand. He bought the hotel in the Spring of 1925. He sold his share to his optimistic partners in 1927 and retired. However, the owner died in 1931, and Mr. Woodfill bought back the hotel that year. He infused massive amounts of money into renovation, lengthened the summer season of the Grand, and business improved, despite the onset of World War II. That trend has never changed, and thirty years later the Hotel is financially solid. Woodfill sold the hotel in July, 1979, to R. D. Musser.

Mackinac Island has a history and a lifestyle all its own. The 2½-by-3½-mile (9 miles around) island is accessible by ferry and air during the summer, and by air, snowmobile, and foot across the frozen Straits of Mackinac during winter. So many people walk across to the mainland on the ice during the winter that the islanders put Christmas trees into the ice to mark a safe path for nighttime and blizzard travel.

The island's permanent population is about 600 to 900 year-round, and reaches 5,000 during the summer months. There are 1,700 acres of horse and bike paths on the island.

America's Best! SURFING

North Shore, Oahu, Hawaii   *For maps of beach areas:*
City and County of Honolulu
Department of Parks and
Recreation
Honolulu, Hawaii 96850

Surfing began as the sport of Hawaiian chiefs, or *alii*, who would paddle out and ride a large wave into shore on a twelve-foot (or longer) board made of koa wood. Most surfers now use foam boards coated with fiberglass and resin, many of which measure under six feet. But to tackle Hawaii's biggest waves, surfers still use long boards and ride the same way the *alii* did.

America's best surfing is on the Hawaiian island of Oahu, and the best of the best is at Waimea Bay on Oahu's north shore. During the summer months you could not find a better spot than these placid waters to skin dive. Then the winter storms roll in from the north (November to March), the waves reach twenty-

Champion Jeff Hakman rides a wave into Oahu's Sunset Beach.

five feet, and the amateurs and the weak of heart are cautioned to keep their distance.

The "Banzai Pipeline" is also on Oahu's north shore. The Pipeline got its name from its unique tubing motion, produced by the peculiar way the waves strike the shoreline and the shallow configuration of the coral reef over which the waves break. When a surfer takes the drop down the steep face of a Pipeline wave, the rugged coral heads loom just beneath the surface like headstones over a watery grave, and a few unfortunate surfers have had them as their markers.

Not all of the best surfing on Oahu is on the north shore. During the summer months, swells sweep in from the south, east and west, and at spots such as Diamond Head, Waikiki, and Ala Moana waves can reach heights of twelve feet or more. The major surfing championships are held at Makaha, on the west shore. Surf there can often rival that on the north shore.

For those purists who eschew boards and get their thrills by sliding down a wave with nothing between themselves and water, Hawaii also has the best bodysurfing. At Makapuu and Sandy Beach, on the southeast shore of Oahu, wave heights are between four and six feet, ideal for bodysurfing.

In surfing circles, however, Waimea Bay is always known as the "giant." When the other major spots on the north shore are closed out, there are still a few surfers at the mouth of the Bay hoping for a long ride and praying a disastrous "wipe-out" won't smash them or their boards to pieces.

209

America's Best! SYMPHONY ORCHESTRA

Chicago Symphony Orchestra

Orchestra Hall
220 South Michigan Avenue
Chicago, Illinois 60604

Box Office: 312-427-7711

Sir Georg Solti, Music Director

October–June
Tickets: $6–$20

London, Angel, DGG, RCA, and
  Mercury Records

"It's harder to get tickets to the Symphony than for a Bears game," said a disappointed gentleman at Chicago's Orchestra Hall box office. "We play better than they do!" retorted the ticket seller. Members of the Chicago Symphony Orchestra can make this proud statement because:

Their Brass Section is the best in the world;

They are very versatile. Their repertoire encompasses works of all periods—Baroque, Pre-classical, Classical, Romantic, Contemporary, and Avant-Garde. Their *forte* is Romantic music (heavy on the Wagner and Mahler);

They undertake very large and ambitious projects, such as Wagner's *Götterdämerung* (Twilight of the Gods) and Brahms's *Deutsches Requiem*. These works may involve an augmented orchestra (perhaps 120), a large chorus (another 120), and several soloists. Even though such productions are very costly, the CSO is not afraid to take them on tour;

They can play with the precision and intimacy of a chamber orchestra, and their phrasing is so tight that the music sounds faster than it actually is (a quality previously ascribed to the music of Toscanini);

They are very pleased with their conductor, Sir Georg Solti. They respect him and are willing to do what he says. (Many

The CSO: A versatile, proud orchestra.

orchestras don't respect their conductors, and will not play well for them.) The CSO is a proud orchestra, and its morale is very high. Consequently, performances are very spirited, ambitious, robust, and sensitive.

Under the direction of Sir Georg Solti (currently the most exciting conductor in the world, with the possible exception of Herbert von Karajan), the CSO has been compared to the American orchestras of the "golden" 30s—the New York Philharmonic under Toscanini and the Boston Symphony under Koussevitzky. No other orchestra has generated so much excitement in recent years.

The CSO has taken its music to the musical capitals of Europe three times, and to Japan once, always to great critical acclaim. Among the honors it has received are twenty Grammy Awards (twelve of them won under Solti's direction) for such recordings as the complete Beethoven Symphonies (Best Album, 1977) and Richard Strauss's *Also Sprach Zarathustra* (Best Orchestral Performance, 1977). Recordings of Mahler's 8th Symphony and Berlioz's *Symphonie Fantastique* each won three Grammys. With Solti, the CSO made its first complete opera recording, Wagner's *Der Fliegende Holländer* (The Flying Dutchman), and a recording of Stravinsky's *Le Sacre du Printemps* (The Rite of Spring), which was a tremendous success immediately upon release. And

211

the critics never stopped talking about the CSO's complete Beethoven Symphonies.

Turnover of orchestra members is slight. Only one or two members join each year, and the average tenure is twenty years. Many of the principles play on valuable instruments that are over 200 years old. Among these are the so-called Baron von der Leyden Stradivarius and the Allegretti Stradivarius, two violins that were built in 1715, and the Braga Stradivarius cello.

The CSO has regularly played in Milwaukee, Wisconsin, since its first season in 1891. Now the orchestra gives about ten concerts per season in Uihlein Hall in the new Center for the Performing Arts. The orchestra also presents Youth Concerts in Chicago for younger people, and a series of "Petites Promenades" which are geared for first, second, and third graders. For these presentations, guest personalities, such as Danny Kaye, join the Orchestra and the children in the ballroom of Orchestra Hall. A chamber music series was established in the 1965–66 season, and under Fritz Reiner a Chicago Symphony Chorus was organized.

The CSO also maintains the Civic Orchestra of Chicago, the only training orchestra affiliated with a major American symphony orchestra. Many current players of the COC are called upon to perform with the CSO when extra players are needed for a particularly large piece, and two-thirds of the Chicago Symphony members were trained in the Civic. Members are chosen through semi-annual auditions; a candidate must be able to perform advanced literature and be engaged in private instrumental study. Members' ages range from fifteen to thirty.

Solti came to the CSO in 1969. He has been conductor of the Bavarian State Opera, Frankfurt City Opera, the Lyric Opera of Chicago, and the Royal Opera House at Covent Garden, London, where, for his ten years of service, Queen Elizabeth knighted him in 1972. Solti assisted Arturo Toscanini (one of his idols) at the 1936 and 1937 Salzburg Festivals in Austria. He has been awarded the French Academy's Grand Prix du Disque eleven times and an honorary Doctorate of Music by Harvard University.

Other conductors of the CSO have included Rafael Kubelik and Fritz Reiner. Many guest conductors such as Daniel Barenboim, Claudio Abbado, and Seiji Ozawa have led the CSO, but some of the great composers who have conducted their own works with this great orchestra have been Saint-Saëns, D'Indy, Elgar,

Richard Strauss, Glazounov, Busoni, Respighi, Ravel, Schönberg, Bloch, Prokofiev, Honegger, Copland, and Tippett.

The CSO was founded by Theodore Thomas in 1891, making it the third oldest symphony orchestra in America (only the New York Philharmonic and the Boston Symphony are older). The Chicago Orchestra, as it was then called, presented daring programs, and its standard of excellence was remarkably high. Thomas was a great proponent of Wagner and of Richard Strauss, at a time when Strauss was hardly known even in Germany! Orchestra Hall, the home of the CSO, was built in 1904 at a cost of $750,000, and it is considered one of the best halls for acoustics in the country.

In 1941, to celebrate its fiftieth season, the CSO commissioned and gave the world premieres of a number of important compositions: Stravinsky's Symphony in C; Milhaud's Symphony No. 1; Kodaly's Concerto for Orchestra; and Walton's *Scapino* Overture. In 1971, the CSO continued its tradition of patronizing the best modern composers by commissioning works by Elliot Carter, Sir Michael Tippett, Hans Werner Henze, and Bruno Maderna. The CSO has given the American premieres of such popular classics as *Also Sprach Zarathustra*, Holst's *The Planets*, and works by Bruckner, Schönberg, Scriabin, Mahler, Bartok, and Vaughn Williams.

America's Best! TRAMWAY

Sandia Peak Aerial Tramway

Sandia Peak Tram Company
10 Tramway Loop North East
Albuquerque, New Mexico 87122

505-296-9585

Ben L. Abruzzo, President

Summer hours: 9:00 A.M.–
  9:00 P.M.; *Tuesdays,* 5:00 P.M.–
  9:00 P.M.
Winter hours: 9:00 A.M.–
  9:00 P.M.; *Tuesdays, noon–*
  9:00 P.M.; *weekends and*
  holidays, 8:00 A.M.–9:00 P.M.

In only twenty minutes you rise from 6,000 feet to the top of a mountain over 10,000 feet above sea level. On a clear day you can see 11,000 square miles of New Mexico. Even sufferers of acro-

Sandia Peak Aerial Tramway rises 4,000 feet in twenty minutes.

phobia delight in a "flight" on the Sandia Peak Aerial Tramway in Albuquerque, New Mexico, the longest (2.7 miles) tramway in the world.

Although the tramway is the best way to get from Albuquerque to the Sandia Peak Ski Area, two-thirds of the 17,000 people who ride it each year are tourists. For your $6, you glide above varied vegetation and rock formations, big horn sheep, mountain lions, and bears. Eagles and hang gliders often pull up alongside for a closer look, and you get an excellent view of the ski slopes. The best time to ride is just before sunset. On your way up you can see for miles; on the way down, the lights of Albuquerque sparkle in the distance.

There are only two towers and three spans on the tramway. One span is 1½ miles long. (Only tramways in Chamonix, France, and Caracas, Venezuela, have longer unsupported spans.) The first tower, the tallest building in New Mexico, provides passengers with a bird's-eye view of the entire state. The next-best American tramway is the Palm Springs Aerial Tramway in California. It's shorter than Sandia Peak, however, and has twice as many towers, which makes the ride less thrilling.

Sandia Peak Tramway was completed in 1966 at a cost of $2 million. Ben Abruzzo, president of the tram company, estimates that it is now worth $5 million. Aerial transport is Mr. Abruzzo's specialty—he crossed the Atlantic in a balloon in 1978. (See p. 99.)

There are restaurants at both the upper and lower terminals. You can purchase a combination tram ride and dinner ticket, as well as a combination tram-chair lift ticket, which allows you to ride over the eastern ski-area side of the mountain before making the return trip.

America's Best! TRUCKS

Kenworth Truck Company

P.O. Box 1000
Kirkland, Washington 98033

206-828-5100

James H. Rutledge, Plant
Manager—South Seattle

206-764-5400

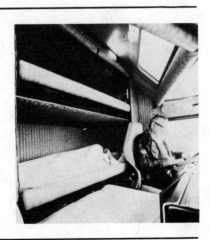

Evel Knievel hauls his equipment in a Kenworth Truck. Another showman tours the U.S. with his Kenworth hauling a frozen whale. He charges 50¢ admission and 50¢ to blow the distinctive air horn. Kenworth engineers once designed a truck that could go over 100 miles per hour, for a client who wanted to use it as the pace vehicle for the Indianapolis 500.

Comfort is so important to truckers that Kenworth will wire the trucks for television and provide closets and luxurious mattresses. Kenworth has also designed revolutionary air-conditioning systems, and all cabs are well insulated to reduce noise and provide protection from temperature extremes. Seats are made of long-lasting heavy-grade Naugahyde and ceilings are upholstered. If you have an ear for music, the unique air horn can be tuned to your taste.

Since the trucks are custom-painted, you can submit a paint sketch and lay out any design you want. Each truck is hand-primed and finished with five coats of epoxy acrylic. You can choose any color or combination and as much chrome and stainless steel as you like.

Kenworth Trucks are custom-designed to ensure you the best engineered truck that will deliver the most weight in the lightest vehicle. Consequently, they are the most economical trucks on the market, and they also have the highest resale value. Kenworths hold up better than other trucks and are generally in greater demand, even after hundreds of thousands of miles. Most owners only sell because of tax depreciation.

Kenworth sells the long-hood and cab-over-engine models through a sales engineer. He will design a vehicle that will enable you to transport your goods for the lowest cost per mile. Since every state has different legal standards and no two owners' requirements are the same, no two vehicles are alike. Kenworth engineers have perfected sturdy suspension systems, utilized computers to help you choose the best drive train for the job, and found ways to maximize horsepower and minimize fuel consumption.

The diesel engines are made by Cummings, General Motors, and Caterpillar, and they are specifically designed to give the best economy with the lowest noise level. The weight of the truck, over 100,000 pounds, is evenly distributed over ten top-quality tires. Each truck is tested on a dynamometer to ensure the proper amount of horsepower, and put through twenty-two miles of rugged road-testing. Kenworth trucks are expected to run over 220,000 miles per year.

Why this attention to detail? Kenworth engineers feel that the way your truck looks is a reflection of your product. They have

Kenworth Trucks are custom-designed for comfort.

proven that a trucker will take better care of a vehicle in which he can take pride. In addition, a first-class "tractor" will often be served first at the loading dock—saving time and money.

Kenworth produces one truck every twenty minutes, or about twenty-four a day. The factory works a single shift, as plant managers feel that quality is impaired by shift work. Order to delivery takes eight weeks.

New models are not introduced annually, but when offered they are presented at regional truck shows. The basic models are the "K" model, which is cab-over-engine, and the "W" model, which has the engine up front.

Kenworth trucks currently comprise 9 percent of the class 8 market of the heaviest duty trucks. A highway vehicle retails for $42,000, more high-powered vehicles for $77,000. Off-highway vehicles, such as logging trucks and oil derricks, sell for up to a quarter of a million dollars.

Mr. Kent and Mr. Worthington, two retired Boeing executives, began Kenworth in 1916. They tackled the problems of logging in the Pacific Northwest, where roads as we know them today did not exist. The special requirements of this area, coupled with the demands for these resources, resulted in the idea of engineering a truck designed to meet each operator's needs. Today there are Kenworth plants in Seattle, Washington; Kansas City, Missouri; Chilicothe, Ohio; and Canada, Australia, and Mexico.

America's Best! TULIPS

Holland, Michigan

Tulip Time, Inc.
Civic Center
8th and Pine
Holland, Michigan 49423

616-396-4221

Pauline Vanderkooy, Office
Manager

Tulip Time Festival starts
the Wednesday closest to
May 15th and runs 4 days

Ever since 1927, when Miss Lida Rogers, a biology teacher at Holland High School, decided to honor a flower and chose the tulip, the streets of Holland, Michigan, have been lined with America's best tulips.

About 100,000 tulips were planted in the city as part of a beautification project in 1928. The reception was so overwhelming that more tulips were planted the following year, and "Tulip Time" has since been an annual event in Holland. Now, each year twelve full-time and five part-time city employees plant 156,000 bulbs, which cost $26,334. Eight miles of roads, as well as parks and gardens, are bedecked with colorful tulips. Nearby Nelis Farms, just a mile north of town, features the largest variety of tulips in the world.

Every May, about 500,000 people visit the Tulip Festival, which is the third largest civic festival (after Mardi Gras and the Pasadena Rose Parade) in the country.

The Festival now runs for four days. It begins the Wednesday nearest May 15th with a "street-cleaning ceremony," in which the Mayor and City Council inspect the streets. Five hundred costumed townfolk participate, some carrying pails of water on wooden shoulder yokes and others wielding brushes and willow brooms. The Folk Parade and a performance of the wooden-shoe dancers follow the opening ceremonies. (Holland has the only authentic wooden shoe factory on the North American continent. Much of the machinery in the factory is over 100 years old.)

Other festivities during the Festival include high school orchestras, marching bands, an all-star brass choir, and a 200-voice mass choir. There's also square dancing, flower shows, art exhibits, and even barbershop quartets.

Why so much enthusiasm for a Dutch custom? Well, two-thirds of Holland's 28,000 people are Dutch. In 1847, a large group of Dutchmen migrated to this part of Michigan for economic and religious reasons. The new settlers were attracted to this area because of its similarity to the Netherlands, right down to the Muk dirt soil and the area's proximity to a large body of water, Lake Michigan.

The Tulip Festival is not the only touch of Holland in this town 180 miles west of Detroit. Dutch chinaware, called Delftware, is manufactured nearby at the only Delft factory in the U.S. A Dutch Village, featuring special gift shops, folk dancing exhibitions, a replica of an 18th-century Dutch farmhouse, and a restaurant, is located just one mile north of town. Windmill Island, opened in 1965, features a 210-year-old "deZwaan" windmill, the only authentic Dutch windmill in the U.S. The City of Holland purchased it with revenue bonds.

America's Best! TURKEYS

Jennie-O-Foods, Inc.

Airport Road
Willmar, Minnesota 56201

612-235-2622

Earl B. Olson, Chairman

Each year, the people at Jennie-O-Foods, Inc., in Willmar, Minnesota, raise three-million turkeys on their twenty-five Minnesota farms, process another four-million turkeys raised by private growers in Minnesota, the Dakotas, Wisconsin, and Iowa, and take in one-million turkeys from partnership operations. All told, they process over eight-million turkeys a year, 50,000 every day. That's 140-million pounds of turkey meat a year, which Jennie-O distributes to every major city in the U.S. and twenty foreign countries.

Jennie-O's program begins with artificial insemination, which ensures that only the best turkeys breed. The hens are fertilized every thirty days and can lay an egg every day during the four-to-five-month laying season. When they are only one day old, the newly hatched turkeys (Jennie-O's hatchery is the largest in the world) are placed on special feed that is prepared by Jennie-O doctors and veterinarians. This consists of soy beans, corn, fish meal, and approximately forty other secret ingredients measured out in precise proportions.

After fifteen weeks on the Jennie-O program, the hens weigh sixteen pounds and are ready for marketing; the toms are ready for marketing after about twenty weeks, when they weigh twenty-five pounds. Turkeys reach their prime at seven months. After that, they grow tough.

The turkeys are electrocuted and bled, then dressed in ice and aged for twenty-four hours before they are frozen. Ten percent of the birds are sold fresh. Jennie-O sells directly and through distributors, and supermarkets, hospitals, and the government are among the best customers.

Among Jennie-O products are self-basting turkeys, two-pound roasts, turkey breasts, turkey pie, drumsticks, and even turkey meat loaf. Jennie-O reprocesses the large toms for pork-substitute products, and makes turkey, hot dogs, hams, bologna, salami, and pastrami with specially cured dark turkey meat. No part of the turkey is wasted. The inedible parts are used for cat food, the blood is extracted for "blood meal" and fed to young turkeys and chickens, and even the feathers are powdered and granulated for grain.

"Eight times out of ten, you can tell a Jennie-O turkey just by taste and succulence," boasts Earl Olson, president and founder of Jennie-O. He also points out that Jennie-O is the largest independent grower of turkeys in the world. Even the Russian government has expressed interest in importing Jennie-O turkeys.

Olson started producing turkeys in 1942 to supplement his $80-a-month income as the manager of a creamery cooperative. That year he made a dollar a head on 300 turkeys. In 1948, he says, he made more than the Governor of Minnesota by collecting $4 a head for his 12,000 turkeys. In 1949, he lost $1 apiece on 30,000 turkeys, making him aware of the flexibility of the poultry market.

But he bought his first processing plant in Willmar, Minnesota, that same year, and now he has four plants: two in Willmar, and one each in Melrose and Litchfield, Minnesota. His wife named the company by combining her daughter's name, Jennie, with the "O" in Olson.

Jennie-O employs 1,500 people in its feed mills, hatcheries, farms, breeder hen farms, and processing operations, not to mention salesmen and truck drivers. Every Thursday, they all get a 50 percent discount on company products.

According to the *Guinness Book of World Records*, the largest turkey ever grown weighed seventy-five pounds. It was *not* a Jennie-O turkey—it might have been the biggest, but it wasn't the best.

America's Best! TWELVE DAYS OF CHRISTMAS FEAST

Jared Coffin House

Nantucket Island
Massachusetts 02554

617-228-2400

Mr. and Mrs. Philip Whitney
Read, Innkeepers

Twelve Days of Christmas:
December 21–January 1

American Express, Diner's Club,
Visa, Master Charge

Room Rates: $45–60 double;
$25–30 single

Breakfast: $2.50–4.95
Lunch: $3.50–6.50
Dinner: $7.95–14.95

Air Service: Air New England,
Hyannis Aviation from Boston;
Gull Air from Hyannis

Boat Service: Steamship
Authority, twice daily from
Hyannis

It's December 21. Peggy Read opens the door, which is decorated with a cranberry wreath, and invites you into her holly- and mistletoe-bedecked parlor to share a cup of Holiday Cheer. Handmade garlands of della robbia, wreaths of holly, sprigs of mistletoe,

221

and old-fashioned kissing balls hang throughout the house. At six sharp, innkeeper Philip Whitney Read calls out "Be Thee Well," pours a dollop of wassail on the yule log, and starts the fire. Thus begins the celebration of the Twelve Days of Christmas at the Jared Coffin House on Nantucket Island, thirty miles off the Massachusetts coast.

Outside, the sound of a distant foghorn mingles with the Christmas carols and the cobblestone sidewalks glisten in the soft December mist. The Christmas tree is lit and you move into the dining room for a dinner of roast suckling pig replete with all the Christmas trimmings. The tables are set with Wedgwood china, pistol-handled silverware, and crystal water goblets. Overhead, a Tole chandelier, handsomely fashioned after an early whale-oil prototype and bearing the eminent Coffin family crest, casts a soft light.

On the Second Night, December 22, the series of candlelit international dinners begins, complete with wines and entrées from different countries for each of the remaining Twelve Days. An Italian feast, for example, might include Zuppa Minestrone d'Astri, Gnocchi a la parigina or Ravioli con Ricotta, Antipasto, Saltimbocca or Gamberi all'Anglio, and Amaretto Torte for dessert.

On Christmas Eve, the Reads ask all guests to join them in the library. Thespians in stovepipe pants, 19th-century morning coats, and ruffled dresses sing Christmas carols on the front steps. Inside, there's eggnog and a gourmet dinner.

After brunch on Christmas morning, you open the presents the Reads have put under the tree for you. There's a traditional dinner in the evening, featuring native pheasant with cream sauce, roast prime rib of beef, Nantucket Bay scallops, native turkey, creamed onions, squash, turnip, potatoes, Christmas pudding, cranberry cordials, parfaits and homemade pies and pastries. Throughout the rest of your stay, wine tastings, wassailing, international-style dinners, eggnog parties, and readings about Yule traditions will bring you together with the other eighty guests, who come for just a few days or stay for the entire twelve days. Many people make their reservations a year ahead of time.

On New Year's Eve, the Reads host a formal dinner and a dance. They serve a New Year's brunch the next day, and on January 6, they celebrate Epiphany with a special dinner.

"Nantucket" is an Indian name for "place of the faraway land." The 3½-by-4-mile island was inhabited by Wampanoag Indians more than 7,000 years ago. Currently, the year-round population stands at 9,000, swelling to 30,000 during the summer months.

Called the "Little Gray Lady," Nantucket has escaped the ravages of the 20th century. Crooked cobblestone streets and the fine 19th-century architecture attest to the fact that the island has not forgotten her past. One of the best ways to explore Nantucket is on Carol's Tour ($5 per person, now in its 32nd year), which winds around the island for an hour and a half in small groups.

Winters on Nantucket are tempered by the Gulf Stream just 300 miles seaward, so you can stroll comfortably as you beach-comb, visit the unique shops, or have a stout or two at one of the old taverns.

The Jared Coffin House was built in 1845 and restored in 1961 by the Nantucket Historical Trust at a cost of $1 million. It reflects the architecture of the other houses on the island, with furled curtains in the shuttered windows, an unpretentious façade, and even a gas lamp next to the front door.

The inn has forty-six rooms, fourteen with four-poster beds. Four of the rooms have crewel embroidered canopies, drapes, and bedspreads. Seven others have canopied double- or queen-sized beds. Philip and Margaret Read bought the inn in 1966.

America's Best! VEAL

Delft Blue-Provimi, Inc.

Provimi Road
Watertown, Wisconsin 53094

414-261-7882, 800-558-9560

Aat Groenevelt, President
Erik Groenevelt, National Sales
Manager

Red Circle Inn
Nashotah, Wisconsin

414-367-2123

Wilhelm H. Karlheim, Executive
Chef-General Manager

The creamy pink color, firm texture, marbling, tenderness, and succulence mark Delft Blue-Provimi as America's best veal.

There are three types of veal in this country. "Bob Veal" is produced from calves less than one week old and lacks color and taste because of insufficient aging. It's plentiful, but Provimi President Aat Groenevelt says it won't do for satisfactory dining. "Grain-fed veal" has some texture, but it isn't creamy pink in color. It tends to be red and "mushy" and could pass as baby beef. "Special Fed Veal" is marketed by Delft Blue and characteristic of the finer veal of Europe.

The big difference is in the Provimi "milk formula" feed that is produced only by the Delft Blue-Provimi plants in Watertown, Wisconsin, and Flanders, New Jersey. "Provimi" combines the words "protein," "vitamins," and "minerals," all contained in the precise blend of skimmed milk, buttermilk, and whey powder that closely resembles the characteristics of whole milk, impractical and expensive to be used as feed.

The feed is produced in powder form and must be carefully mixed with hot and cold water so that its temperature will be as close as possible to 100 degrees F. when fed to the calf. It was first developed by Aat Groenevelt twenty years ago in New Jersey and is based upon a "milk replacer" feed formula used in European veal production. Aat moved to Wisconsin to start Delft Blue because the necessary dairy by-products and calves were readily available there.

Only Holstein dairy bull calves are used. They are put on the special Delft Blue-Provimi program when just a few days old and are allowed to grow to a weight of between 325 and 350 pounds, larger than any other calves raised for veal production in the U.S.

Delft Blue-Provimi Veal uses 160,000 calves a year. They're raised around the country by farmers who adhere to the strict guidelines of the Delft Blue-Provimi program. In return, Delft Blue agrees to buy the calves at a set price and market the veal through extensive promotional programs and a nationwide warehouse and distribution system.

The calves are raised in heated barns ventilated by special fans and all equipment is sanitized daily to protect the animals' health. They are fed only the Delft Blue feed twice a day for fifteen weeks on a rigid, precise schedule. At the end of the fifteen weeks, they are graded by government and company standards. Over 90 percent of the veal meets the highest government and company grades of quality.

Since the company opened its own packing house in 1974, Delft Blue-Provimi has been vacuum packed. This means that the veal

Delft Blue uses the Red Circle Inn as a test kitchen.

can be shipped by box rather than on the rail, handling is easier, the shelf life is prolonged, and freezer burn and weight loss due to dehydration is avoided. Distribution points around the country can maintain inventories without spoilage.

The veal is sold to restaurants and institutions, and most of the primal cuts are offered to butcher shops and exclusive retail veal outlets in America. Hearts, tongues, livers, and other offal are flown out of the country to Europe, where they are considered to be delicacies.

In 1976, Delft Blue bought the Red Circle Inn in Nashotah, Wisconsin. Built in 1848, it is the oldest restaurant in Wisconsin and was owned for years by the Pabst Blue Ribbon Brewery as a showplace. The name "Red Circle" comes from the red circle on the Pabst insignia. Argie Pabst is still a regular customer. Delft Blue uses the restaurant as a test kitchen for its veal products and menu suggestions. Seventy-five percent of the menu contains veal dishes, including veal meatballs and veal schnitzel. Many customers come regularly from Milwaukee, thirty miles away, and the restaurant even chauffeurs special customers from Chicago.

Delft Blue Veal is also served in such fine restaurants as the Commander's Palace in New Orleans, Petite Marmite in Palm Beach, Florida, and the main dining room of the Ritz-Carlton Hotel in Boston.

Ever since Delft Blue-Provimi Special Fed Veal Company was founded in 1964, Aat Groenevelt has tried to counter American confusion and disenchantment with veal. He explains that twenty years ago the only veal available in America was "slimy, red meat" from calves slaughtered too young. They didn't have the marbling and "conformation" for texture of a fifteen-week-old, "milk-fed" calf. Naturally, Americans became disenchanted with veal.

That image, however, has changed as the quality of American veal has improved. Aat Groenevelt, who started with a little feed mill in New Jersey, has expanded his operation to meet the demand for high-quality veal. Delft Blue now has a slaughterhouse in Mentone, Indiana, a slaughter and "breaking" facility (where the slaughtered calves are portioned into the proper cuts) in New Jersey, another breaking facility in Pleasanton, California, and a slaughterhouse and breaking operation in San Juan, Puerto Rico, where the stable climate is ideal for raising the calves.

America's Best! VEGIMALS

Freemountain Toys, Inc.

at the Vegimill
Bristol, Vermont 05443

802-453-2462

Beverly Red, Proprietor

If you have never snuggled up to an eggplant or become close friends with an ear of corn, the people at the Vegimill in Bristol, Vermont, can introduce you to a number of very personable vegetables.

Colorful, soft, and provocative in their extraordinary design, the Vegimals are unique among stuffed toys. "Most other stuffed toys are just two-dimensional, and the only thing that makes them three-dimensional is the stuffing," explains Beverly Red, their creator. "The Vegimals are more expressive because they are distinctly three-dimensional—the back is as interesting as the front, the inside is as interesting as the outside."

If you crack open the soft, tan-colored shell of Peanuts, you'll find two golden velour peanuts (with faces) wrapped up in their removable brown velour skins. You can actually pick the seeds out of Watermelon, or pluck off Daisy's petals one by one (then stick them back on with their Velcro fasteners).

The Vegimill sells about 50,000 Vegimals each year. The most popular is Peas ($19), five wistful-faced green velour spheres nestled within a velour pod with a zipper. Usually, the Vegimill sells more Peas than all the other Vegimals together. The other Vegimals include Butternut (winter) Squash (with a muff to warm his hands), Tomato, Cauliflower, Broccoli, Celery, and Olive (with a removable pimento).

Nutritionists think that Vegimals are good for teaching children a healthy attitude toward vegetables that they often resist eating. Health food stores like them for display purposes. Vegimals have even made two guest appearances on the *Today Show* where shuckable Corn charmed Gene Shalit by coming out of its husk. Barry Manilow is very much taken with his blue-eyed Banana.

Beverly Red studied art at Bennington College, Vermont, where she developed an interest in soft sculpture. She began making toys for her friends (Carrot was her first), and finally she was asked to create a whole line of stuffed vegetables. In 1975, she began an unusual cottage industry that now involves forty workers. Vegimals are sewn by seamstresses in their homes, and then are stuffed and finished in the Vegimill. Freemountain Toys employs women with young children, those who lack means of transportation, the aged, the handicapped, and others who are not able to hold full-time jobs.

The Vegimals are made of fine materials such as velour and synthetic furs. Their high-quality resilient Polyfil makes them durable, safe, fire-resistant, and entirely machine washable. They have even been awarded a certificate of commendation from the Public Action Coalition on Toys (PACT) because they are imaginative and safe, they inspire constructive, nonviolent activity, their packaging is non-sexist and non-racist, and they are merchandised in a non-exploitative manner.

Beverly has extended her talents beyond Vegimals and directed them toward the cosmos—she has created Earth, with movable continents, Galaxy, filled with blue, yellow, and red stars, and Saturn, with quilted rings. She has also designed Lamb, with a white coat of synthetic fur, Furry Worm, with felt collar and print tie, Pig, who gives birth to Piglet, and Redman, who is a terrific success ("If you knew him you'd understand," says Beverly). Her current personal favorite is the Fish in a Fish in a Fish—three fishes of increasing size who swallow each other. Since the fall of 1978, Beverly and the Vegimill workers have been sewing wings, horns, antennae, feelers, ears, antlers, and lightning bolts onto baseball caps to make Freemountain Hats ($9 to $10), which are being donned by fun-loving kids and adults all over the country. In fact, the Vegimill sold 250,000 hats during the first year of production.

Vegimals and other Freemountain products—forty-three in all—are available by mail order from the Vegimal and in retail stores. They range in size from eight to twenty-six inches and are priced from $6.50 to $32.

America's Best! VOLCANO

Kilauea Volcano	*Recorded Eruption Information:* 808-967-7977
Hawaii Island	
	Kona Flight Service
Hawaii Volcanoes National Park	*Kona Airport*
Volcano, Hawaii 96785	
	808-329-1474
808-967-7311	
	5-passenger Aztec or 3-passenger Warrior aircraft; 90-minute flight; $54 per passenger
Dave Ames, Superintendent	

For centuries, Hawaiians have considered Kilauea Volcano on Hawaii Island to be the home of Pele, goddess of fire. Pele still reigns supreme there, and if you happened to be at the Volcano

Kilauea is one of the world's most active and observable volcanoes.

House Hotel overlooking Kilauea Crater in 1974, you could have sipped a mai tai at the bar while watching some of her fiery antics. Three spectacular eruptions took place in July, September, and December (New Year's Eve) of 1974, and Mauna Ulu, a vent of Kilauea, was active constantly from January to late July of 1974. Even when Kilauea sleeps, a visit there is an unforgettable experience.

Kilauea, one of the world's most active volcanoes, is also the most observable. When it is erupting, scientists from all over the world take advantage of its relatively unexplosive nature to examine it closely. Scientists attribute Kilauea's "safeness" to the composition of the molten rock beneath the Hawaiian Islands. The basaltic rock is hotter and less viscous (more fluid) than in other volcanoes that are more explosive, such as Vesuvius and Etna. Instead of exploding, Kilauea is more apt to erupt in a series of fountains and flows, which release some of the gaseous pressure.

When Kilauea erupts, earth tremors occur with great frequency in the volcano area, sometimes on the order of thousands in a single day. However, most of these tremors cannot be felt or measured except with the most sensitive instruments.

The Hawaii Volcano Observatory, located on the rim of the Kilauea caldera, monitors all volcano activity in order to forecast volcanic eruptions. In the core of the earth, many heavy elements such as lead, iron, and nickel are producing heat from radioactive decay. A stream, called a "mantle plume," of this concentrated material rises 2,000 miles to the earth's crust. Forty miles below the Pacific crust, the pressure and temperature are ideal for the rock to melt, forming magma (unerupted lava). The magma rises to within three miles of the surface where it is stored in a magma reservoir until enough pressure builds up for an eruption.

Hours before the eruption, a harmonic tremor, a continuous earthquake of a distinctive pattern, occurs in the volcano. Immediately before the eruption, the volcano summit deflates rapidly and the ground level drops several feet as the magma moves out of the mountain to the surface where the ground will crack open at the point of eruption.

Sensitive instruments, such as seismographs and tilt meters, are used to detect these warning signs. A tilt meter measures the tilting of a volcano's slope. If the tilt becomes steeper, the volcano is swelling with magma. If the tilt becomes more gradual, the magma is moving out from the mountain and towards the surface.

The Hawaii Volcano Observatory is the ideal place to study active volcanoes. The weather is usually good, and the volcanoes are very accessible—you can even walk right up to the vent.

For those lucky enough to be in the area during an eruption, charter companies occasionally fly tours over the active volcano area. The small planes swoop down so close that the acrid smell of sulphur permeates the shivering crafts, which shake from the volcanic "wind," while the exterior paint blisters from the heat. Depending on the nature of the eruption and its location, visitors can often get to within a few hundred feet of the site, affording them a spectacular view of these primeval forces at work.

A sea of molten lava still surges beneath the hardened basalt surface at Kilauea, as is evidenced by the billowing clouds of steam which continuously rise from the central Halemaumau Crater and surrounding areas. Kilauea is actually a three-by-two-mile caldera, a crater enlarged through collapse.

Halemaumau, more than a half mile in diameter, is the principal active vent. Originally called "Kalua a Pele" (Pit of Pele), Halemaumau has erupted seventeen times in the last fifty years, and erupted continuously between 1969 and 1974. Between 1905 and 1924, Halemaumau was a raging sea of lava and erupted almost continuously. It has made the area so famous for volcanic activity that Congress developed the site into a National Park.

Don't wait, however, for an eruption to visit the volcano. The stark landscape alone is awesome, and there are more than twenty-four miles of trails in and around the crater maintained by the Hawaii Volcanoes National Park Service. Park rangers and naturalists knowledgeable in geologic history and the flora and fauna of the area conduct organized hikes. There are also slide shows, films, lectures, and other programs.

The Park Service recommends the early fall as a good time to visit the volcanoes, because visitation has slacked off, the flowers are in bloom, and, statistically at least, the rain isn't as heavy. Explore the volcano on foot rather than by auto, as the experience of hiking on what was once molten lava of 2,000 degrees F. is unforgettable. Walking along the half-mile Devastation Trail, behind a recently active vent of Kilauea Iki Crater, you can see the stark remains of a native ohia tree forest obliterated by an eruption in 1959. The trail leads you around the cinder hill to witness an occasional tree skeleton or cylindrical mold in the ground where a tree was surrounded by cinder before it burned. Tree ferns, which grow only in Hawaii, are found in the Tree Fern Forest next to Kilauea Iki Crater. Nearby Thurston Lava Tube surged with molten lava nearly 500 years ago.

There has been an observatory at Kilauea since 1912, and the records show continuous volcanic activity since then. Hawaiian volcanoes erupt so often, a volcanologist doesn't have to spend a lifetime waiting for an eruption. Even a casual visitor has a chance of seeing America's best volcano in action.

America's Best! WILDERNESS LODGE

Kachemak Bay Wilderness Lodge

China Poot Bay
via Homer, Alaska 99603

Michael and Diane McBride,
Proprietors

$150 per day (3-day minimum);
$750 at Brown Bear Camp
(3-day minimum; air fare
included)

At Kachemak Bay Wilderness Lodge, 225 miles from Anchorage, seals herd on the sand bar out front, Ollie the sea otter frolics on the beach, and eagles nest within walking distance. You can ride the incoming tides past wildflower cliff gardens, streams, and waterfalls. Or you can trace the line of ancient *barabaras* (sod houses) to reconstruct the past lives of ancient man. Most exciting of all is a bush flight into the northern camp to look for and photograph the magnificent brown bear, with an incomparable ice-blue glacier as your scenic backdrop.

Owners Mike and Diane McBride operate one of the few Alaskan lodges where guests join a year-round resident family. They have kept the camp small and usually accommodate only eight people at a time. The McBrides will meet you on a Thursday or a Sunday at the Homer Small Boat Landing. There they will show you something of the commercial fishing industry of the area, then head for the lodge in an open dory. On a clear day, you can see the mountains of Cape Douglas in the distance. Seals, porpoises, and whales help guide your way, and passing Gull Island, you'll see a rare nesting ground teeming with thousands of sea birds.

When you reach China Poot Bay, the area will be bustling with red-face cormorants, puffins, and guillemots playing in the waves. One of the hiking trails on the shore leads to the sea caves, which archaeologists think were used as the site of ancient burials.

The McBrides schedule their visitors according to the rhythms of nature—the salmon run, the extremely low tides, summer activity at the bird rookery, the concentrations of brown bears at the salmon streams.

The log lodge is dominated by a massive stone fireplace and is decorated with material the McBrides have salvaged and restored. (The kitchen cabinets came from an old halibut schooner.) Stone ledges in the living room walls lead to sleeping lofts.

Meals always include home-baked bread and are served family-style in the dining room, where you can watch the ever-changing tidal pools from huge picture windows. Occasionally, a black bear will mosey by the window to check out the diners.

There are two guest rooms in the lodge, and private accommodations in three nearby cabins. They are considered deluxe by bush standards, containing electricity, wood stoves, and outside privies. There is also a community bathroom in the lodge with a tub and shower, and a large sod-roofed Finnish sauna.

The McBrides recommend visits of at least three days to become familiar with the territory. A typical day might include a trip to Grewingk Glacier, where you can sit and listen to the groaning of the ice and watch terns nest on the shoreline. You can also kayak, fish for salmon, trout, and halibut, hike through the dense forests, study the marine life—the possibilities are endless.

By special arrangement you can visit the Brown Bear Camp, 100 miles north of Kachemak Bay. This area has the largest concentration of brown bears in the world, and it's not unusual to see twenty bears at one time. The McBrides consider man to be the intruder in these parts. They feel he must be an unobtrusive visitor, and they will not allow you to take photographs unless you can guarantee that you will not interfere with the life patterns of the animals. The rustic tent cabins lie at the base of a great peninsular land bridge stretching toward Siberia. Archaeologists think this area may have been a link in man's earliest migrations.

The China Poot Bay area has had no permanent residents (except for a few scattered settlers) since the Athabaskans and the Eskimos, who flourished there centuries ago. Temperatures are rarely below freezing, and the proximity of the Japanese current makes the winter extremely warm. Mike fell in love with the area when he was stationed there with the Air Force. In 1969 he and Diane sailed across the Bay from Homer to settle their new home.

They hauled ten-foot logs to build a seawall, reconstructed the lodge out of a heap of ruins, and learned to live on moose, berries, and fish.

America's Best! ZOO AND WILD ANIMAL PARK

San Diego Zoo	San Diego Wild Animal Park
P.O. Box 551 San Diego, California 92112	Route 1, Box 725 E Escondido, California 92025
714-231-1515	Andrew Y. Grant, General Manager
Charles Bieler, Executive Director Carole Towne, Public Relations Manager	Carole Towne, Public Relations and Marketing Director Suzanne Strassburger, Public Relations Manager
7 days a week: July–Labor Day, 9:00 A.M.–7:00 P.M.; Labor Day–October, 9:00 A.M.– 5:00 P.M.; November–February, 9:00 A.M.–4:00 P.M.; March– June, 9:00 A.M.–5:00 P.M.; adults, $6.25; children 3–15, $4; under 2, free	7 days a week: November– February, 9:00 A.M.–4:00 P.M.; March–June 12, 9:00 A.M.– 5:00 P.M.; June 13–September 1, 9:00 A.M.–9:00 P.M.; September 2–October 1, 9:00 A.M.–5:00 P.M.; adults, $6.25; children 3–15, $4; under 3, free (includes monorail ticket)

The San Diego Zoo offers you a glimpse of 6,500 specimens of 1,813 species, including many you've never heard of, in a beautifully landscaped subtropical environment sprawling over 1,900 acres.

The Zoo houses one of the finest collections of exotic animals in the world, and serves an important conservational purpose for the entire world community. It owns specimens of many endangered

The fishing camp is built over a cascading waterfall.

species and has mated animals that usually will not reproduce in captivity. This is especially important, since many of the Zoo's animals live nowhere else in the world.

One of the Zoo's rarest exhibits is a herd of Przewalski's Mongolian wild horses. These are the world's only true wild horses, and they have not been seen in the wild in the past ten years. There are only 260 left in the world, and they are all in zoos. (This is the kind of horse that Genghis Khan and his Mongolian army rode over 1,000 years ago.)

The San Diego Zoo is the only zoo outside Australia that has koala bears. San Diego is one of the few places in the world with the food that koalas need: their diet consists solely of eucalyptus leaves.

Among the other rare creatures that call the Zoo home are okapis, horse-like animals that have the coloring of a giraffe, the stripes of a zebra on their hind legs, and velvet-soft skin. The Zoo also possesses Komodo dragons, the largest lizards in the world, and pygmy chimpanzees, the animals that are most closely related to man. The Zoo is patrolled by a squad of red jungle fowl from India (they look like domesticated chickens). Hundreds of them run about freely to keep the insect population down. The Zoo also has the largest collection of parrots and their relatives ever assembled in the history of the world, and the only zoo in the world with Tahitian blue lories (now extinct in Tahiti).

Much of what the animals eat is raised on the grounds. Alfalfa and barley are grown through a sophisticated new technique called "hydroponics," which saves growing time and doesn't require soil—the plants are grown in water. The Zoo also raises mice, crickets, and rats to feed the animals.

The 100-acre Zoo is the only self-supporting nonprofit organization of its size and dimension in the world. Founded in 1916 as part of the California exposition at Balboa Park, all of its assets are the property of the city, although the administration operates independent of municipal government.

Special features of the Zoo include guided bus tours, an aerial tramway, and a children's zoo. Among the most interesting visitors are the thousands of migrating ducks, swans, and geese that come through the city each year between October and February and stay a few days to enjoy the hospitality (and food) of the Zoo's Migratory Bird Ponds—free of charge, of course.

The $15,000,000 Wild Animal Park opened in 1972. Thousands of visitors have flocked there ever since, and annual attendance figures now top one million. Since its conception, the Park has emerged as a major animal research center, and fourteen of its nineteen endangered species have reproduced with an astounding 85 percent survival rate.

The Park is home to over 3,000 animals from all over the world, more than $1 million worth of plants and trees, and 100 kinds of rare and colorful birds. More than 200 species of wildlife, including elephants, tigers, giraffes, gazelles, and hippos, roam in relative freedom over 1,800 acres of a meticulously planned landscape that closely resembles the animals' natural habitats. Rare and endangered species, such as the white rhino, the Arabian oryx, and the Bengal tiger, live here in peace. Lush landscaped gardens filled with rare and exotic plants surround the animal habitats and aviaries.

Visitors enter a world of exotic sights, sounds, colors, and smells. Perhaps the most innovative part of the Park's design is the WGASA Bushline monorail system, built specially by the Westinghouse Airbrake Company. Visitors travel safari-like along five miles of track aboard electric monorail cars, which wind silently through the eastern half of the Park. During the fifty-minute ride, a driver-guide points out many of the Park's 3,000 animals and explains their characteristics and habits.

For those who want to take in the same sights at a more leisurely pace, there is the Kilimanjaro Hiking Trail. Panoramic viewpoints, observation platforms, and log suspension bridges allow visitors ideal locations from which to observe and photograph the animals.

One of the liveliest spots in the preserve is the seventeen-acre Nairobi Village, designed and constructed with exacting detail and authenticity in an attempt to give visitors the flavor of the original environment from which the exhibits were taken. Aside from the vast array of wildlife and botanical exhibits, a Gorilla Grotto, animal shows, and even musical performances, Nairobi Village has shopping bazaars, restaurants, picnic areas, and photo shops. Lush landscaped gardens filled with rare and exotic plants surround animal habitats and aviaries. Over 100 species of colorful birds fly overhead.

The Congo River fishing camp, built over a cascading waterfall, is an authentic reproduction of a native fishing village. At the animal kraal, children are allowed to pet and feed deer, antelope, gazelles, and goats. The glass-fronted Animal Care Center offers visitors an opportunity to watch food preparation and care of infant animals.

Most of the Park is accessible to those in wheelchairs. Visually handicapped visitors can enjoy a special botanical garden filled with plants of different textures. Trails and walkways all have braille signs and rope trail guides.

For shoppers, the Park Bazaar offers handcrafted African artifacts, jewelry, pictures, clothes, and other souvenirs. The Thorn Tree Terrace and the Mombasa Cooker serve up a variety of dishes. Other service facilities include binocular rental shops ($1 for the day), lockers, drinking fountains and restrooms, public phones, lectures and Park literature, first-aid stations, and parking for 2,000 cars.

Index

Shops, restaurants, hotels, individuals, and the other suppliers of America's best, as well as the cities and towns in which you'll find them, are indicated by boldface type.

K

Kachemak Bay, Alaska, 233
Kachemak Bay Wilderness Lodge, 232–234
Kahalui, Maui, Hawaii, 169–171
Kamuela, Hawaii, 175–177
Kansas
    jogging rollers skates, 120–123
Karlheim, Wilhelm H., 223
Kaye, Danny, 212
Keeshin Charter Service, 45–46
Keeshin, Paul A., 45–46
Kelly, Grace, 104
Kennedy, John F., 71, 166
Kennedy, Rose, 104
Kennedy, Ted, 74
Kent Valley, Washington, 180
Kenworth Truck Company, 215–217
Khrushchev, Nikita, 70
Kilauea Volcano, 228–231
King Salmon fishing, 126–127
Kings Island, 183
Kings Mills, Ohio, 183–184
Kirkland, Washington, 215–217
Kissinger, Henry, 175
Kitch'n Cook'd potato chips, 169–171
kites, 127–130
Kittredge, George, 160–163
Kittredge Industries, Inc., 160–163
Klein, David, 112
Knievel, Evel, 215
Knoud, M. J., 185–186
Knox County, Maine, 130–132
Kobayashi, Dewey, 169–171
Kohala Coast, 176
Kona Flight Service, 228
Kreuz Market, 27–29
Kurdi, Shelly, 172, 174

L

Lacombes, Jacques, 180
Lacoste, Pierre, 41–42
Lafayette, General, 147

La Jolla, California, 202
Lake Havasu City, Arizona, 62
Lames, Missouri, 148
Lane, Brian, 106
Langhirano, Italy, 187
Lateef, Yusef, 90
La Tona, Tony, 192–193
Laurel and Hardy, 35
Lawrence, Steve, 104
Lemmon, Jack, 71
Le Petit Bar, 93–94
Lerner, Alan J., 71
Le Sacre du Printemps, 211
Liberty Banjo Company, 24–27
Lincoln, Abraham, 166
Linnean House, 40
L. L. Bean, Inc., 53–55
Lobel, Leon, 47–49
Lobel, Morris, 49
Lobel, Stanley, 47–49
lobster, 130–132
Lockhart, Texas, 27–29
London Bridge, 62
Loren, Sophia, 108–109
Los Angeles, California, 61–63
Los Angeles Children's Hospital, 62
Los Angeles Rams, 62
Los Angeles Times, 63
Louis XIV, 149
Louis Phillipe, 17
Louisiana
    appetizers, 16–18
    Bouillabaisse Orleans, 41–42
    bread pudding, 42–43
    fresh fruit frozen daiquiris, 93–94
    fried chicken, 94–95
    pousse café, 171–172
luau, 133–135
luminarias, 135–137
luxury sports automobile, 138–141

M

MacAlister, Paul T., 11
McBride, Diana, 232–234

Photo Credits

Front cover, Bachrach *page 7*, Werner J. Kuhn *page 10*, Hawaii Visitors Bureau *page 12*, Skip Gandy *page 15*, Prince Studios *pages 47 and 48*, Lawrence Fried *page 57*, Don Kellogg *page 70*, Cindy Cates *page 81*, Lampel *page 89*, CBS *page 134*, A. Boccaccio *page 137*, Dick Kent *page 151*, Wilson H. Browneld *page 155*, Nancy Simmerman *page 166 (top)*, Fabian Bachrach *page 166 (bottom)*, Bradford Bachrach *page 167*, Bachrach *pages 178 and 179*, Bob Peterson *page 199*, Douglas Hopkins *pages 210 and 211*, Robert M. Lightfoot III *page 229 (top and bottom)*, National Park Service *page 235*, San Diego Wild Animal Park.